Spatial Modernities

This collection of essays offers a series of reflections on the specific literary and cultural forms that can be seen as the product of modernity's spatial transformations, which have taken on new urgency in today's world of ever increasing mobility and global networks. The book offers a broad perspective on the narrative and poetic dimensions of the modern discourses and imaginaries that have shaped our current geographical sensibilities. In the early twenty-first century, we are still grappling with the spatial effects of 'early' and 'high' modern developments, and the contemporary crises revolving around political boundaries and geopolitical orders in many parts of the world have intensified spatial anxieties. They call for a sustained analysis of individual perceptions, cultural constructions and political implications of spatial processes, movements and relations.

The contributors of this book focus both on the spatial orders of modernity and on the various dynamic processes that have shaped our engagement with modern space. They creatively engage in a dialogue between literature, cinema, art history, geography, architecture, cultural semiotics and political science, and they transform twentieth- and twenty-first-century theory and philosophy to examine the textual forms of different spatial modernities. The chapters do not only engage with the cartographies, crossings and displacements represented *within* different texts and media, but are also attentive to the ways in which the latter produce space and perform mobility. Tracing an arc from Thomas More's *Utopia* to the digital spatiality of contemporary autobiographical film, they treat texts as active cultural forces that crystallize, reinforce, interrogate or complicate the spatial imaginaries of modernity through their own narrative and poetic form.

Johannes Riquet is Associate Professor of English Literature at the University of Tampere. His research focuses on spatiality, the multiple relations between literature and geography, travel writing, phenomenology and film studies. He has published on island narratives, railway literature and cinema, the poetics of snow and ice, and Shakespeare.

Elizabeth Kollmann studied in Port Elizabeth and Zurich and completed her PhD in English Literature at the University of Zurich in 2014. Her research interests include life writing, exile, postcolonialism and South African literature. She is a Lecturer in English at the ZHAW Zurich University of Applied Sciences.

Routledge Interdisciplinary Perspectives on Literature

For a full list of titles in this series, please visit www.routledge.com.

Spatial Modernities
Geography, Narrative, Imaginaries

Edited by Johannes Riquet and
Elizabeth Kollmann

Routledge
Taylor & Francis Group

NEW YORK AND LONDON

First published 2018
by Routledge
711 Third Avenue, New York, NY 10017

and by Routledge
2 Park Square, Milton Park, Abingdon, Oxon OX14 4RN

Routledge is an imprint of the Taylor & Francis Group, an informa business

Library of Congress Cataloging-in-Publication Data
CIP data has been applied for.

ISBN: 978-1-138-30455-0 (hbk)
ISBN: 978-0-203-73004-1 (ebk)

Typeset in Sabon
by codeMantra

Contents

Figures

Acknowledgements

Our thanks go first and foremost to the participants of the conference "Travelling Narratives: Modernity and the Spatial Imaginary," which took place in Zurich in 2013. The stimulating presentations and conversations we had at the conference prepared the ground for the writing of this book. We would also like to thank our former colleagues from the English Department at the University of Zurich for their support at different stages of the project. Special thanks go to the members of the research group "Space/Phenomenology and Embodied Experience," among others, Martin Heusser, Ana Sobral, Rahel Rivera Godoy-Benesch, Michelle Dreiding, Stefanie Strebel, Martino Oleggini and Gabi Neuhaus. The many workshops and discussions with this group have been formative for our understanding of the poetics of space and the idea of spatial modernities. We would also like to thank Hanne Juntunen for her assistance in the final stages of the project. Finally, our thanks go to Jennifer Abbott and Veronica Haggar at Routledge for their support and guidance.

Notes on Contributors

Tom Conley is the Abbott Lawrence Lowell Professor of Visual and Environmental Studies and of Romance Languages and Literatures at Harvard University. He studies relations of space and writing in literature, cartography and cinema. His work moves to and from early modern France and issues in theory and interpretation in visual media. His books include *Film Hieroglyphs* (1991, new edition 2006), *The Graphic Unconscious in Early Modern Writing* (1992), *The Self-Made Map: Cartographic Writing in Early Modern France* (1996, new edition 2010), *L'inconscient graphique: Essai sur l'écriture de la Renaissance* (2000), *Cartographic Cinema* (2007), *An Errant Eye: Topography and Poetry in Early Modern France* (2011) and *À fleur de page: Voir et lire le texte de la Renaissance* (2014).

Jean-Paul Forster has taught English and American literature in Lausanne as well as at the Centre de Télé-enseignement, University of Nancy II, of which he is an Honorary Professor. He is the author of *Jonathan Swift: The Fictions of the Satirist* (1991), *A First Approach to English Literatures: From Beowulf to Salman Rushdie* (2003), a short introduction to English, American and Commonwealth literatures, and *Eighteenth-Century Geography and Representations of Space in English Fiction and Poetry* (2013).

Ina Habermann has been Professor of English at the University of Basel since 2007. Her main fields of interest include Shakespeare and the early modern period, literature and film in the interwar period and the Second World War, Irish literature, cultural and literary history and theory as well as gender studies. She is the author of *Staging Slander and Gender in Early Modern England* (Ashgate, 2003) and of *Myth, Memory and the Middlebrow: Priestley, du Maurier and the Symbolic Form of Englishness* (Palgrave, 2010). Her current research projects deal with British literary discourses of Europe and the literary representation of otherworldly spaces. She has initiated and is Chairwoman of the *Centre of Competence of Cultural Topographies*.

Britta Hartmann holds a PhD in English Literature from the University of Tasmania. Her doctoral dissertation examined island fiction from Daniel Defoe's *Robinson Crusoe* (1719) to the present day. She has taught English literature and film at the University of Vechta (Germany) and the University of Tasmania (Australia). Her research interests include the cultural representation of islands, oceans and pirates, along with theories of place, spatiality and belonging. She also explores these themes through the writing of fiction and is currently working on an island novel.

Elizabeth Kollmann studied in Port Elizabeth and Zurich and completed her PhD in English Literature at the University of Zurich in 2014. Her research interests include life writing, exile, postcolonialism and South African literature. She is a Lecturer in English at the ZHAW Zurich University of Applied Sciences.

Christina Ljungberg is Adjunct Professor of English and American Literature at the University of Zurich with several years of media experience in Swedish and Canadian film and television. Her many books and articles, most recently *Creative Dynamics* (John Benjamins, 2012) and *Thinking with Diagrams* (with Sybille Krämer, De Gruyter, 2016), focus mainly on ways of mapping knowledge and the intermedial function of maps and photographs in literature and art. Her current research project (with Olga Fischer, Amsterdam) concerns iconicity in language and literature.

Maarja Ojamaa is currently working as a Postdoctoral Researcher at the Baltic Film, Media, Arts, and Communication School (BFM) at Tallinn University in Estonia. She is also affiliated with the Department of Semiotics at the University of Tartu, where she defended her PhD thesis on the transmedial aspects of cultural autocommunication. Her primary research interests lie in transmedial mechanisms of cultural memory and in the reusage of cultural heritage. In addition to the research work, she has been teaching semiotics-related courses at all stages of the Estonian higher education system as well as in high schools.

Caroline Rabourdin is an architect, essayist and academic. She graduated from INSA Strasbourg, the Bartlett School of Architecture (UCL), and holds a PhD from Chelsea College of Arts (UAL). Her research interests include spatial theory, phenomenology, geometry, spatial literature, art writing, translation studies and comparative literature. She is Teaching Fellow in History and Theory at the Bartlett School of Architecture, UCL, Course Lecturer for the MA in History and Critical Thinking at the AA School of Architecture, and runs the Printed Matter course on artists' books. She is also

Head of the AA Visiting School Paris, which celebrates writing as a critical and creative practice.

Johannes Riquet is Associate Professor of English Literature at the University of Tampere. His research focuses on spatiality, the multiple relations between literature and geography, travel writing, phenomenology and film studies. His is currently preparing his first monograph, *The Aesthetics of Island Space: Perception, Ideology, Geopoetics*, for publication (under contract with Oxford University Press). He is also working on a second book on interrupted railway journeys in British literature and cinema as well as a collaborative project on representations of the transnational Arctic in contemporary fiction. He co-founded the international research group Island Poetics and is on the editorial board of the *Island Studies Journal*.

Deirdre Russell is Lecturer in Film Studies at the University of South Wales, where she teaches film theory, French cinema, documentary and autobiographical film. Her publications and current research interests include narrative theory, contemporary documentary film and media convergence.

Barney Samson lectures at the University of Essex, where he completed his PhD in 2017. His doctoral thesis, supervised by Jeffrey Geiger and Marina Warner, examined the desert island in popular culture since the Second World War, using Bauman's conceptions of seduction and repression. He is currently adapting the thesis for publication and writing a book with the Island Poetics Research Group, of which he is a founder member. Barney has previously written about superheroes as sufferers of psychological trauma and on the *Harry Potter* novels as sites of Foucauldian heterotopia. As an undergraduate, he studied Music at Girton College, Cambridge and continues to work in music education and as a freelance musician alongside his academic work.

David Shim is Assistant Professor at the Department of International Relations and International Organization at the University of Groningen. He is interested in the visual and spatial dimension of global politics and works at the intersection of International Relations, Geography and Area Studies. His work has appeared, among others, in *International Political Sociology*, *International Studies Review*, *Geoforum*, *International Relations of the Asia-Pacific* and *Review of International Studies*. His book *Visual Politics and North Korea* (2013) is available at Routledge. David has translated some of his research activities into teaching practice, which can be viewed on his blog "Visual Global Politics."

Robert T. Tally Jr. is Professor of English at Texas State University. His books include *Topophrenia: Place, Narrative, and the Spatial Imagination* (2018), *Fredric Jameson: The Project of Dialectic Criticism* (2014), *Poe and the Subversion of American Literature* (2014), *Spatiality* (2013) and *Utopia in the Age of Globalization* (2013); and, as editor, *Teaching Space, Place, and Literature* (2017), *The Routledge Handbook of Literature and Space* (2017) and *The Geocritical Legacies of Edward W. Said* (2015). Tally is also the General Editor of "Geocriticism and Spatial Literary Studies," a Palgrave Macmillan book series.

Framing the Debate
Spatial Modernities, Travelling Narratives

Johannes Riquet

Setting the Scene: Spatial Stories of Modernity

This is a book about spatial modernities, and the geographical narratives and imaginaries by which they are woven together. When Michel Foucault, in 1967, proclaimed that "[t]he present epoch will perhaps be above all the epoch of space" (1986, 22), he was thinking about the twentieth century, whose preoccupation with networks, simultaneity, data and global relations he opposed to the nineteenth century's obsession with time: with beginnings, origins, linearity and the past. Fifty years after Foucault's influential words, and with half a century of spatial theory in the humanities in between, it is time to return to the idea of an "epoch of space" from the perspective of a time in which Foucault's view of a networked world operating via the storage and instantaneous dispersal of data along multiple paths, still partly prophetic in 1967, has become a daily reality. Yet this book does not focus exclusively on the twentieth and twenty-first centuries, nor does it claim that space is necessarily more important than time in any given period. Rather, its focus is on the spaces of modernity, understood in the broadest sense of the term, and its aim is to trace an arc from the spatial imaginaries resulting from the early modern voyages of discovery to the spatial orders and disorders of late modernity. There are as many conceptions of modernity as theorists writing about it, and they variously emphasize rationalization and disenchantment (Weber, Horkheimer and Adorno, Habermas), differentiation and individualization (Durkheim), the emergence of the risk society (Giddens, Beck), nihilism (Nietzsche) and fleeting aesthetic experiences (Baudelaire, Simmel), as well as the rise of bureaucracy and capitalism (Marx, Bauman), state power (Foucault), science (Luhmann, Gaukroger) and – importantly for this book – cartography (Bulson, Cosgrove, Conley).

Rather than subscribing to one definition of *modernity*, conceived of in the singular, the contributors of this volume probe the usefulness of spatiality as an analytical category to understand the literary and cultural production of different *modernities*. I would like to set the scene by briefly presenting three stories that will serve as vignettes illustrating, each in its own way, what is meant by spatial modernities and the entanglement of geography, narrative and imaginaries through which they come to be.

The first of these takes us to the Pacific. In April 2013, the journal of the American Geophysical Union, *Eos*, published an unusual obituary (Seton et al. 2013) – not for a person, but for a geographical entity: "Obituary: Sandy Island (1876–2012)." In this short article, four geoscientists from Australia offered their final conclusions on a case that had attracted worldwide public attention and caused a minor stir in the scientific community in 2012. When the R/V *Southern Surveyor* was cruising in the eastern Coral Sea somewhere between New Caledonia and Australia, the scientists on board the ship were looking out for a 25-km-long island that appeared on various maps and data sets including Google Earth (but not on their hydrographic charts). They found nothing but water of a minimum depth of 1400 m. Sandy Island, it turned out, did not exist – and, in all likelihood, never had. The 'undiscovery' of the island provoked intense debates about the reliability of digital information technology and global scientific data, and various scientists tried to rationalize the error by suggesting that Sandy Island might exist after all or might have existed in the past; others suggested that it could have entered the maps through an error in digitization.[1] It soon transpired that the island had appeared on British admiralty charts since 1908, and that it had supposedly been sighted by the crew of a whaling ship, the *Velocity*, in 1876 (Seton et al. 2013, 141). For Maria Seton, leader of the 2012 expedition, and her co-authors, the Sandy Island case "called into question how well humanity really knows our own planet" (2013, 141), and geologist Sabin Zahirovic, who was also part of the expedition, pointed out in an interview that the maps of the surface of the Moon and of Mars are more detailed than the maps of our oceans.[2]

Yet what is really remarkable about this story is not that a non-existent island managed to remain on the maps until the twenty-first century, but rather that this error should have provoked such surprise. The early modern impulse to map the world entailed the blending of 'real' and 'imaginary' geographies; many of the countless phantom islands of early modern cartography remained on the maps well into the nineteenth and even twentieth century, and a good number were added along the way. Some of these islands, like "Friesland" (believed to exist south of Greenland) and "Davis Island" (a large island thought to be located near the Galápagos Islands), entered the maps because of navigational errors, erroneous sightings (such as clouds mistaken for land) or simply the invention of navigators (Benjamin Morrell is a case in point). Others came from mythical, legendary and fictional accounts; thus, islands like Thule, Hy-Brasil and the Isle of Saint Brendan appeared on maps as late as the nineteenth century. The early modern discoveries themselves were sometimes the result of imaginary cartographies as Columbus and others looked for the islands described in partly or entirely fictitious accounts like Marco Polo's and John Mandeville's travelogues (Gillis 45–61), and the immensely popular island books or *isolarii* of early modernity, studied by scholars such as Frank Lestringant (2002) and Tom Conley (1996, 167–201), contained maps and descriptions of islands without differentiating between fact and fiction (a distinction that was itself spurious). When the existence of those islands could not be confirmed, they were frequently just moved elsewhere. The naval authorities were well aware of the problem of phantom islands. In 1828, Ohio journalist Jeremiah N. Reynolds compiled the United States' first official list of doubtful islands (Stommel 1984, xix), and in 1878, a British ocean surveyor deleted 128 islands from the map, including three that actually existed (Marsden 2015, par. 3). Robert H. Fuson's *Legendary Islands of the Ocean Sea* (1995) studies these wandering and phantom islands, and Henry M. Stommel (1984) has devoted an entire book to *Lost Islands*. With this context in mind, Sandy Island is not a strange aberration, but simply belongs to a long history of the partly imaginary cartographies of modernity.

The second story takes us to the Arctic. In the summer of 2016, the passengers of a Dutch sailing ship, the *Rembrandt van Rijn*, found an old bottle on the coast of a remote fjord in East Greenland. The bottle contained a letter dating from 1997 that described the writers' journey from Ittoqqortoormiit to Ammassalik (more than 800 km) written in Kalaallisut (Western Greenlandic):

> So far, we have been stuck in ice and fog for 12 days altogether. All in all, we have rowed a total of 58.5 hours. Today, we are taking a break and preparing for the continuation of our journey as the waves are currently too strong. We are all very well.[3]

A few months later, the letter found its way back to one of the senders in the form of a digital image with a detour via Switzerland; posting the names of the four expedition members on a Greenlandic Facebook forum resulted in four replies within less than two hours, including one that specified the telephone number of one of the expeditioners, the only one still alive today. A Skype connection from Switzerland to Greenland was soon established, and a Swiss journalist who had been on board the *Rembrandt van Rijn* is currently writing up the story of the bottle and its sender,[4] Piitaaraq Brandt, himself a former journalist with a remarkable career: he worked for the Greenlandic broadcasting company KNR, won the Danish-Greenlandic cross-country championships eight times and also translated George Orwell's *Animal Farm* to Greenlandic ("Peter Brandt, tusagassiortoq" 1990, 2). In 1958, Brandt started a lifelong project of circling the Greenlandic coast in sections without a motor by boat, dog sledge and on skis – sometimes alone, sometimes in the company of others (cf. Andersen 2010). The 1997 expedition which left the bottle in the fjord was part of this project.[5]

Yet the 2016 cruise during which the bottle was found is interesting for another reason, which connects it to a long history of Arctic exploration and resource extraction. The *Rembrandt van Rijn* transported journalists, tourists and scientists, among them a Swiss geologist who owns a company specializing in geological exploration for mineral extraction in the Arctic by Greenlandic and international companies. He worked, among other projects, for the Nalunaq gold mine, which was operated by a Greenland-based company from 2004–2008 and sold to a British company in 2009 (www.helvetica-exploration.ch/personnel/). The passengers of the sailing ship found the bottle near the remains of a hut, which, as they later found out, had been built in 1932 during an expedition to East Greenland headed by Ejnar Mikkelsen, a well-known Danish polar explorer who had captained the Anglo-American Polar Expedition of 1906–1908 (Mikkelsen 1933). The Danish Geodætisk Institut played an important role in the 1932 expedition in the interest of surveying and mapping the coast of East Greenland (Higgins 2010, 10). Research in Greenland intensified during the Cold War, especially by the United States and Denmark; science was closely entangled with military and economic interests. Denmark sought to consolidate its own geopolitical hold over Greenland, and cartography played an important role in this endeavour (Doel, Harper and Heymann 2016). Scientific exploration was tied to economic exploitation; in the 1950s, a new mining company, the Nordisk Mineselskab, took up operations in East Greenland and used the 1930s hut as a fuel depot. The geological consultant of the company, Lauge Koch, hired geologists from Switzerland, Britain and Sweden. The Swiss connection was thereby of particular importance as Swiss universities (unlike their Danish counterparts) produced a great number of geologists, many of whom went on to work for international mineral and oil companies (Ries 2016, 127–133). The message in a bottle, sent in 1997 and retrieved in 2016, is thus connected to an episode in the long human history of the Arctic that began with Martin Frobisher's voyages in search of the Northwest Passage in the 1570s. Frobisher's encounters with the Inuit of Baffin Island and (fleetingly) Greenland mark the beginning of European colonization of the Arctic, and Piitaaraq Brandt's unmotorized circling of Greenland coincides (and resonates) with the decolonization of the island (cf. Andersen 2010). Concurrently, the recent opening of the Northwest Passage and the global interest in Arctic resources echoes early modern geospatial orders and investments in Arctic geography (cf. Craciun 2009; Dodds and Nuttall 2016).

The third story takes us to Eastern Europe – more specifically, to the backyard of the Cultural Centre of Novi Sad, the second largest city of Serbia. A gigantic cinema screen made of concrete looms over the ruinous space, which is currently a kind of no man's land. It functioned as an

outdoor cinema until 2008, when the Cultural Centre went into reconstruction; by the time it was reopened, the company that had operated
the cinema had gone bankrupt. Currently, ownership of the area is contested. In the meantime, the neighbouring priest has partly taken over
the space by building a ramp and using it to access his own backyard by
car; similarly, an adjoining restaurant has started to use part of the space
as a parking lot for delivery vehicles.[6] The backyard of the Cultural
Centre has thus been subject to various social forces that produce space
(along the lines theorized by Henri Lefebvre [1991]). Politically, the
summer cinema is closely connected to the history of Yugoslavia and
its former leader Josip Broz Tito, a cinephile who was responsible for
the construction of similar cinemas all over the country.[7] The forgotten
summer cinema of Novi Sad is thus a spatial reminder of the tumul-
tuous political history of the city and the various spatial orders it has
been connected to; the very idea of the modern state of Yugoslavia is
entangled with the region's complex history of Ottoman and Habsburg
occupation and the displacements and migrations it entailed, and the
foundation of Novi Sad in 1694 was a direct consequence of the beginnings of Habsburg rule.

Towards a Poetics of Modern Space

The deserted summer cinema was temporarily reanimated in January
2017 when the artists' collective Ephemera used the space for the Novi
Sad edition of the poetry festival "50 Poems for Snow," an international initiative whose aim is the organization of poetry readings on
the first day of snowfall in different cities.[8] The members of the same
collective, which consists mainly of architects as well as architecture
students from Novi Sad, had already turned the outdoor cinema into a
performance space in 2012 for a series of activities in the context of the
39th International Festival of Alternative and New Theatre (INFANT).
The aim of the project, titled "Backyard," was to revitalize the decay-
ing space "in the old core of the city" through "provocative ephemeral
transformations" that included multimedia installations, screenings of
videos about the space by students of architecture, physical transformations of the site and various other events (Zeković and Žugić 2018,
par. 1). In line with the general aims of the Ephemera Collective, these
events were meant to foreground the dynamic and transient nature of
space in its material, medial and experiential dimensions. Their objective was to transform a site that is itself visibly undergoing transformation and, as such, draws attention to the ongoing transformations that
structure the city and space in general. In this sense, "50 Poems for
Snow" was a suitable follow-up event: the site's transformation by the
first snowfall tied in with the collective's emphasis on the ephemerality
of space.

The other two stories, too, have their poetic correlatives. The entanglement of the Arctic with the global spatialities of modernity is foregrounded and performed in a short video entitled "Dolor ártico / Arctic Ache" by the Spanish (UK-based) filmmaker Diego Barraza. "Arctic Ache" (2015) is a video essay on a poem by the Greenlandic poet Jessie Kleemann, read by Claire Wilkinson. The poem gives us what seems to be a series of childhood reminiscences about the Arctic from the position of an exiled poetic speaker: "Moving glaciers," "jolted molecules of seals whales [sic]," "running polar bears and she-wolves / my brothers' games / dog sleds pulling time backwards / melting the hearts of men at war."[9] The image of "dog sleds pulling time backwards" combines spatial progression with the retrogressive movement of memory; in chronotopic intersection, a physical experience of space functions as a metaphor for time. Conversely, the metaphorical "melting" of hearts obliquely gestures towards the very real melting of Arctic ice. Throughout the poem, the profound transformative effects of modernity on the Arctic are subtly hinted at. Towards the end of the text, the poem gestures towards the links between modern capitalism and Arctic resource extraction: "uranium gold aluminium / beaded diamond collars of PU-lammelled couture / designed trains of / excess." Without stating it explicitly, the text here evokes the scramble for Arctic resources that started with Frobisher's delusionary search for gold on Baffin Island and is currently entering a new phase in the context of the potential freeing of mineral resources due to the melting of Arctic ice; the image of "beaded diamond collars" creates a connection between Arctic spaces and the excesses of global consumer culture. This interconnection between the Arctic and the world is poetically achieved by placing seemingly unrelated processes and spaces side by side.

This juxtaposition of different spaces is even more striking when the video is included in the analysis. As we watch it, we experience a disjunction between the words of the poem and the images, which never show us the Arctic but (reversing the logic of the spoken words) only hint at it through a shot of a plush polar bear and (perhaps) the presence of snow. Yet the apparent disconnection between the images and the poem is precisely the point as it makes the viewer think about their relation. Repeated images of trains (one of which is a goods train, possibly transporting coal) and a shot of busy city life point to the processes of industrialization and urbanization that have had a very direct impact on the Arctic – and transformed its landscapes as remembered by the speaker. "Arctic Ache" thus makes the viewers feel the transnational entanglement of the Arctic by spatially unsettling and dislocating them. This is accentuated by the transnational production of the video: the journey of the poem itself from Greenland to the UK, from the page to the screen, itself performs this spatial entanglement. It is telling that the video begins with a shot of a bottle in water, an image of spatial mobility and circulation that can be read as signifying the global interconnectedness of modernity. The sea, in this image, has messages to carry and stories to tell, and the spatial imaginary constructed by "Arctic Ache" is a poetic response to these stories.

The story of Sandy Island, the island that was 'lost' in the 2010s, also resonates with similar stories in the realm of fiction. This is not surprising given that its existence was probably fictitious from the start, and that the history of modern cartography itself is closely intertwined with the history of fictional travel accounts. The recent television series *Lost* (2004–2010), which tells the story of a group of castaways on a mysterious island in the Pacific after a plane crash, can be read as a late modern reappraisal of the shifting cartographies of island and ocean space that had such a profound impact on the early modern imagination (cf. Lestringant 2002; Gillis 2004; Kiening 2006). *Lost* can be (and has been) read in many different ways – the sheer inexhaustibility of the island can make it function as an allegory of almost anything – but it can also be understood as a comment on the Western investment in imaginary island geographies, and the malleability of these geographies on real, imaginary and mental maps. The island of *Lost* is mobile in space and time, defies comprehensive exploration and final understanding and contains so many contradictory traces from numerous spaces and historical events (such as a polar bear and a Beechcraft airplane from Nigeria) that it ceases to make any referential sense; its intertextual links to other island narratives range from More's *Utopia* and William Shakespeare's *The Tempest* to William Golding's *Lord of the Flies* and Steven Spielberg's *Jurassic Park* (cf. Graziadei et al. 2017, 263). Ultimately, one might argue that its very existence is predicated on the countless island imaginations that preceded it. The war on the island between the castaways and the so-called "Others" places the series in a tradition of island narratives that begins with early modernity's narratives of encounters between Europeans and islanders in different parts of the world, but the Others are as little 'of the island' as the castaways. *Lost* is thus part of, but also critically interrogates, a tradition in which Pacific islands have functioned as "ideological testing ground[s]" onto which Western fantasies and anxieties are projected (Howe 2000, 2). Throughout the series, *Lost* disorients its viewers through spatial and temporal shifts, complexities and inconsistencies; flash-forwards, flashbacks and flash-sideways create an ever more complicated filmic time-space rather than a gradual reduction of spatio-temporal uncertainty. In many ways, and despite its conservative ending (cf. Samson 2017, 208–209), *Lost* resists modernity's narratives of exploration, discovery and spatial control; ultimately, one could argue that it is not the castaways who are lost in the series, but the island itself, which, like Sandy Island, reveals itself to be an elusive phantasm created by the geographies of modernity.

Taken together, the three stories are illustrative of the spatial dimensions of modernity. If we take modernity to mean "a determinate rupture with what came before" (Aguiar 2011, 1), then the geographical dimension of this rupture is a transformation of spatial orders and experiences. While the spatial modernities exemplified by the three stories are not identical, there are important overlaps between them. They are contemporary stories that take us back to the beginnings of modern cartography, global interconnectedness, capitalism, colonial exploitation, the so-called 'Westphalian' state system and nationalism, but they also testify to the partial dissolution and interrogation of these modernities. All three are connected to the *longue durée* of space, crystallizing complex spatial histories and alerting us to the continued after-effects of important spatio-temporal ruptures and transformations; all of them connect 'local' spatial stories to larger geopolitical processes of global significance; all of them demand an entangled and multi-layered understanding and analysis of spatiality; all of them ask us to think about space alongside mobility, relationality and difference; finally, and perhaps most importantly for this book, all of them are inseparable from narrative and poetic forms that construct distinctly modern spatial and geographical imaginaries. This, in short, is the aim of *Spatial Modernities*: to unpack specific literary and cultural forms that can be seen as the product of modernity's spatial transformations. The literary and cultural texts examined here, however, should not be seen as passive responses that merely *reflect* the spatial preoccupations of modernity. Rather, they actively negotiate these spatialities in different ways; they generate their own forms of spatial expression to make sense of, manage, expose, critique or contest modern spaces and spatial modernities.

Confronting the Spatial Turn

Recent decades have seen an explosion of spatial theories in the humanities and spatially oriented analyses in literary and cultural studies. Predated by a range of other approaches (such as the theories of Mikhail Bakhtin [1981] and the spatial phenomenologies of Maurice Merleau-Ponty [2002] and Gaston Bachelard [1957]), the foundational works of the so-called 'spatial turn' range from sociology (Henri Lefebvre's [1991] study of the social production of space) and critical geography (Edward Soja's [1989] postmodern take on Marxist and materialist geography) to semiotics (Yuri Lotman's [1990] work on semiospheres and boundaries and the meaning-making processes that structure them), philosophy (the rhizomatic geo-philosophy of Gilles Deleuze and Félix Guattari [1980]) and cultural history (Paul Carter's [1987] revisionist spatial history of the settlement of Australia). Within literary and cultural studies, interdisciplinary approaches to literature and other forms of cultural production have reoriented the discipline towards the spatial since the late twentieth century. J. Hillis Miller's *Topographies* (1995) examines the intersection of language and place in a series of analyses of how "topographical descriptions or terms function in novels, poems, and philosophical texts" (1995, 4); Franco Moretti's *Atlas of the European Novel: 1800* (1998) uses maps to "[place] literary phenomen[a] in [their] specific space" (1998, 7), adding a geographical dimension to the discussion of the relationship between the novel and ideological developments such as the construction of the nation-state; more recently, Bertrand Westphal's geocriticism has advocated a multifocal and multi-layered analysis whose objects are not individual novels and authors but real and imaginary spaces and places, or rather the entanglement of 'real' and 'fictional' geographies; within film studies, Fredric Jameson's *The Geopolitical Aesthetic: Cinema and Space in the World-System* (1992) examines cinema's attempts to allegorically represent the complexities of global space, while Conley's *Cartographic Cinema* (2007) develops film's "implicit relationship with cartography" (2007, 1) through a series of essays on individual works. In theatre studies, Chris Morash and Shaun Richards's *Mapping Irish Theatre: Theories of Space and Place* (2013) draws on the work of Yi-Fu Tuan to explore the poetics of space in drama in general and in Irish theatre specifically.

There are countless other examples. Space, it would seem, is everywhere; recent handbooks like *The Routledge Handbook of Literature and Space* (Tally 2017) and book series like Palgrave's Geocriticism and Spatial Literary Studies (since 2014) testify to the trend. These new approaches announce interdisciplinarity in their very names: composite terms like *literary geography*, *literary cartography*, *cultural cartography* and *spatial humanities* signal a commitment to dialogue between disciplines that is shared by the contributors of this volume. The language of space has become so pervasive in some of these discourses that their very concepts deploy spatial metaphors. Deleuze and Guattari's *A Thousand Plateaus* (1980) relies on the language of stratigraphy; Westphal, who is heavily influenced by Deleuze and Guattari, posits that "[a]ny study of a space must take its geological or archaeological turns" and believes in the power of fiction to "[bring] out all the folds of time relating to a place" (2011, 143); Kenneth White's geopoetics is interested in a "style of writing" that he refers to as "*textonics*" (2006, 19; emphasis in original), a textual form that is analogous to the irregular, chaotic and complex processes that shape physical space. These innovative approaches have added much to the study of literary and cultural spaces, even if their metaphorical deployments of the language of geography, geology and cartography have sometimes led to vagueness and conceptual imprecision.[10]

This collection does not seek to devise a radically new approach to literary and cultural spaces per se, nor does it claim to offer a comprehensive overview of spatial theories and theorists.[11] Its innovation, as stated initially, lies in its broad – though necessarily selective – perspective on the narrative and poetic dimensions of modernity's spatial imaginaries. Its contributors creatively engage in a dialogue between literature, cinema, art history, geography, architecture, cultural semiotics and political science, and they draw on and transform twentieth- and twenty-first-century spatial theory and philosophy to examine the textual forms of different spatial modernities. This approach implies a historical dimension, and several chapters are explicitly or implicitly indebted to Mikhail Bakhtin's notion of the *chronotope* (1981). Using the concept to analyze the specific intersections of time and space (such as the spatialization of time in the chronotope of the road) in a number of literary genres from Greek romance to different forms of the European novel, Bakhtin not only examines how time is spatialized and space is temporalized within those genres, but his approach also implies a *historicity* of spatial form. Like Bakhtin's chronotopic criticism, this collection is thus neither purely historicist nor purely formalist.[12]

Spatial Orders/Dynamic Spatialities

I began this introductory chapter by approaching the idea of spatial modernity through three stories. In the following, I will turn to a number of theorists and philosophers whose work engages with modernity through space in order to conceptualize the notion of spatial modernity in a more systematic fashion. The work of Doreen Massey is a good starting point. For Massey, the history of Western thought is characterized by a long-standing bias that privileges time over space as the more 'living' dimension. In this philosophical tradition, exemplified for instance by the thought of Henri Bergson (2002), dividing up time into segments and points is viewed as taking the life out of time by treating it like space (this is why, for Bergson, Zeno's paradoxes are flawed: the tortoise can only catch up with Achilles if the dynamic flow of time is interrupted and time is, impossibly, divided). Without denying the life of time, Massey notes a tacit assumption at work in this view, namely the treatment of space as a priori static, rigid and fixed:

> this is the idea that there is an association between the spatial and the fixation of meaning. Representation – indeed conceptualisation – has been conceived of as spatialisation. [...] Of course, the argument is usually [...] that through representation we spatialise time. It is space which is said to thereby tame the temporal.
>
> (2005, 20)

For Massey, this frequently unquestioned assumption in turn tames the spatial and "takes the life out of space" (2005, 71), precluding a more adequate – if more challenging – understanding of space as dynamic, relational and intersectional:

> On the road map you won't drive off the edge of your known world. In space as I want to imagine it, you just might. […] For such a space entails the unexpected. The specifically spatial within time-space is produced by that – sometimes happenstance, sometimes not – arrangement-in-relation-to-each-other that is the result of there being a multiplicity of trajectories.
>
> (2005, 111)

For Massey, this taming of space takes on special significance in Western modernity. In a chapter entitled "Spatialising the History of Modernity" (2005, 62–71), Massey argues that the construction of a (colonial) geography of power and knowledge, whose aim was the production of Western modernity as the natural destiny of the globe, went hand in hand with a view of space as territorial, bounded and divided (2005, 64–65). Modernity, for Massey, depended on the spatial imaginary of the nation-state and bounded societies tied to specific places and regions. The modern story of space is thus

> a story about space which in its period of hegemony not only legit-imised a whole imperialist era of territorialisation but which also, in a much deeper sense, was a way of taming the spatial. This is a representation *of* space, a particular form of ordering and organis-ing space which refused (refuses) to acknowledge its multiplicities, its fractures and its dynamism.
>
> (2005, 65; emphasis in original)

In this view, modernity's drive towards spatial ordering and territorial control entailed a freezing of the very *concept* of space.

Massey is not alone in associating modernity with the production of rigid spatial orders and a view of space as abstract and bounded. For Michel de Certeau, this is the space of modern cartography, which grad-ually rendered the dynamics of space invisible:

> Between the fifteenth and the seventeenth centuries, the map be-came more autonomous. No doubt the proliferation of the 'narra-tive' figures that have long been its stock-in-trade (ships, animals, and characters of all kinds) still had the function of indicating the operations – travelling, military, architectural – that make possible the fabrication of a geographical plan.
>
> (1984, 121)

Early modern cartography gradually eliminated movement from space:

> Thus the sailing ship painted on the sea indicated the maritime ex-
> pedition that made it possible to represent the coastlines. It is equiv-
> alent to a describer of the 'tour' type. But the map gradually wins
> out over these figures; it colonizes space; it eliminates little by little
> the pictural figurations of the practices that produce it.
>
> (1984, 121)

Tim Ingold takes a similar stance. For him, cartography is one of the
fields in which modernity has domesticated the life of lines; other examples include the replacement of the art of the medieval scribe with the
mechanics of the printing press and the substitution of modern transportation for practices of wayfaring:

> Once the trace of a continuous gesture, the line has been fragmented –
> under the sway of modernity – into a succession of points or dots. This
> fragmentation [...] has taken place in the related fields of travel, where
> wayfaring is replaced by destination-oriented transport, mapping,
> where the drawn sketch is replaced by the route-plan, and textuality,
> where storytelling is replaced by the pre-composed plot.
>
> (2007, 75)

In Ingold's view, then, modernity is marked by the imposition of mechani-
cal networks, a static geometrical order consisting of straight lines connect-
ing dots. This order reaches its epitome with the advent of steam-powered
machines. The assembly line and the railway are two prominent examples;
Wolfgang Schivelbusch (1986) offers a powerful account of how the machine ensemble of the railroad regularized both time and space in the nineteenth century, and how the railway network, gravitating around fixed
points and effacing the space in between, extended from the railroad itself
to the structure of everyday life. For Franco Moretti, early detective fiction's reliance on a modern fantasy of organized and transparent space
that leaves no room for deviant (i.e., individualized) behaviour is tied to
this network: "All Holmes's investigations are accompanied and supported
by the new and perfect mechanisms of transportation and communication.
Carriages, trains, letters, telegrams, in Conan Doyle's world, are all crucial
and *always* live up to expectations" (1990, 247; emphasis in original).

These theorists focus on different time spans in their spatial analyses
of modernity. The advent of steam power and mechanization certainly
inaugurated a new phase of modernity, but the early modern period is a
useful starting point for thinking about the spatial transformations in the
centuries that followed. For Zygmunt Bauman, the modern impulse to fix
and control space is announced in the thought of René Descartes in the
seventeenth century: "At the threshold of the modern conquest of space

Descartes, looking forward, identified existence with spatiality, defining whatever exists materially as *res extensa*" (2000, 113). In fact, Bauman argues that the spatial conquests that started in early modernity and were accelerated by the machines of high modernity could serve as one of many valid starting points for the modern period: "Modernity was born under the stars of acceleration and land conquest [...]. In this chase, spatial expansion was the name of the game and space was the stake; space was value, time was the tool" (2000, 112–113). Thinking about modernity in spatial terms, in other words, cannot be disentangled from engaging with capitalist as well as colonialist and imperialist ideologies. Edward Said does the latter in his analysis of the geographies of empire in *Culture and Imperialism* (1993), as does Mary Louise Pratt in her study of the visual appropriation of space by "imperial eyes" (2008). Pacific scholar Epeli Hau'ofa has critiqued the spatial imagination of lines and surfaces underlying colonial ideologies: "[...] it was continental men, Europeans and Americans, who drew imaginary lines across the sea, making the colonial boundaries that, for the first time, confined ocean peoples to tiny spaces" (1994, 7). Critiquing the static spatial orders brought to the Pacific by Western powers, Hau'ofa proposes instead an oceanic view of an interconnected "sea of islands," a "perspective in which things are seen in the totality of their relationships" (1994, 7) that resonates with Édouard Glissant's (2007) relational philosophy of space in the Caribbean context. These critics offer powerful alternatives to the rigid spatial models of Western modernity.

But the conquest and taming of space is not the only story to be told about modernity. A second, equally prevalent story connects modernity to mobility. This is the aspect of modernity that Tim Cresswell studies so admirably in *On the Move: Mobility in the Modern Western World*. For Cresswell, the pervasive experience and positive valuation of mobility is a defining feature of Western modernity and distinguishes it from medieval Europe, where mobility had a very different status (2006, 9–21). Conley's *The Self-Made Map: Cartographic Writing in Early Modern France* studies the interplay of cartography and writing in the construction of early modern subjectivities, but cartography does not equal the freezing of space in his account. On the contrary, he argues that these cartographic writings "are fictions with mobile and ever expanding possibilities" that perform "a process of discovery that *maps its movement as it goes*" (1996, 5; emphasis in original). Thus, for instance, the early modern *isolarii* are sites of spatial experimentation that produce a "sense of a world that is in congress, multiplication, and dispersion" (1996, 187) even while they (impossibly) aspire to represent the world in its totality. For Daniel Cosgrove, too, these island books "reflected a nonhierarchical conception of the world" (2001, 99). Focusing on a later period, Eric Bulson's *Novels, Maps, Modernity: The Spatial Imagination, 1850–2000* draws on Georg Lukács's discussion of the novel as an expression of modernity's "transcendental homelessness" to think about cartography in terms of dislocation and disorientation as much as order and orientation: "This oriented disorientation of readers [...] is precisely where we see the novel responding to many of the processes we identify more general [sic] with modernization and modernity (empire, urbanization, and technology)" (2007, 2). Andrew Thacker's *Moving through Modernity: Space and Geography in Modernism* (2003) reorients the study of literary modernism towards space and examines the perspectives on modernity as an experience of multiple movements articulated in texts by E. M. Forster, James Joyce, Virginia Woolf and others. While discussions of modernity's preoccupation with movement and a flux of experiences and encounters often focus on high modernity and the experience of the city – Walter Benjamin's (1982) and Georg Simmel's (2006) responses to Baudelaire's *flâneur* as a paradigmatically modern figure are cases in point – in many ways the global circulation of people, goods and ideas that marks high and late modernity was inaugurated by early modernity's voyages of discovery and the concurrent confrontations with alterity.

Thinking about spatial modernities, then, also means considering the relationships between contradictory spatialities; it means responding to what Cresswell refers to as "the tension between a spatialized ordering principle seen by many to be central to modernity, and a sense of fluidity and mobility emphasized by others" (2006, 16). Yet the contradiction is only an apparent one. For one thing, mobility itself is not always dynamic: as Cresswell points out, mobility "became increasingly regulated and regular" and "marked by timetables and mechanization" in high modernity (2006, 10). Further, the mobility of some (citizens, tourists, men, colonizers) depended (and continues to depend) on the immobility of others (aliens, the service industry, women, the colonized) (Cresswell 2006, 15). And finally, static and dynamic spatialities respond to and generate each other as often as not. The spatial theorists of modernity are aware of this, even if they tend to emphasize one aspect over the other. Thus, Conley argues that cartography offered the subject an "*illusion* of autonomy and self-possession" (1996, 2; emphasis added), a fiction of control and totality that rested on a foundation of dispersal and spatial uncertainty. For de Certeau (1984), the order of the map is a fiction that is challenged from below by the spatial practices of individuals, who reshape space through their movements and actions. Ingold, too, while lamenting what he considers modernity's march towards abstract geometries and rigid structures, concludes (citing de Certeau) by recognizing that "the structures that confine, channel and contain are not immutable" (2007, 102–103), but continually subverted by the movements of both human and non-human actors.

Massey offers a particularly insightful account of these spatial contradictions. For her, modernity's taming of the spatial is a "suppression of the real challenges of space" (2005, 70). Implicit in her argument is the suggestion that the static spatial imaginaries of modernity can be seen as a compensatory response to an experience of space as mobile and dynamic, containing the threats of the latter. The modern experience of difference and cultural contact was met by a refusal "to acknowledge [the] multiplicities, [...] fractures and [...] dynamism [of space]" (2005, 65). Drawing on the work of Eric Wolf and Johannes Fabian, Massey argues that anthropological visions of a pre-modern past of place-bound and isolated societies are fantasies that are belied by a historical reality of cultural contact and exchange (2005, 67–70). Similarly, the retreat into "nationalisms and parochialisms and localisms of all sorts" in contemporary responses to anxieties around globalization should be read as a nostalgia that "mourn[s] the loss of the old spatial coherences" but actually "[looks] backwards to a past that never was" (2005, 65). And yet, for Massey, the "increasing global contacts and flows" (2005, 65) of modernity could also imply "a different view of space," one that decentres "the European trajectory" and

> [moves] away from that imagination of space as a continuous surface that the coloniser, as the only active agent, crosses to find the to-be-colonised simply 'there'. This would be space not as a smooth surface but as the sphere of coexistence of a multiplicity of trajectories.
>
> (2005, 63)

I would like to close this section by briefly reflecting on the distinctive spatialities of late modernity as theorized by a number of philosophers whose positions help us to further unpack the complex relationships between uniform and dynamic spatialities that Massey addresses. Some of these accounts are marked by a sense of loss. Thus, Marc Augé's hypothesis is that what he calls *supermodernity* erodes places and instead "produces non-places, meaning spaces which are not themselves anthropological places" (1995, 78); these non-places are anonymous spaces of transit that people do not dwell in but pass through, such as shopping malls and airports. Drawing on Claude Lévi-Strauss and Augé, Bauman in *Liquid Modernity* (2000) offers a typology of public spaces in late capitalism. These spaces (such as the "temples of consumption" and spaces that architecturally discourage people from spending time in them, like La Défense in Paris) are designed to create a culture of uniformity and minimize contact with strangers. Where Augé's argument implies a certain nostalgia for place, however, Bauman, not unlike Massey, views these spatial structures as compensatory mechanisms to ward off the threat of too much exposure to alterity:

> Efforts to keep 'the other', the different, the strange and the foreign at a distance, the decision to preclude the need for communication, negotiation and mutual commitment, is not the only conceivable, but the expectable response to the existential uncertainty rooted in the new fragility of fluidity of social bonds.
>
> (2000, 108)

For Bauman, late modernity is generally characterized by liquidity and lightness. If "heavy modernity" was marked by place-bound heavy machinery and the drive to occupy and conquer more and more space (the era of "hardware" where size mattered), late capitalism is marked by spatial flexibility and transience, delocalization, insubstantiality and instantaneity (the era of "software" and digital networks): "In 'liquid' modernity, it is the most elusive, those free to move without notice, who rule" (2000, 120).

Yet Bauman does not see liquid modernity as an absolute break with earlier forms of modernity. Rather, he views it as a continuation and transformation of processes that characterize modernity in general. Capitalism's ideology of free flow and open exchange has its roots in the emergence of global trade networks in early modernity; if, as Bauman implies, liquidity and fluidity are both structuring principles of late capitalism and sources of social anxiety, this "existential uncertainty" is prefigured by the spatial shifts and cultural dislocations of the early modern period (cf. Mentz 2015). Michel Serres's reflections in *Atlas* (1994) on the role of cartography in the age of simultaneity, virtual reality and communication networks, where geographical distance ceases to be meaningful in many contexts, address the problem of orientation in the complexity of contemporary global culture, but the analyses of Conley, Lestringant, Cosgrove, Mentz and others have shown that early modernity, too, was marked by a profound sense of disorientation. Focusing on the early *and* late stages of modernity can therefore draw our attention to the fragility and contingency of modernity's supposedly stable spatial orders and, at least in some cases, serve to unmask them as (compensatory) fictions. When Theodor W. Adorno discusses the disintegration of subjectivity in Beethoven's late works through a spatial metaphor that evokes the imagery of T. S. Eliot's *The Waste Land* ("Of the works themselves it leaves only fragments behind, and communicates itself [...] only through the blank spaces from which it has disengaged itself" [Adorno 2002, 566]), he simultaneously comments, as Said puts it, on the "fallen, unredeemed reality" of modernity (2006, 18). There are different 'early' and 'late' phases of modernity (Adorno's late modernity is very different from Bauman's), and like modernity itself, they are better understood as a plurality of processes and perspectives rather than a clearly demarcated period, but focusing on different 'earlinesses' and 'latenesses' sheds light on the tensions and contradictions of modernity's spatial imaginaries.

Travelling Narratives, Mobile Texts

Like the three stories introduced initially, the spatial imaginaries analyzed by the contributors of *Spatial Modernities* testify to the *longue durée* of space, the multiplicity of spatial trajectories and the contradictory spatialities in different manifestations of modernity. The different chapters examine spatiality through contemporary culture and/or cast a retrospective look at a variety of modern discourses and imaginaries that have shaped our current spatial and geographical sensibilities, going back to early modernity and its cartographic imaginaries. In the early twenty-first century, we are still grappling with the spatial effects of 'early' and 'high' modern developments; after the decolonization of Pacific and Caribbean islands and other colonial spaces, as well as the late-twentieth-century (and ongoing) reshuffling of geography in Europe, the contemporary crises revolving around political boundaries and geopolitical orders in many parts of the world have intensified spatial anxieties. They call for a sustained analysis of individual perceptions, cultural constructions and political implications of spatial processes and movements.

The contributors of this book focus both on the spatial orders of modernity and on the various dynamic processes that have shaped our engagement with modern space. They do so through the analysis of literary and cultural texts, which, as outlined above, they view as active responses to these spatial modernities. Accordingly, the chapters do not only engage with cartographies, boundaries, movements, transfers, transports and crossings as represented *within* texts, but are also, with varying emphasis, attentive to the ways in which these texts produce their own spaces, and how they perform and generate movement and mobility. It is in this sense that the narratives examined here are not just narratives about travel, displacement and spatial relations, but also *travelling narratives* that act out the very spatial processes they engage with. In doing so, they crystallize, reinforce, interrogate, expose, critique or complicate the geographical and spatial imaginaries of modernity through their own narrative and poetic form.

Spatial Modernities is divided into five parts. Part I, "Mapping Modernity," examines the cartographic narratives and imaginaries of modernity. Robert T. Tally Jr.'s opening chapter ("In the Suburbs of Amaurotum: Spatiality, Fantasy, Modernity") traces an arc from early modern to contemporary cartographies by providing a theoretical discussion of how the intersection of mapping and fantasy in Sir Thomas More's *Utopia* speaks to (late) modern struggles to map the world system. As Tally argues, the seemingly rational cartographic order of modernity in fact rests on foundations that are partly fantastic. In Chapter 2 ("Mapping Utopia"), Christina Ljungberg stays with More's influential text, excavating its experimental cartographies through a careful study of the 1516 and 1518 frontispiece maps. For Ljungberg, the content of More's utopian society is less important than the structure in which it is presented; in her reading of the text and the maps, cartography does not create closed spatial orders but responds to the early modern experience of cultural difference by relativizing positions and generating fresh thought. Jean-Paul Forster's contribution ("Of the Novelty of Bird's-Eye Views in Eighteenth-Century Travelling Narratives") discusses the intersection of scientific and imaginative gazes in the mapping of unfamiliar and familiar territories in novels by Daniel Defoe, Jonathan Swift and Tobias Smollett. As Forster shows, the descriptions of bird's-eye views in these novels testify to the mathematization of space in the eighteenth century, resonating with (and, in the case of Swift, mocking) emerging cartographic practices. In the final chapter of Part I, "Satellite Vision and Geographical Imagination," David Shim takes the well-known nocturnal satellite images of the Korean peninsula as a case study to address the geopolitical implications of entanglement of ideology, remote sensing and visual imagination. Shim's analysis of the ideological framing of darkness in these images offers new perspectives on the politics of contemporary mapping technologies and their constructions of alterity.

It is fitting that three of the four chapters of Part I discuss islands, which have a special place in the Western spatial imagination and have exerted a fascination on cartographers and writers of fiction alike. Accordingly, Part II, "Island Spaces," examines the West's preoccupation with these landforms in three chapters that explicitly focus on the poetics of island space in texts ranging from Defoe's *Robinson Crusoe* to contemporary island fiction. In Chapter 5 ("Crossing the Sand: The Arrival on the Desert Island"), Barney Samson examines the ideological import of the castaways' initial movements on the islands in *Robinson Crusoe* and *Lord of the Flies*. His careful analysis of the poetics of crossing, traversing and exploring distinguishes between static (or closed) and dynamic (or open) forms of movement, and links them to different perspectives on modernity that either endorse or challenge its spatial orders. Britta Hartmann's contribution ("Two Centuries of Spatial 'Island' Assumptions: *The Swiss Family Robinson* and the *Robinson Crusoe* Legacy") interrogates the spatial assumptions in scholarly and fictional responses to Johann David Wyss's *The Swiss Family Robinson*. As she demonstrates, these responses follow the characters of the novel in assuming – against sensory evidence – that they are shipwrecked on an island. For Hartmann, these assumptions are evidence of the ongoing effects of nineteenth-century imperialism in the twentieth and twenty-first centuries. Chapter 7 by Johannes Riquet ("Island Stills and Island Movements: Un/freezing the Island in 1920s and 1930s Hollywood Cinema") examines static island representations in the credit sequences of a number of island films, reading them in relation to modern visual regimes and early anthropological fantasies. Focusing on W. S. Van Dyke's *White Shadows in the South Seas* (1928), he argues that the spatial freezing of the island is ultimately undone by various forms of movement, including those generated by the cinematic apparatus itself.

The two chapters of Part III, "Shorelines/Borderlines," further explore the ambivalence of boundaries evident in Part II's discussion of island narratives, turning to the imaginative relevance of the sea(shore) in the context of the shifting geopolitical orders of modernity. Both chapters are attentive to the role of the sea as a liminal space with variable associations. In Chapter 8 ("Words and Images of Flight: Representations of the Seashore in the Texts about the Overseas Flight of Estonians during the Autumn of 1944"), Maarja Ojamaa offers a semiotic analysis of the changing significations of the seashore in the Estonian cultural imaginary occasioned by the Second World War. Examining a novel, a painting and a film, she sheds light on the mediation of a historical experience that invested the seashore, previously linked to openness and cultural exchange, with a poetics of profound loss. Chapter 9 by Ina Habermann ("The Literary Channel: Identity and Liminal Space in Island Fictions") focuses on the English Channel as an Anglo-French in-between space in G. B. Edwards's *The Book of Ebenezer Le Page* and Julian Barnes's *England, England*. Her geocritical study demonstrates that these two novels mobilize the different associations of their respective settings – Guernsey and the Isle of Wight – to construct different cultural topographies that articulate different forms of liminality and in-betweenness.

The remaining chapters of the book shift the emphasis to the dynamics of textual space itself. All of them are guided by a phenomenological or experiential perspective; the spatialities they examine are subjective and linked to the processes of writing and reading (as well as filming and viewing). The two chapters of Part IV, "Modernity on the Move," deal with texts that explore modernity's mobilities through the movement of writing itself. Tom Conley's discussion of Montaigne's essay "De la vanité" as a paradigmatically modern travelling narrative in Chapter 10 ("Montaigne: Travel and Travail") argues that the essay substitutes the transports effected by writing for the hardships (or *travail*) of physical travel. He shows how Montaigne's text engages motion and displacement through the spatio-temporal shifts and rifts of its very form as well as through the psychic energies produced by the textual mapping and interweaving of different spatial memories. Caroline Rabourdin's discussion of a fictional train journey ("The Expanding Space of the Train Carriage: A Phenomenological Reading of Michel Butor's *La Modification*") traces the capacity of literary texts to move between different spatialities, sometimes within a single sentence. She demonstrates that Butor's text explores the mobility of the train through the body of the reader, effecting a number of shifts – from the landscape to the compartment and from the space of the train to the space of reading.

The last two chapters of the book form Part V, "Late Modernity and the Spatialized Self." They turn to the role of spatiality in contemporary autobiographic writing and film. In Chapter 12 ("The Reader, the Writer, the Text: Traversing Spaces in Frank McCourt's *Angela's*

Ashes"), Elizabeth Kollmann engages with the affective transfer of spatiality through texts by discussing how the experience of exile and spatial dislocation travels from the narrator to the reader in McCourt's memoir. She argues that the vehement reactions unleashed by the publication of the book should be read as evidence of the readers' own sense of dislocation created by the hybrid space of the text. The final chapter of the book by Deirdre Russell ("Narrative, Space and Autobiographical Film in the Digital Age: An Analysis of *The Beaches of Agnès* [2008]") asks to what extent the spatial forms characteristic of new media – such as the hypertext and the database – challenge narrative conceptions of identity. Using an autobiographical film by Agnès Varda as her case study, she ultimately suggests that narrativity is transformed (rather than abolished) by the interaction with digital spatiality. The book thus aptly ends with a discussion of the ongoing spatial transformations of the narratives that surround us. We may not live in an "epoch of space," but certainly in a time where space takes ever new turns.

Notes

1 The Sandy Island story was first reported in *The Sydney Morning Herald* (Robertson 2012). For some journalistic responses to the debate, among many others, see Harding (2012) and Pearlman (2012).
2 A video of the interview can be found on the website of *The Guardian* at www. theguardian.com/science/video/2012/nov/23/pacific-sandy-island-video.
3 Photo of original (personal communication from Melanie Trüssel, November 2, 2016). My translation.
4 I am indebted to Helmi Sigg for sharing the details of the expedition and the subsequent enquiries with me.
5 Personal communication, February 22, 2017. I am grateful to Piitaaraq Brandt for filling me in on the details of the 1997 expedition and his lifelong project of circling the coast of Greenland.
6 Miljana Zeković and Višnja Žugić, personal communication, October 21 and 23, 2017.
7 Mila Turajlic's documentary film *Cinema Komunisto* (2010) sheds light on the role of cinema in Tito's Yugoslavia and on Tito's personal love for the screen, suggesting that Yugoslavia itself might be viewed as a cinematic illusion.
8 The announcement for the Novi Sad event in January 2017 can be found at www.facebook.com/pg/ephemeracollective/photos/?tab=album&album_id=1736393883053354; details about the poetry festival are available at http://50poemsforsnow.tumblr.com/.
9 The citations refer to an online version of Kleemann's poem at forfatternesk limaaksjon.no/moving glaciers/.
10 Thus, Tania Rossetto (2014) calls for a more precise study of the links between literature and cartography.
11 An excellent overview of key theorists of spatiality is provided in *Thinking Space* (2000), edited by Mike Crang and Nigel Thrift.
12 A purely historical approach to space is offered in John R. Gillis's cultural histories of island and ocean space (2004, 2012). Conversely, Marie-Laure Ryan, Kenneth Foote and Maoz Azaryahu's spatial narratology in *Narrating Space/Spatializing Narrative: Where Narrative Theory and Geography Meet*

(2016) provides a primarily formalist approach to spatiality. For another recent example of a narratological approach to literary space, see Elana Gomel's *Narrative Space and Time: Representing Impossible Topologies in Literature* (2014).

References

Abrams, J. J., Jeffrey Lieber, and Damon Lindelof, creators. *Lost*. 2004–2010. Burbank: Buena Vista, 2005–2010. DVD.

Adorno, Theodor W. 2002. "Late Style in Beethoven." In *Essays on Music*, edited by Richard Leppert and translated by Susan H. Gillespie, 564–568. Berkeley: University of California Press.

Aguiar, Marian. 2011. *Tracking Modernity: India's Railway and the Culture of Mobility*. Minneapolis: University of Minnesota Press.

Andersen, Jette. 2010. "Grønlandseventyreren Peter Brandt på ny tur." Nuuk: Kalaallit Nunaata Radioa (website). August 17, 2010. knr.gl/kl/node/114526.

Augé, Marc. 1995. *Non-Places: Introduction to an Anthropology of Supermodernity*. Translated by John Howe. London: Verso.

Bachelard, Gaston. 1957. *La poétique de l'espace*. Paris: Quadrige.

Bakhtin, Mikhail M. (1937) 1981. "Forms of Time and of the Chronotope in the Novel." In *The Dialogic Imagination*, translated by Caryl Emerson and Michael Holquist, 84–258. Austin: University of Texas Press.

Baudelaire, Charles. 1955. *The Painter of Modern Life and Other Essays*. Edited and translated by Jonathan Mayne. London: Phaidon.

Barraza, Diego and Jessie Kleemann. February 10, 2015. "Dolor ártico / Arctic Ache." *Moving Poems*. http://movingpoems.com/2015/02/poem-no-6-by-jessie-kleemann/.

Bauman, Zygmunt. 2000. *Liquid Modernity*. Cambridge: Polity.

Benjamin, Walter. 1982. *Das Passagen-Werk*. Edited by Rolf Tiedemann. Two volumes. Frankfurt am Main: Suhrkamp.

Bergson, Henri. 2002. "The Perception of Change." In *Henri Bergson: Key Writings*, edited by John Mullarkey and Keith Ansell Pearson, 303–326. London: Bloomsbury.

Bulson, Eric. 2007. *Novels, Maps, Modernity: The Spatial Imagination, 1850–2000*. New York: Routledge.

Carter, Paul. 1987. *The Road to Botany Bay: An Essay in Spatial History*. London: Faber and Faber.

Crang, Mike, and Nigel Thrift, eds. 2000. *Thinking Space*. London: Routledge.

Cresswell, Tim. 2006. *On the Move: Mobility in the Modern Western World*. New York: Routledge.

Cosgrove, Denis. 2001. *Apollo's Eye: A Cartographic Genealogy of the Earth in the Western Imagination*. Baltimore: Johns Hopkins University Press.

Conley, Tom. 1996. *The Self-Made Map: Cartographic Writing in Early Modern France*. Minneapolis: The University of Minnesota Press.

———. 2007. *Cartographic Cinema*. Minneapolis: University of Minnesota Press.

Craciun, Adriana. 2009. "The Scramble for the Arctic." *Interventions* 11 (1): 103–114.

de Certeau, Michel. 1984. *The Practice of Everyday Life*. Translated by Steven Randall. Berkeley: University of California Press.

Deleuze, Gilles and Félix Guattari. 1980. *A Thousand Plateaus: Capitalism and Schizophrenia*. Translated by Brian Massumi. London: Continuum.

Dodds, Klaus, and Mark Nuttall. 2016. *The Scramble for the Poles: The Geopolitics of the Arctic and Antarctic*. Cambridge: Polity.

Doel, Ronald E., Kristine C. Harper, and Matthias Heymann, eds. 2016. *Exploring Greenland: Cold War Science and Technology on Ice*. New York: Palgrave.

Foucault, Michel. (1967) 1986. "Of Other Spaces." Translated by Jay Miskowiec. *Diacritics* 16 (1): 22–27.

Fuson, Robert H. 1995. *Legendary Islands of the Ocean Sea*. Sarasota: Pineapple Press.

Gomel, Elana. 2014. *Narrative Space and Time: Representing Impossible Topologies in Literature*. New York: Routledge.

Gillis, John R. 2004. *Islands of the Mind: How the Human Imagination Created the Atlantic World*. New York: Palgrave Macmillan.

———. 2012. *The Human Shore: Seacoasts in History*. Chicago: University of Chicago Press.

Glissant, Édouard. 2007. *Poetics of Relation*. Translated by Betsy Wing. Ann Arbor: University of Michigan Press.

Graziadei, Daniel, Britta Hartmann, Ian Kinane, Johannes Riquet, and Barney Samson. 2017. "Island Metapoetics and Beyond: Introducing Island Poetics, Part II." *Island Studies Journal* 12 (2): 253–266.

Harding, Luke. 2012. "The Pacific Island that Never Was." *The Guardian* (international edition). November 22, 2012. www.theguardian.com/world/2012/nov/22/sandy-island-missing-google-earth.

Hauʻofa, Epeli. 1994. "Our Sea of Islands." *The Contemporary Pacific* 6 (1): 147–161.

Higgins, Anthony K. 2010. "Exploration History and Place Names of Northern East Greenland." *Geological Survey of Denmark and Greenland Bulletin* 21: 1–10.

Howe, K. R. 2000. *Nature, Culture, and History: The "Knowing" of Oceania*. Honolulu: University of Hawaiʻi Press.

Ingold, Tim. 2007. *Lines: A Brief History*. London: Routledge.

Jameson, Fredric. 1992. *The Geopolitical Aesthetic: Cinema and Space in the World System*. Bloomington: Indiana University Press.

Kiening, Christian. 2006. *Das wilde Subjekt. Kleine Poetik der Neuen Welt*. Göttingen: Vandenhoeck & Ruprecht.

Lefebvre, Henri. 1991. *The Production of Space*. Translated by Donald Nicholson-Smith. Malden: Blackwell.

Lestringant, Frank. 2002. *Le livre des îles*. Genève: Librairie Droz.

Lotman, Yuri M. 1990. *Universe of the Mind: A Semiotic Theory of Culture*. Translated by Ann Shukman. London: I. B. Tauris.

Marsden, Philip. 2015. "Deleted Islands." *1843* (magazine), *The Economist*. September/October, 2015. www.1843magazine.com/places/cartophilia/deleted-islands.

Massey, Doreen. 2005. *For Space*. London: SAGE.

Mentz, Steve. 2015. *Shipwreck Modernity: Ecologies of Globalization, 1550–1719*. Minneapolis: University of Minnesota Press.

Merleau-Ponty, Maurice. (1945) 2002. *Phenomenology of Perception*. Translated by Colin Smith. London and New York: Routledge.

Mikkelsen, Ejnar. 1933. *Report on the Expedition by Ejnar Mikkelsen. Meddelelser om Grønland* 104 (1).

Miller, J. Hillis. 1995. *Topographies*. Stanford: Stanford University Press.

Morash, Chris and Shaun Richards. 2013. *Mapping Irish Theatre: Theories of Space and Place*. Cambridge: Cambridge University Press.

Moretti, Franco. 1990. "Clues." In *Popular Fiction: Technology, Ideology, Production, Reading*, edited by Tony Bennett, 238–251. London: Routledge.

———. 1998. *Atlas of the European Novel, 1800–1900*. London: Verso.

Marie-Laure, Ryan, Kenneth Foote, and Maoz Azaryahu. 2016. *Narrating Space/Spatializing Narrative: Where Narrative Theory and Geography Meet*. Columbus: Ohio State University Press.

Pearlman, Jonathan. 2012. "Missing Pacific Island Riddle 'Solved.'" *The Telegraph*. December 2, 2012. www.telegraph.co.uk/news/worldnews/australia andthepacific /9718177/Missing-Pacific-island-riddle-solved.html.

"Peter Brandt, tusagassiortoq." *Atuagagdliutit/Grønlandsposten* 130 (54, May 12, 1990): 2.

Pratt, Mary Louise. 2008. *Imperial Eyes: Travel Writing and Transculturation*. Second edition. New York: Routledge.

Ries, Christopher Jacob. 2016. "Uncommon Grounds: Danish and American Perspectives on Greenland's Geology (1946–1960)." In *Exploring Greenland: Cold War Science and Technology on Ice*, edited by Ronald E. Doel, Kristine C. Harper, and Matthias Heymann, 119–142. New York: Palgrave.

Robertson, James. 2002. "Where Did It Go? Scientists 'Undiscover' Pacific Island." *The Sydney Morning Herald*. November 22, 2012. www.smh. com.au/technology/technology-news/where-did-it-go-scientists-undiscover-pacific-island-20121122-29ro4.html.

Rossetto, Tania. 2014. "Theorizing Maps with Literature." *Progress in Human Geography* 38 (4): 513–530.

Said, Edward. 1993. *Culture and Imperialism*. New York: Knopf.

———. 2006. *On Late Style: Music and Literature against the Grain*. New York: Pantheon.

Samson, Barney. 2017. *Islands in the (Main)stream: Post-War Popular Representations of the Desert Island*. Unpublished doctoral dissertation. Colchester: University of Essex.

Schivelbusch, Wolfgang. 1986. *The Railway Journey: The Industrialization of Time and Space in the 19th Century*. Leamington Spa: Berg.

Serres, Michel. 1994. *Atlas*. Paris: Julliard.

Seton, Maria et al. 2013. "Obituary: Sandy Island, 1876–2012." *Eos* 94 (15): 141–142.

Simmel, Georg. 2006. *Die Großstädte und das Geistesleben*. Frankfurt am Main: Suhrkamp.

Soja, Edward W. 1989. *Postmodern Geographies: The Reassertion of Space in Critical Social Theory*. London: Verso.

Stommel, Henry M. 1984. *Lost Islands: The Story of Islands that Have Vanished from Nautical Charts*. Vancouver: University of British Columbia Press.

Tally, Robert T. Jr. 2017. *The Routledge Handbook of Literature and Space*. London: Routledge.

Thacker, Andrew. 2003. *Moving through Modernity: Space and Geography in Modernism*. Manchester: Manchester University Press.

Turajlic, Mila, dir. *Cinema Komunisto*. 2010. San Francisco: Kanopy Streaming, 2015. E-video.

Westphal, Bertrand. 2011. *Geocriticism: Real and Fictional Spaces*. Translated by Robert T. Tally Jr. New York: Palgrave Macmillan.

White, Kenneth. 2006. *On the Atlantic Edge: A Geopoetics Project*. Dingwall: Sandstone Press.

Zeković, Miljana and Višnja Žugić. 2018. "Backyard." SCEN: Centre for Scene Design, Architecture and Technology (website). www.scen.uns.ac.rs/eng/?page_id=1871.

Part I
Mapping Modernity

1 In the Suburbs of Amaurotum
Fantasy, Utopia and Literary Cartography[*]

Robert T. Tally Jr.

Utopiae Insulae Figura, an illustration included in the original 1516 publication of Thomas More's *Utopia*, depicts the form of More's fanciful but ideal nation-state. In this woodcut, Utopia's capital city, Amaurotum, is placed in a suitably central position, but even more prominent in the foregrounding is a ship at anchor, presumably the one that brought Raphael Hythlodaeus to the island. A sailor stands on the deck and appears to be gazing off at the Utopian landscape, and one could argue that this figure represents the position of More's own readers, who vicariously take part in a travel narrative, exploring the spaces of this strange country.[1] It is a peculiarly modern image, and the careful ordering of its elements reflects the rational order of Utopian society, which in turn discloses a perhaps unconscious desire for order, symmetry and reason in early modern European societies as well. The mere historical and geographical accident of Hythlodaeus's discovery of Utopia is duly compensated for in the methodical, logical and rational organization of the society. More's *Utopia* supplies a fantastic vision of how a society can reorganize itself, spatially and socially, as a thoroughly modern state.

Utopia, as well as the genre it helped to establish and the mode of thought it exemplifies and popularizes, represents a critical node at which conceptions of fantasy, spatiality and modernity intersect. In this vision of the utopian place (or *no-place*),[2] More enacts a reorganization of social spaces that anticipates the changing spatiality of the Baroque epoch and the project of Enlightenment rationality, thus forming a certain image of modern social organization. If, as Phillip E. Wegner has convincingly argued in *Imaginary Communities* (2002), utopia is inextricably tied to the spatial histories of modernity, then More's literary cartography of the ideal *insula* might be seen as a prototype for the imaginary maps of modern societies. These are fundamentally fantastic, at least as much as the imaginary community of Utopia is, since they are both fictional and imaginary. However, the term *fantasy* has often been freighted with unfavourable associations and must overcome critiques from at least two fronts: the somewhat scientific or philosophical

bias towards a kind of narrative realism, on the one hand, and the politically charged critique of fantasy as an escapist genre, on the other.
Traditionally, the critical discourse of modernity has envisioned a de-
mystification of the world, such that the repression or elimination of
those elements deemed fantastic has appeared to be almost an imperative of a distinctly modern world view, as in that archetypical narrative
of Western modernity, *Don Quixote*, where the fantasies promulgated
by chivalric romances and embraced as facts by the mad knight are
repeatedly and humorously shown to be false in the face of an all-too-
realistic real world. But, because all utopias are necessarily always fantastic, inasmuch as they project an entirely imaginary and by definition
not (or not yet) real place, utopian discourse has itself at various times
been dismissed as unrealistic, impractical or romantic, perhaps most
famously by Marx and Engels in *The Communist Manifesto*. From
the perspective of a sober realism, both works of fantasy and utopia
might be dismissed as fanciful, if not childish or silly. Yet a number
of anti-fantasy critics have embraced utopia, granted special status to
this particular form of fantasy, owing to its cognitive, quasi-scientific
projection of a rational order.[3] In this view, utopia is the progressive,
future-oriented and modern genre or mode par excellence, while fantasy
appears as backward-looking, nostalgic or anti-modern.

However, viewed from the perspective of a *longue durée*, the experience of modernity has also been imbued with a profoundly fantastic content, whether in the sense of a utopian projection of idealized societies,
or later by a sort of Gothic return of the repressed (perhaps best emblem-
atized by Goya's famous "Sleep of Reason"), the speculative projection
of alternative futures or places in what emerges as the genre of science
fiction, or the historical vision of radically different pasts or presents in
the fantasy genre. The dialectic of mimesis and fantasy in literature, as
Kathryn Hume has analyzed in some detail, does not resolve itself as a
simple victory for one mode or the other, but both continue to inform
works of the imagination (see Hume 1984). This dialectic has undoubtedly played itself out in narrative throughout history, but many scholars have observed an increasing tendency towards the fantastic in the
past century, as even the most high-minded of serious literature (such as
Ulysses or *One Hundred Years of Solitude*) has drawn upon myth, magic
or other apparently unrealistic modes of discourse in their production.
Although readers and scholars differ as to the merits of fantasy as a literary genre, there is little question that, as Tom Shippey has put it, "[t]he
dominant literary mode of the twentieth century has been the fantastic"
(2000, vii). Between More's *Utopia* of the early sixteenth century and
what China Miéville has characterized as the literature of estrangement
in the twenty-first century (see Crown 2011), a persistent if discontinuous line of fantastic thought runs through modern literary history.

Realism itself, one could argue, is not exempt from fantasy's influence. Even for those whose aim is to produce a pragmatic and realistic representation of the people, events and spaces under consideration in a given work, the fantastic mode has become a necessary part of any literary cartography. If narratives are among the principal means by which writers and readers project imaginary maps of their world, these may or may not also be utopian, and the degree to which their representational techniques may be deemed realistic or unrealistic may vary wildly from work to work. However, the basic grounding in a certain mode of alterity makes possible the innovative and critical apprehension of reality itself, as I discuss below. Unlike in More's canonical version or even in the modern utopias of the industrial age (such as Edward Bellamy's *Looking Backward*, William Morris's *News from Nowhere* or H. G. Wells's *A Modern Utopia*), the utopian imagination in the age of globalization is not concerned with discovering a hidden island or future ideal state in the world; rather, it involves a figurative projection and representation of the world itself. Yet these earlier versions share with the more recent productions a fundamentally fantastic approach to the reality they seek simultaneously to represent and to transform. Utopias such as More's, then, might be said to provide fantastic maps in which the given social system's other spaces – those liminal and hybrid zones in which the strange, seemingly fantastic, but possibly liberating elements of this world make themselves visible – may be discerned. No less than a writer interested in a realistic depiction of the society in which the narrative takes place, the utopian or fantasist addresses the condition of the 'real' world, but does so while thinking that the improbable or impossible might be true. In these otherworldly spaces, the radical alterity associated with the fantastic mode establishes a conceptual and affective break with the present state of things. The city of Amaurotum, whose name is etymologically suggestive of shadows or dreams,[4] offers one kind of fantasy for imagining the social spaces of modernity, but in the mist-enveloped realms of fantasy, we may discover some of modernity's other spaces as well.

Utopian Spatiality

More's fictional Utopia establishes an ideal image of how social spaces are to be organized in a modern nation-state. Among the many marvellous scientific and social achievements in this country that is at once a no-place (*ou-topos*) and a good place (*eu-topos*), urban planning must be counted near the top. "There are fifty-four splendid big towns on the island, all with the same language, laws, customs and institutions. They're all built on the same plan, and, so far as the sites will allow, they all look exactly alike" (More 2003, 50). Such standardization of the Utopian urban space is part of what makes it utopian:

> But let me tell you some more about the towns. Well, when you've seen one of them, you've seen all of them, for they are as nearly identical as local conditions will permit. So I'll just give you one example – it doesn't matter which. However, the obvious choice is Amaurotum.
>
> (50, translation modified)

The centrality of this imaginary city and its role in the idealized state accord it some privilege in the world of imaginary places. The fantastic metropolis of Amaurotum appears as a representative space of modernity.

In projecting this rational, standardized space of the capital city, More and the utopians who followed in his wake anticipate the massive social and spatial transformations associated with the emergence of the modern nation-state. The rationalization of social space he envisions partakes of the same sorts of revolutionary spatial transformations that have been famously described and analyzed in Michel Foucault's archaeologies of the medical "gaze" or genealogy of disciplinary societies. Sounding a good deal more ominous than the utopians, Foucault describes the "disciplinary mechanism" that this political reorganization of social space establishes:

> This enclosed, segmented space, observed at every point, in which the individuals are inserted in a fixed place, in which the slightest movements are supervised, in which all events are recorded, in which an uninterrupted work of writing links the centre and the periphery, in which power is exercised without division, according to a continuous hierarchical figure, in which each individual is constantly located, examined and distributed among the living beings, the sick and the dead – all this constitutes a compact model of the disciplinary mechanism.
>
> (1977, 197)

The plague-stricken, late seventeenth-century society Foucault describes in *Discipline and Punish* would seem to be rather far removed from the humanistic ideals of More's Utopia, and yet Foucault concludes that "[t]he plague-stricken town [...] is the utopia of the perfectly governed city" (1977, 198). In Foucault, the shadows of Amaurotum appear a good deal darker.

More's idealized description of the social ordering of Utopia anticipates the revolutionary reorganizations of power and knowledge in the Enlightenment.[5] This new spatial order of the modern urban geography, which increasingly extends its conceptual reach to the national and international spatio-political ensembles as well, has been historically associated with a philosophical discourse of modernity connected to the multimodal phenomenon of *Aufklärung*, which for Immanuel Kant entailed mankind's emancipation from a childish or minor status and which itself cannot be wholly separated from the material basis in the transformations of political economy or, in other words, the capitalist mode of production (Kant 1963, 3).[6] The capitalist reorganization of time had a tendency to spatialize the temporal mode through what Marx understood as the fetishism of the commodity, in which (subjective) labour time congealed into the (objective) form of the physical commodity. "Thus," according to Georg Lukács in his famous meditation on reification, "time sheds its qualitative, variable, flowing nature; it freezes into an exactly delimited, quantifiable continuum filled with quantifiable 'things' (the reified, mechanically objectified human personality): in short, it becomes space" (1971a, 90). From a more general, philosophical point of view, the Enlightenment project is also characterized by a sort of spatialization of experience, such that every aspect of human and inhuman existence could somehow be ordered into a rational and orderly diagram.

Max Horkheimer and Theodor W. Adorno in *Dialectic of Enlightenment* (1987) notoriously observed that the crucial aspect of Enlightenment rationality was the meticulous coordination and classification of the elements of existence, which extends to its apprehension of geographical space, obviously, in rationalizing the spaces of the world with new geometric and geographic precision. But it also tends to spatialize knowledge itself, making everything increasingly measurable and mappable. Referring the bizarrely resonant conceptual parallels between Kant's transcendental aesthetic and the Marquis de Sade's gymnastic sexual concatenations, Adorno and Horkheimer argue that "[w]hat Kant grounded transcendentally, the affinity of knowledge and planning, which impressed the stamp of inescapable expediency on every aspect of a bourgeois existence that was wholly rationalized, even in every breathing-space, Sade realized empirically" (1987, 88). Not only space but all human activity becomes measurable, quantifiable and ordered, such that even the extravaganzas of Sadean pornography can appear as dully categorical as the periodic table of elements. But, in terms of the Enlightenment's great modern injunction – *Sapere aude* – enunciated by Kant himself in his answer to the question, "What is Enlightenment?" (1963), such drily methodical ordering is a sign of mankind's maturity (3). It is evidence that humankind, having overcome the chimeras of superstition and affiliated phantasmagoria, can now embrace the coolly rational understanding of the world. This is itself a utopian vision, reflecting the aspirations of a rationalist thinker whose optimism with respect to mankind's self-emancipation from religious or political charlatans would be sorely tested in the coming years and centuries.

More's perfectly laid out social spaces and standardized cities, the Baroque reorganization of social space in terms of mathematical precision or the Cartesian grid, the ordering of spaces according to the exigencies of a disciplinary society à la Foucault's genealogy of power, the transformation of time and experience into a spatial framework in a capitalist mode of production, the Enlightenment project of rationalization and the desacralization of the world – all of these are themselves the real-world results of what may well be considered, ironically or otherwise, a fantastic mode of thought. The dream of a perfectly rational organization of social space, like utopia itself, is after all a fantasy, and the utopian philosophical order, political policies, economic processes or urban planning that attempt to realize these fantasies are, in some ways, also fantastic. The literary or figurative mappings produced by such processes disclose fantastic spaces.

The paradigm shifts associated with the advent of a modern social organization require the imaginative projection of an almost mathematical order that is quite unreal, bringing the chaotic and vicissitudinous elements of nature, culture and society into an orderly whole that cannot but be artificial. The utopian project of modern philosophy and science is to imagine an alternative reality in which reason and order prevail, if only provisionally, or as a means of making more sense of our own, intransigently irrational or disorderly experience of the world. In this manner, one could liken the utopian project to that of cartography itself, which imposes an obviously artificial order, often in the form of a Cartesian grid, complete with coordinates and trajectories, upon a space that in one's 'real-world' experience frequently resists the map's logical order, as smooth spaces become striated, deterritorialized and reterritorialized (see Deleuze and Guattari 1987, 361–362). The distinctive spatiality of this modern vision is marked in the figure of the map itself, which is inherently modern while also exceeding its own attempts to confine the spaces it represents to the limits of its frame. Although some sort of orienting or mapping activity seems essential to the human condition itself, the rise of cartography in Europe during the 'Age of Discovery' is far from coincidental. As Tom Conley points out in *The Self-Made Map* (1996), aside from the *portolan* charts used by Mediterranean navigators to help locate harbours, "at the beginning of the fifteenth century, maps were practically nonexistent, whereas only two centuries later they were the bedrock of most professions and disciplines" (1). There is something simultaneously fantastic and real about the map, particularly the world map, in which an abstract representation of an impossibly vast space— the world itself—is to be grasped in almost banally practical terms, as a mere tool for navigation, or, in a more sublime sense, as a work of art. The map, then, like the fantastic vision of an ideal social organization, is itself utopian.

The Need for Fantasy

One might argue that the fantastic, broadly conceived as a mode but also encompassing the literary genre of fantasy – a genre that would include utopian writing as a subset –[7] is constitutive of the "unfinished project" of modernity itself (see Habermas 1987). That is, the attempt to apprehend critically the diverse spaces in which we live requires a fantastic literary or figurative cartography. Such a project concerns both the daily, lived experience of individuals in modern societies and the broader structural totality, the mode of production or the spaces of the world system, which lie beyond the ken of the individual subject, but which may be figured forth in the aesthetic sphere. The practical value of fantasy lies in its ways of simultaneously making sense of the world and imagining alternatives to it.

However, since "fantasy" is frequently used to dismiss whatever it purports to represent, any aesthetic or critical project in the fantastic mode must address the stringent critiques of those who oppose fantasy in all of its forms.[8] Even more so than with the often maligned *utopia*, a word and concept that continues to need to be defended against those forces that militate in favour of the sociopolitical status quo, *fantasy* is freighted with a rather pejorative sense in modern criticism and theory. Fantasy is opposed not only to mimetic realism in literature or art, but sometimes to reality itself. Fantasy's apparent rejection of the real, the possible and even the probable, is perhaps reason enough for some to reject it outright. Moreover, as noted above, fantasy also finds enemies from within the realm of non-mimetic or anti-realistic literature and criticism. Some of its most influential and vocal foes today are critics who themselves embrace utopia and science fiction, but who argue that the estrangements of fantasy are politically suspect, at best offering mere escapism or reinforcing the status quo, at worst actively supporting reactionary politics. Following Darko Suvin's influential notion of "cognitive estrangement" in science fiction (1979, 4), such theorists as Fredric Jameson, Carl Freedman and others have dismissed fantasy as a genre (taken to be distinct from science fiction and utopia) on the grounds that it is characterized by irrational, non-cognitive or mythic estrangement, which then leaves it open to the potentially reactionary politics of nostalgia or romanticism.

While a number of spatially oriented critics have embraced utopia, many of these same critics have been openly hostile to fantasy. For example, Fredric Jameson has long defended utopian thinking against those, both within a leftist intellectual tradition and outside of it, who would use the term *utopia* to defame cultural projects intended to imagine radical alternatives to the present social or political system. Referring particularly to the utopianism of Herbert Marcuse in the 1960s and defending it against the charges of Marx's own anti-utopian arguments, Jameson contends that, whereas in the older society (as in Marx's classic analysis) Utopian thought represented a diversion of revolutionary energy into idle wish-fulfillments and imaginary satisfactions, in our own time the very nature of the Utopian concept has undergone a dialectical reversal. Now it is practical thinking which everywhere represents a capitulation to the system itself, and stands as a testimony to the power of that system to transform even its adversaries into its own mirror image.

(1971, 110–111)

If practical thinking, perhaps including a certain philosophical or literary realism, has become the enemy of the imagination, the faculty that resists the gravitational force field of the merely actual in favour of speculative projections of the distantly possible, virtual or even impossible, then one might argue for the necessity of fantasy for rethinking the world. Yet Jameson joins Suvin, Freedman and a number of other prominent utopians in rejecting fantasy. Indeed, in his own extensive statement on "the desire called utopia," Jameson condemns any confusion between the generic modes of utopia (here understood as a "socio-economic subset" of science fiction) and fantasy by stating that "[w]e must now lay this misunderstanding to rest" (2005, 56).[9] Here, then, the antagonism is not between fantasy and some favoured form of realism but between fantasy and a still-preferable but non-realistic form, that of utopia or, more generally, science fiction.

Although the fantasy-versus-SF antagonism, with its strident partisans and passionate arguments, undoubtedly antedates academic criticism on the subject, a key point of departure for scholars remains Suvin's trailblazing 1979 study, *Metamorphoses of Science Fiction*. In that book, Suvin both champions and carefully analyzes the broad-based and expansive genre of science fiction, while also establishing the terms by which fantasy would be dismissed. Drawing upon the Brechtian concept of "estrangement," Suvin argues that science fiction is a genre of "cognitive estrangement," whereas fantasy relies on irrational, mythic or metaphysical estrangement. Suvin finds that fantasy as a genre is fundamentally anti-scientific, using religious themes, magic and other fanciful elements to project a different world, but one which has little direct bearing on the world in which we live. As such, fantasy is not useful for those who wish to *think* the world, and even less useful for those who wish to change it (Suvin 1979, 4). Fantasy is thus escapist and reactionary, as the world into which the reader is expected to escape is often that of a mythical, often pastoral, past. For example, Michael Moorcock has argued that

[s]ince the beginnings of the Industrial Revolution, at least, people have been yearning for an ideal rural world they believe to have vanished—yearning for a mythical state of innocence [...]. This

refusal to face or derive any pleasure from the realities of urban industrial life, this longing to possess, again, the infant's eye view of the countryside, is a fundamental theme in popular English literature.

(1987, 126)

Fantasy thus is deemed to be either useless or harmful for any progressive political project.

It probably does not help that the most inescapable figure in twentieth-century fantasy literature, J. R. R. Tolkien, whose own political views were not exactly revolutionary, defended fantasy precisely *as* an escapist practice. Complaining that readers opposed to fantasy have confused "the escape of the prisoner with the flight of the deserter," Tolkien asks: "Why should a man be scorned if, finding himself in prison, he tries to get out and go home? Or if, when he cannot do so, he thinks and talks about other topics than jailers and prison-walls?" (1966, 79). Although, it might be noted, Moorcock has observed that jailers most certainly do not hate *escapism*; what they hate is actual escape (quoted in Miéville 2002b). Indeed, Tolkien goes so far as to claim that the world outside this prison is just as 'real,' whether the prisoner can see it or not, which suggests a view of fantasy as an imaginative method for apprehending the 'real world' rather than a means of escaping from it. That is, in imagining an otherworld like Middle-earth and populating it with histories, persons, events and so on, fantasists like Tolkien provide readers with means of making sense of their all-too-real worlds, in a manner consistent with the most realistic of fiction but also going beyond the merely realistic. The literary cartography of Middle-earth can aid us in giving shape to our own views of this world, drawing on the lessons of the fantastic narratives that may not be accessible or even possible in strictly mimetic representations of 'real' everyday life.

Coming from an entirely different political and philosophical tradition, China Miéville has also defended fantasy against its detractors on both the right and the left. A committed socialist and activist, as well as an important author of fantasy and science fiction (a distinction he does not think is very useful), Miéville has said some rather mischievous things about Tolkien, most famously, that the Oxford professor's influential presence was "a wen on the arse of fantasy literature," although he has repented of this view in recent years (see Miéville 2009b). Miéville is undoubtedly opposed to the retrogressive politics of such fantasists as Tolkien or C. S. Lewis, but he finds in the Marxist critique of capitalism evidence for fantasy's critical value. Indeed, Miéville asserts that fantasy offers a better approach than even realism for getting at the truth of the 'real world' under capitalism. After discussing Marx's analysis in *Capital* of the fetishism of the commodity and the hidden social relations embedded in it, Miéville explains that "'[r]eal' life under capitalism *is a fantasy*: 'realism,' narrowly defined, is therefore a 'realistic' depiction of 'an absurdity which is true,' but no less absurd for that. Narrow 'realism' is as partial and ideological as 'reality' itself" (2002a, 42). Furthermore, Miéville insists, the "apparent epistemological radicalism of the fantastic mode's basic predicate," namely that "the impossible is true," makes it well suited to the task of an oppositional or critical project (2002a, 42–43). It should be noted, however, that Miéville quite rightly does not claim that fantasy is itself a revolutionary mode or "acts as a guide to political action" (2002a, 46). The value of fantasy lies less in its politics, which could fall anywhere along the political spectrum, after all, than in its imaginative encounter with alterity. As Miéville concludes,

> the fantastic might be a mode peculiarly suited to and resonant with the forms of modernity. [...] Fantasy is a mode that, in constructing an internally coherent but actually impossible totality—constructed on the basis that the impossible is, for this work, *true*—mimics the 'absurdity' of capitalist modernity.
>
> (2002a, 42; emphasis in original)

That is, where the so-called 'real' world of capitalist modernity is in fact false, masking the underlying social relations of production, the fantastic mode, precisely because it calls this so-called 'real world' into question from the start, makes possible novel, imaginative and radically different representations.

Miéville decries the attitude that has allowed "generations of readers and writers to treat, say, faster-than-light drives as science-fictional in a way that dragons are not, despite repeated assurances from the great majority of physicists that the former are no less impossible than the latter" (2009a, 234).[10] Against the anti-fantasy sentiments of the spaceship enthusiasts or dragon detractors, Miéville files all of these genres – science fiction, utopia and fantasy – within a larger, but perhaps more helpful, category that he terms the literature of alterity. This intensive regard for otherness, whether presented in terms of the past or future, the earthly or the interstellar, the monstrous or the alien, is shared by all forms of the fiction of estrangement, including some, like *Moby-Dick*, that are inexpressibly 'strange' even while they present absolutely realistic (or, at least, possible) persons, places and events. The conception of a fiction of "estrangement" enables the fantastic mode to exceed the boundaries of its more tightly circumscribed genre. The supreme value of fantasy lies in its meditation on the impossible, which can enable a radically different vantage point from which to view reality. As Miéville puts it, "we need fantasy to think the world, and to change it" (2002a, 48).

In this sense, Miéville's defence of fantasy as a critical mode with which to map the world connects neatly with the argument of one of the leading utopian theorists of the past century. Marcuse saw in the power of the imagination and, specifically, in the products of the aesthetic sphere an opportunity to 'refuse' the limitations of the spatio-temporal conditions of modern life:

> The Great Refusal is the protest against unnecessary repression, the struggle for the ultimate form of freedom – to live without anxiety.' But this idea could be formulated without punishment only in the language of art. In the more realistic realm of political theory and even philosophy, it was almost universally defamed as utopia.
>
> (1966, 149–150)

Of course, Marcuse does not intend this last word as a pejorative, but acknowledges the way in which utopia, like fantasy, is normally dismissed by those with a vested interest in the 'reality principle' or the sociopolitical status quo. But, as Marcuse concludes, "[i]n its refusal to accept as final the limitations imposed on freedom and happiness by the reality principle, in its refusal to forget what *can be*, lies the critical function of phantasy" (1966, 148–149). Here utopia and fantasy come together as a single theoretical practice in the service of a literary cartography of both the existing world system and potential alternatives formations.

Conclusion: *Plus Ultra*

The value of this fantastic effort seems to me to be confirmed in the imaginative endeavour involved in mapping our own 'real world,' particularly the postmodern world system in which the traditional guideposts are no longer trustworthy or desirable. "Happy are those ages when the starry sky is a map of all possible paths," writes Lukács of the age of the epic, using language that sounds not much different from Tolkien's: "The world is wide and yet it is like a home" (1971b, 19). Today, the celestial charts are not so reliable or *heimlich*, and the literary cartography of the present world system has to be, in some ways, otherworldly. In theory and in practice, the alterity of fantasy makes possible new ways of seeing, and thus of interpreting and, perhaps, even changing, the world in which we actually live, for better and for worse. In the era of globalization, an age which has witnessed a remarkable resurgence of fantasy in the arts and literature, perhaps not coincidentally, the world system forms what Jameson, following Sartre, has called the "untranscendable horizon" of any critical project, such that "all thinking today is *also*, whatever else it is, an attempt to think the world system as such" (1992, 4; emphasis in original). This global space requires a sort of abstraction and imaginative projection that makes a literature of estrangement the form potentially best suited to the present condition. The fantastic mode allows us, among other things, to see the world anew and to imagine different approaches to representing and otherwise engaging with it. As Miéville asserts pointedly, "fantasy [...] is *good to think with*" (2002a, 46, emphasis in original).

In More's case, the 'discovery' of the island of Utopia signalled the possibility, if only in the form of satire or social critique, of a radically transformed society, even if the main thrust of the narrative is less prescriptive than critical. New spaces are possible, if only they can be imagined. Famously, More's island nation was not originally an island. Before it could function as an ideal society, the conqueror-king Utopus had ordered a fifteen-mile-wide trench to be dug in order to separate the nation from the mainland. The radical break, of course, becomes symbolic of the spatio-temporal rupture that signals the emergence of the modern state. That is, it involves both the delineation of a distinctive national space, with all the concomitant ideological freight of borders and boundaries, enclosure, subdivisions and so on, and the marked disjunction between the viscerally experienced present and a soon-to-be-forgotten or romanticized past.[11] It is a spatio-temporal metaphor for what Marcuse would call "the scandal of qualitative difference" (1970, 69). More's capital city and prototype of the modern state are imaginary, but their effects are all too real. The utopian space to be found in the organization of Amaurotum is perhaps quintessentially modern, fit for the world system emerging in the wake of voyages of discovery, ordered and rational and, above all, sensible. But the fantastic or otherworldly spaces to be found in the suburbs of Amaurotum are where we might see glimmers of another modernity or a postmodernity. In the troubled waters surrounding Utopia on the map, we might discern the old warning, *hic sunt dracones*.[12] But that is a zone where the modern Imaginary grapples with an unrepresentable Real, where bureaucrats and monsters jostle each other, and the fantastic mode of mapping such fictional spaces may disclose an image of the world we live in and, perhaps, of other worlds not yet visible on the horizon.

Notes

* An earlier version of this chapter was published in *English Language Notes* 52.1: *Imaginary Cartographies*, ed. Karen Jacobs (Spring/Summer 2014): 57–66.
1 In a subsequent, more detailed illustration attached to the 1518 edition of *Utopia*, the sailor is looking out toward the viewer, rather than at the island. In the foreground, Hythlodaeus lectures a man (More himself, who stands in for the reader) while gesturing towards the island nation in the distance.
2 Famously, More's coinage of the word *utopia* from Greek roots involved a homophonic pun, combining in the same pronunciation the *eu*-topos (good place) and the *ou*-topos (no place).
3 Darko Suvin's influential conception of science fiction, of which utopia is a "socio-economic subset," as a genre of "cognitive estrangement" accounts for part of this reaction to fantasy as a genre or mode. In Suvin's view, the

estrangements of fantasy are non-cognitive, irrational or specifically "meta-physical," and therefore retrogressive (Suvin 1979, 4). Carl Freedman offers an updated and somewhat more nuanced account, but he also embraces the distinction, dismissing the estrangements of fantasy as "irrationalist" and therefore "theoretically illegitimate" (Freedman 2000, 17). But, see also China Miéville (2009a).

4 Like other names in *Utopia*, such as the river Anydrus (which suggests "no water"), Amaurotum contains an amusing double meaning for those who know Greek; its Greek root means "made dark or dim," which implies a state of being shadowy or unseen.

5 The timeline is not as important as the development and dissemination of ideas and practices, such that the early modern transformations of both abstract (Cartesian) and social space may be seen as part of the radical reordering of urban spaces in the Baroque and later epochs, along with the restructuring of social spaces along ever more striated, segmented and coordinated lines.

6 Here one might also mention the sociological interventions of Max Weber and Georg Simmel, whose work established the relations between rational-ization and social spaces long before the definitive work of Henri Lefebvre in *The Production of Space* (1991), among other writings.

7 See Miéville, "Cognition as Ideology" (2009a, 243–244).

8 For example, Ursula K. LeGuin has recently criticized Kazuo Ishiguro for apparently belittling fantasy in explaining that his novel *The Buried Giant* merely used "surface elements of fantasy," but was not itself a work of fan-tasy. Le Guin defends fantasy as "probably the oldest literary device for talking about reality," and notes that the presence or absence of "surface elements" is not what constitutes fantasy. Rather, "[l]iterary fantasy is the result of a vivid, powerful, coherent imagination drawing plausible im-possibilities together into a vivid, powerful and coherent story" (Le Guin 2015).

9 The chapter of *Archaeologies of the Future* in which Jameson attempts to definitively distinguish science fiction from fantasy is titled, aptly enough, "The Great Schism" (Jameson 2005, 57–71).

10 Compare Tolkien's comment in "On Fairy-stories": "The notion that motor-cars are more 'alive' than, say, centaurs or dragons is curious; that they are more 'real' than, say, horses is pathetically absurd" (1966, 81).

11 In More's Utopia, the past is not romanticized.

12 See, e.g., Balasopoulos (2008). *Hic sunt dracones* has its own fantastic back-story. Despite its influence on the popular imagination, the phrase "Here be Dragons" appeared on no known historical world maps (except the Hunt-Lenox Globe, perhaps); see my *Utopia in the Age of Globalization: Space, Representation, and the World System* (2013, 95–96).

References

Balasopoulos, Antonis. 2008. "'*Utopiae Insulae Figura*': Utopian Insularity and the Politics of Form." *Transtext(e)s/Transcultures: Journal of Global Cultural Studies*, special issue, 22–38.

Conley, Tom. 1996. *The Self-Made Map: Cartographic Writing in Early Modern France*. Minneapolis: University of Minnesota Press.

Crown, Sarah. 2011. "What the Booker Prize Really Excludes." *Books* (blog), *The Guardian*. October 17, 2011. www.theguardian.com/books/booksblog/2011/oct/17/science-fiction-china-mieville.

Deleuze, Gilles, and Félix Guattari. 1987. *A Thousand Plateaus*. Translated by Brian Massumi. Minneapolis: University of Minnesota Press.

Foucault, Michel. 1977. *Discipline and Punish: The Birth of the Prison*. Translated by Alan Sheridan. New York: Vintage.

Freedman, Carl. 2000. *Critical Theory and Science Fiction*. Middletown: Wesleyan University Press.

Habermas, Jürgen. 1987. *The Philosophical Discourse of Modernity: Twelve Lectures*. Translated by Thomas McCarthy. Cambridge, MA: The MIT Press.

Horkheimer, Max, and Theodor W. Adorno. 1987. *Dialectic of Enlightenment*. Translated by John Cumming. New York: Continuum.

Hume, Kathryn. 1984. *Fantasy and Mimesis: Responses to Reality in Western Literature*. New York: Methuen.

Jameson, Fredric. 1971. *Marxism and Form: Twentieth-Century Dialectical Theories of Literature*. Princeton: Princeton University Press.

———. 1992. *The Geopolitical Aesthetic: Cinema and Space in the World System*. Bloomington: Indiana University Press and the British Film Institute.

———. 2005. *Archaeologies of the Future: The Desire Called Utopia and Other Science Fictions*. London: Verso.

Kant, Immanuel. 1963. "What is Enlightenment?" In *On History*, edited and translated by Lewis White Beck, 3–10. Indianapolis: Bobbs-Merrill.

Le Guin, Ursula. 2015. "95. 'Are they going to say this is fantasy?'" *Ursula K. Le Guin's Blog*. March 5, 2015. www.ursulakleguin.com/Blog2015.html.

Lefebvre, Henri. 1991. *The Production of Space*. Translated by Donald Nicholson-Smith. Oxford: Blackwell.

Lukács, Georg. 1971a. *History and Class Consciousness: Studies in Marxist Dialectics*. Translated by Rodney Livingstone. Cambridge: The MIT Press.

———. 1971b. *The Theory of the Novel*. Translated by Anna Bostock. Cambridge: The MIT Press.

Marcuse, Herbert. 1966. *Eros and Civilization: A Philosophical Inquiry into Freud*. Boston, MA: Beacon Press.

———. 1970. "The End of Utopia." In *Five Lectures: Psychoanalysis, Politics, and Utopia*, translated by J. Shapiro and S. Weber, 62–82. Boston: Beacon Press.

Miéville, China. 2002a. "Editorial Introduction." Symposium: Marxism and Fantasy. *Historical Materialism* 10 (4): 39–49.

———. 2002b. "Tolkien – Middle-earth Meets Middle England," *Socialist Review* 259 (January). http://socialistreview.org.uk/259/tolkien-middle-earth-meets-middle-england.

———. 2009a. "Cognition as Ideology: A Dialectic of SF Theory." In *Red Planets: Marxism and Science Fiction*, edited by Mark Bould and China Miéville. Middletown: Wesleyan University Press. 231–248.

———. 2009b. "There and Back Again." *Omnivoracious* (blog, guest post). June 15, 2009. www.omnivoracious.com/2009/06/there-and-back-again-five-reasons-tolkien-rocks.html.

Moorcock, Michael. 1987. *Wizardry and Wild Romance: A Study of Epic Fantasy*. London: Victor Gollancz Ltd.

More, Sir Thomas. (1516) 2003. *Utopia*. Translated by Paul Turner. New York: Penguin.

Shippey, Thomas A. 2000. *J. R. R. Tolkien: Author of the Century*. Boston: Houghton Mifflin.

Suvin, Darko. 1979. *Metamorphoses of Science Fiction: On the Poetics and History of a Literary Genre*. New Haven: Yale University Press.

Tally, Robert T., Jr. 2013. *Utopia in the Age of Globalization: Space, Representation, and the World System*. New York: Palgrave Macmillan.

Tolkien, J. R. R. 1966. "On Fairy-stories." In *The Tolkien Reader*, 33–99. New York: Ballantine Books.

Wegner, Phillip E. 2002. *Imaginary Communities: Utopia, the Nation, and the Spatial Histories of Modernity*. Berkeley: University of California Press.

2 Mapping Utopia

Christina Ljungberg

Narratives of geographical imaginaries have populated literature and culture since time immemorial. However, it was with the advent of printing that discourse became located between meaning and its spatial form. For suddenly, the relationship between rhetorical order and mapping processes became visible, allowing writers to 'pilot' or 'navigate' the worlds they were creating in words. This relationship had been known since antiquity, but it was only now – laid out and diagrammatized on the printed page – that its visibility came into play. For the first time, historical processes, cartography and geographic discovery were manifestly linked to literature, which they both inspired and were inspired by. Texts appeared that, as Tom Conley has observed, "betray[ed] the touch of the architect, the stage designer, the painter, and, no less, the cartographer" (1996, 4). Often accompanied by maps, as frontispieces or inserted into books, they visibly situated the literary text in a geographical context.

What happens to a text when its space is represented both verbally and cartographically? How do writing and mapping interact, and how does this influence our reading? One of the effects is that, by juxtaposing writing and cartography, writers force readers to switch between the two and compare two kinds of representation. This shift, leapfrogging between text and map and back to the text again, calls attention to the constructed nature of both fictional and cartographic space, signalling that what we are looking at is but one way among many to represent spatial relationships. Secondly, maps help readers to visualize and move within the text's fictional space by drawing them into the space-time continuum of the narrative, helping them to move mentally with and *within* the story. Thirdly, being an abstract diagram depicting selected spatial relationships, a geographical map also has a performative function. What constitutes its performative character is the following: when the mapmaker presents various data to be abstracted into a systematic code, a new reality is created, which is then interpreted by the readers from their diverse perspectives. As Dodge, Kitchin and Perkins point out, information on a map always emerges in rather different ways, depending on the "knowledge, experience and skill of the individual to perform mappings and apply them to the world" (2009, 21). This is why every new reading creates a new state of affairs, according to the viewpoint chosen. Fourthly, by making its fictional space material and real, the map lends the text a sense of authenticity, making it a useful instrument for claiming authority as well as authenticating the narrative's truthfulness.

Yet, as an imaginary construct, a map also allows writers to implicitly and ingeniously criticize political and social wrongs by opening up a dialogue that might bring about change or, at least, show potential alternatives. As we will see, this becomes particularly important for reading Thomas More's *Utopia* (1516). This seminal work still serves as the *urtext* for the almost endlessly proliferating concept of utopia, often widely diverging from More's brilliant original. What makes his text so remarkable is that it juxtaposes map and text, thereby highlighting how precisely the collocation of various perspectives can influence acts of viewing and describing.

Spatial Strategies in Narrative

As printing helped verbal descriptions of space acquire a figural and almost material quality, verbal texts started to become what Michel de Certeau has called "spatial stories" (1984, 115). According to de Certeau, stories are "spatial trajectories" since they "traverse and organize places; they select and link them together, [and] make sentences and itineraries out of them" (1984, 115). De Certeau sees a link between language and physical movement: physical movements are themselves symbolic performances and produce other symbolic performances, generating various forms of utterance that are written, oral or gestural. They are performative, partly because they are actions in themselves and partly because they produce new spatial realities in which events can take place. Thus, "[e]very story is a travel story – a spatial practice" (1984, 115); similarly, Tom Conley argues that any work of writing that transports its readers into new realms can be considered a 'travelling narrative' (see Chapter 10 of this volume).

Stories could therefore be called "narrative maps" or "narrative tours" (1984, 117). They perform the task of transforming places into spaces and vice versa; they "organize the play of changing relationships" between them, thereby staging an interplay that spans everything from descriptions of static scenes to rapid successions of events which "multiply" spaces, as in detective stories or folk tales. This interplay of relationships applies fundamentally to both literary and cartographic representations, which alternate between the presentation of a tableau or scene, which implies previous knowledge of a place, and the spatialization of action through movements (de Certeau 1984, 119). This "chain of spatializing operations," as de Certeau calls it, is characterized by "references to what it produces (a representation of places) or to what it implies (a local order)." It generates the structure of the "travel story" that makes use of certain locations performatively by naming them, or by sanctioning them (1984, 120).

Once upon a time, discursive itineraries – de Certeau calls them "tours" – and maps were closely intertwined. It was the advent of modern scientific discourse and modern cartography that separated them, with the map increasingly distancing itself from the itinerary that once was "the condition of its possibility" (de Certeau 1984, 121). The plotting of modern maps produced a new subject that was partly defined by the relationship of the self to space. In contrast to medieval maps, which represented both an ideographic and a mythographic space (cf. Nöth 2012; Ljungberg 2016), this new subject was forced to develop new strategies to deal with the Cartesian space embodied in Western maps. Due to the increasingly scientific cartographic representation, which required constant visual simplification of complex sets of data, a completely new type of map emerged. Instead of representing natural processes such as itineraries or patterns, maps became visual documents, reflecting and even reinforcing patterns of control. This made those who possessed and used the maps omniscient spectators since they alone were able to survey the space projected and represented by maps as objects of art, science and technology.

This development coincided with Christopher Columbus's, Amerigo Vespucci's and John Cabot's new discoveries, published in their travel stories, which documented the conquests of new space. A new genre of literature emerged, orienting the reader within the geographical spatial contexts in which these discoveries took place and which were becoming increasingly important. Famous sea captains and merchants wrote about their explorations and, in order to both illustrate and authenticate their narratives for their readers and financiers, provided them with maps (Mayer 1997, 184). Thanks to the development of printing (Brotton 1998, 35), maps changed from being exclusive to monarchs and nobility, the clergy or scholars to a medium accessible to a wider audience. The new readership not only acquired new geographical knowledge, but was also persuaded of the authenticity of these new territories by means of maps, which gave credibility to the existence of the terrains depicted, an impression that was reinforced by the 'documentary' quality and authority of the printed page.

The map's usefulness as a document was quickly taken up by literary authors who realized its value as a way of supporting the validity of their imaginary stories. They hoped to match the fabulous experiences described in the 'real' travel narratives, in which maps were often as much products of imagination and conjecture as of solid geographical knowledge. The new literary genre – travel literature – developed further into stories of imaginary voyages and places, offering writers additional advantages. Firstly, it gave them the opportunity to express ideas and opinions that were not officially allowed for political or religious reasons;

secondly, it prompted their readers to discover and 'see' for themselves alternatives to the prevailing social, political or religious structures by means of texts and maps depicting alternative worlds.

It is in this context that the first edition of Sir Thomas More's speculative political essay *Utopia* (1516) appeared. The essay included a map that was revised in the 1518 edition, with telling differences between the two. As is well known, Utopia literally means "nowhere" and designates a place that does not exist. As More declared ironically in a letter to his friend Peter Giles, the location of the island is not shown on the map because it must have been overlooked. It must have been, he muses, that Giles and himself "forgot to ask" Raphael Hythloday, the narrator of the tale of Utopia, about its actual whereabouts, which is why Hythloday probably "forgot to say, in what part of the New World Utopia lies" (7). The fictional account is that Hythloday knew the place, since he – as Peter Giles tells Morus in Book I – took service with Amerigo Vespucci and was "Vespucci's constant companion on the last three of his four voyages, accounts of which are now common reading everywhere" (More 1992, 11). And Hythloday did not, in fact, try to hide the location of Utopia. He simply "mentioned it only briefly and in passing," as Giles writes in his letter to Jerome Busleiden, in which he goes on to claim that "an unlucky accident caused both of [them, i.e. Giles and More] to miss what [Hythloday] had said" (1992, 112).

As Jeremy Harwood suggests, More's reference to Vespucci's *Novus Mundus* or *The Four Voyages of Amerigo Vespucci* is illuminating. At the time, it was *the* travel book to read. Vespucci's travel narratives had first been published in Florence in 1503 and then quickly spread throughout Europe (2011, 67). Enormously popular and widely circulated, they made him much better known to his contemporaries than, for example, Columbus or Cabot. By 1510, there were as many as twenty-four editions of Vespucci's accounts. It was even in his honour that Martin Waldseemüller made his famous world map (Figure 2.1), which was the first ever to name "America" and to literally put the continent on the map since Amerigo Vespucci was the first to realize that a new continent had been discovered (Harwood 2011, 68).

Although Vespucci's book was partly a forgery, based on parts of his three letters from the discoverer's *two* voyages, *Novus Mundus* was not entirely invention. As Gerhard Wegemer points out, "[l]ike most preposterous tales, *Novus Mundus* was based on some fact" (1998, 101). However, Hythloday's narration takes the most outrageous parts of Vespucci's stories even further, trying the reader on for size. Thus, More has Peter Giles claim that Hythloday travelled with Vespucci on three of his four voyages but then left Vespucci to discover the island of Utopia; yet scholars believe that only two of Vespucci's voyages actually took place (Almagià 2014). In fact, More gives his readers a handful of reasons to make us cautious of Hythloday's narrative, even letting Hythloday boast

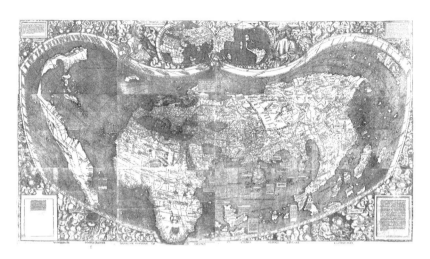

Figure 2.1 Universalis Cosmographia (Martin Waldseemüller, 1507). Library
of Congress.

to have sailed around the globe several years before the expedition organized by Ferdinand Magellan (1519–1522) resulted in the first known
circumnavigation.[1] In addition, in the 1518 edition, More has (the 'real,'
historical) Peter Giles write a letter to a common friend, elaborating the
joke about the imprecision of Utopian geography by drawing a special
Utopian alphabet and even remembering some verses in 'Utopian' that
Hythloday had recited to him, although he is not quite sure that he re-
members them correctly (1992, 114) (Figure 2.2).

The document shown in Figure 2.3 is, as Peter Giles puts it, "a little
scrap of verse, written in the Utopian tongue" that Hythloday showed
him after More had left them, and which, in translation, reads as follows:

> Me, once a peninsula, Utopus the king made an island
> Alone among all the nations, and without complex abstractions
> I set before me the philosophical city.
> What I give is free, what is better I am not slow to take from
> others.
>
> (More 1992, 114)

The notion of reciprocal exchange of ideas and thoughts proposed in
the poem becomes evident when reading *Utopia*. The text seems to
seek dialogue and exchange in a pragmatic and context-related setting,
transforming rigid philosophical positions into manifest change, not unlike the poem's hands-on dynamics that transforms a peninsula into an
island. Rather than dealing in theoretical concepts, it seems as if More

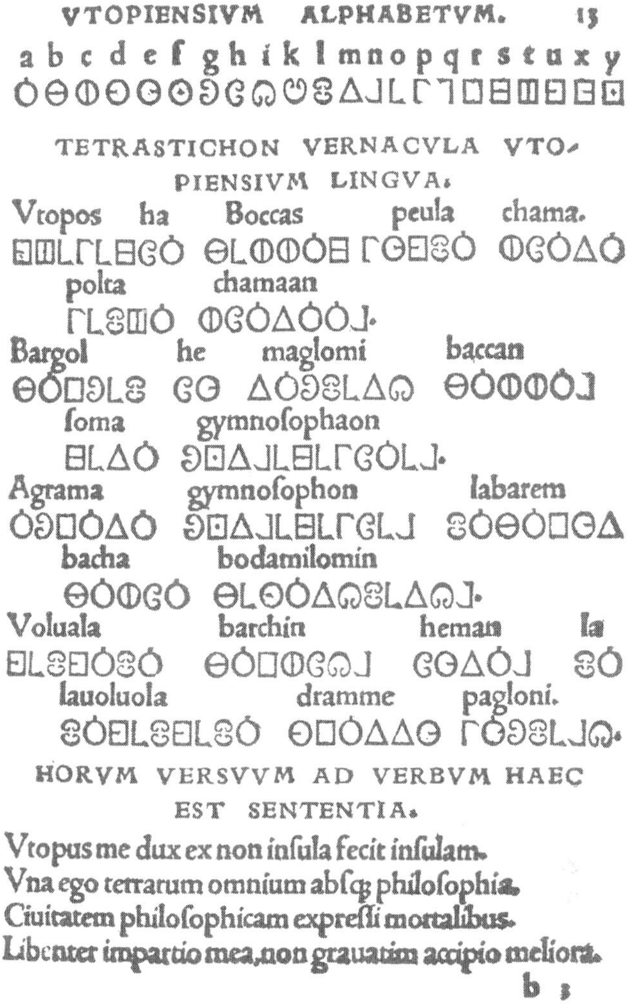

VTOPIENSIVM ALPHABETVM. 13

a b c d e f g h i k l m n o p q r s t u x y

TETRASTICHON VERNACVLA VTO-
PIENSIVM LINGVA.

Vtopos ha Boccas peula chama.

polta chamaan

Bargol he maglomi baccan

foma gymnofophaon

Agrama gymnofophon labarem

bacha bodamilomin

Voluala barchin heman la

lauoluola dramme pagloni.

HORVM VERSVVM AD VERBVM HAEC
EST SENTENTIA.

Vtopus me dux ex non infula fecit infulam.
Vna ego terrarum omnium abfcp philofophia.
Ciuitatem philofophicam exprefli mortalibus.
Libenter impartio mea, non grauatim accipio meliora.

b ;

Figure 2.2 "Tetrastichon Vernacula Utopiensium Lingua," by Peter Giles, published in the 1516 and 1518 editions of Sir Thomas More's *Utopia*.

wants *Utopia* to function as a critique of abstract philosophy with its
theoretical, universal terms and instigate change of the real, dynamic
and concrete world of people and actions. Hence, as Warren Wooden
and John Wall point out, More wants us to examine the island of Utopia
as a place in constant process that is open to "change, to dialectic, to the
give and take of discussion" (1985, 32). His readers should understand
Utopia as a means of insight, "not as an object of knowledge but as an
occasion for an act of perception, an instrument for 'seeing' designed

to call attention to what is involved in perception" (Wooden and Wall 1985, 233). As Wooden and Wall point out,

> In *Utopia*, we believe, More takes one step beyond Erasmus's concept of didactic fiction by presenting an image which cannot be copied in England but which works, nonetheless, to enable its readers to move from where they are to somewhere else.
>
> (1985, 236)

More does this ironically. He constructs *Utopia* as a hoax with pitfalls for the inattentive reader, and this is where the addition of the maps to the text proves to be of vital importance. Maps are hybrid systems since they include both graphic and textual elements; they provide geographical as well as cultural information (Nöth 2012, 349). Their capacity to abstract and to generalize makes them ideal for making experimental journeys on the map – or in the mind. This makes them spatial embodiments of knowledge with the peculiar potential to stimulate new cognitive engagements and experiments. Building a fictional world that resembles our life world, a map allows such experimentation; this not only enables us to lose ourselves to our imaginary travels but also encourages us to try out and test ideas and actions that we otherwise would not dare to perform, such as criticizing authorities, tracing adventurous journeys or simply helping us understand complex relationships.

Writers have exploited this potential in a very sophisticated fashion from very early on (on the use of maps in More's *Utopia*, see also Ljungberg 2012, 41–47). Mapping imaginary spaces like Utopia, the attentive reader is able to form a mental diagram by following Hythloday's description of the island's spatial relations as well as to explore the diagrammatically ordered information provided by the map. Diagrams are formidable instruments for interpreting both texts and maps since they help us get an abstract systematic overview and "[read] for the plot" (Brooks 1984) – without getting lost in the details. They allow the reader of a map or a text to control the meaning of the various elements and to trace changes as a kind of abstract operation that affects the relations between the individual parts of the text or between objects on the map such as rivers, mountains, roads or cities. Diagrammatization is hence the process that creates a comprehensible connection between the dimensions, levels and elements of both text and map. By making clear the relationships between the diverse components of the phenomena that concern us, diagrammatization facilitates various interpretations and so opens up the text or map to different readings.

This process becomes especially important in *Utopia*, which is a travel narrative as well as a complex philosophical treatise. More seems to have succeeded in leading readers to believe in the existence of the island since, when the book appeared, many readers took his account literally and believed that *Utopia* was just another travel narrative about the New World (Adams 1992, viii), a place located somewhere in Vespucci's *Novus Mundus*. Hythloday fits into this scheme since, as we saw earlier, he is introduced as having discovered America together with Vespucci but to then have parted company with the latter when he sailed on. In addition, in his introductory letter to Peter Giles, More mentions a certain clergyman who had declared his intention to go to Utopia as a missionary. However, *Utopia* is also presented to us as a travel story in de Certeau's sense. It contains all the necessary components: it includes physical journeys and offers readers divergent notions and perspectives, intending to transport them from one perspective to new and different viewpoints, including the introduction of the idea of a society that is entirely different from the autocratic one of their contemporaries. More achieves this by staging *Utopia* as a travel story about a trip to Flanders, Bruges and Antwerp, where he meets his friend Peter Giles. Giles then introduces him to Raphael Hythloday, the world traveller who happened to land in Utopia on his way from South America and ended up spending five years among the Utopians. By using actual geographical locations, More enables readers to locate themselves, to put themselves on the map, as it were, and get used to the idea of another unknown island. In what follows, More uses the island of Utopia to introduce different notions and perspectives to those current in the writer's own society: More, Giles and Hythloday all discuss social and political issues from different viewpoints, re-appropriating space in de Certeau's sense since More tactically presents his view of an alternative state. Explicitly avoiding questions about "the routine of the traveller's tales" such as "monsters [...] Scyllas, ravenous Celaenos, man-eating Lestrygonians," More and Giles instead ask Hythloday about "wise and sensible institutions that he has observed among the civilized nations" (More 1992, 7). What interests them are "governments solidly established and sensibly ruled," which, as they point out, are rather the exception to the rule (More 1992, 7).

The distinctly different society that *Utopia* asks the reader to imagine is presented as being "quite absurd" (More 1992, 45). In Utopia, great efforts are made not only to avoid war unless absolutely necessary, but also to spare as many lives as possible. Utopians also insist on religious tolerance, an issue that was to become increasingly thorny in Henry VIII's England. Most absurd, however, is "[the Utopians'] communal living and their moneyless economy" (84), a notion that was entirely opposed to the behaviour of the English élite in More's time and especially to that of its totalitarian monarch. As R. W. Chambers has suggested, *Utopia* is partly a protest against New Statesmanship, which allowed a despotic prince more or less everything (1992, 142). More here contests the imposition of these various forms of power by an autocratic ruler and "grabbing superman" and, instead, depicts a state where "all things in common do rest" (Chambers 1992, 142). Since this easily could have landed him in great trouble with the authorities, More chooses the elegant strategy of shaping *Utopia* as a travel narrative with its typical narrative format of a first-hand traveller-narrator: first, More himself, then his informers and, finally, the main narrator of Utopian geography and customs, Raphael Hythloday. The book thereby appears as a factual narrative and actual story about a real place. In his endeavour, More was supported by the so-called Humanist Circle which included himself, Erasmus of Rotterdam, Peter Giles and Jerome Busleiden, who all supplied him with suitable letters (Adams 1992, 108).

Providing this 'travel narrative' with a map was, thus, crucial for More, not only to authenticate his narrative but also to make his readers aware of the various perspectives and possibilities of government available in theory, if not yet in practice. This is why the maps become crucial for an understanding of the narrative investment in *Utopia*. If we look at the first map of 1516, it appears to be an almost 'literal' representation of the island of Utopia as More has his narrator, Raphael Hythloday, describe it at the beginning of Book II:

> The island of the Utopians is two hundred miles across in the middle part where it is widest, and is nowhere much narrower than this except toward the two ends, where it gradually tapers. These ends, drawn toward one another as if in a five-hundred-mile circle, make the island crescent-shaped like a new moon. Between the horns of the crescent, which are about eleven miles apart, the sea enters and spreads into a broad bay. Being sheltered from the wind by the surrounding land, the bay is never rough, but quiet and smooth instead, like a big lake. Thus, nearly the whole inner coast is one great harbour, across which ships pass in every direction, to the great advantage of the people. What with shallows on one side, and rocks on the other, the entrance into the bay is perilous. Near the middle of the channel, there is one rock that rises above the water, and so presents no dangers in itself; on top of it a tower has been built, and there a garrison is kept. (1992, 31)

The map seems to be following Hythloday's description of Utopian geographical space closely, albeit in a conventionalized manner. It certainly conjures up "the stage designer, the painter, and [...] the cartographer," (Conley 1996, 5). It also evokes the architect, especially on reading Hythloday's description of the architecture of its principal city, Amaurot, or Ciuitas Amaurotum, as it is called on this map, which More places at the omphalus or "navel of the land" (1992, 32), and which designates the island's spiritual as well as physical centre. In contrast, the island's other fifty-four cities are mainly represented by a few stylized singular castles and churches. However, the island's

Figure 2.3 Map of Utopia. Woodcut by [Ambrosius Holbein] in the 1516 edition of Sir Thomas More's *Utopia*.

"crescent-shaped" form is clearly discernible on this map, as is the river Anyder, which follows the shape of the island up to its estuary, the Ostium Anydri.

If we now look at the later map in the edition of 1518, we see some significant changes from the earlier version, although the map is obviously related to the one in the 1516 edition.

On this map (Figure 2.4), the watchtower by the bay appears to have been elaborated into an ornate fortification that guides the viewer's eye into the entrance to the island. The second river mentioned in the text – which is not marked on the 1516 map – is now seen flowing through the city portal, whereas the large bay at the sea-approach to the island has entirely disappeared. Mountains, hills and forests – which are not

Figure 2.4 Map of Utopia. Woodcut by Ambrosius Holbein in the 1518 edition of Sir
Thomas More's *Utopia*.

mentioned in the text – fill the empty spaces on the map where, in the
earlier version, there were only very stylized depictions of buildings and
the river Anyder. In addition, whereas the names Fons Anydri, Ostium
Anydri and Ciuitas Amaurotum (Amaurotum urbs on the 1518 map)
were written *into* the map space on the earlier map, they have now been
provided with ornate frames in a garland-like arrangement that appears
superimposed upon the island.

The three-dimensionality created by this frame-like arrangement gives the impression of depicting a realistic landscape in which the viewer has to position him- or herself. As Wooden and Wall remark, it is precisely the effort to make the map more 'realistic,' lending it a more 'correct' image, which makes the 1518 map "more problematic" (1985, 243). However, even more interesting is that this frame-like arrangement actually reflects the structure of the narrative as it promotes the illusion created by the text's narrative perspectives. Book I opens with the initial first-person narrator, the "Most Distinguished and Eloquent Author THOMAS MORE, Citizen and Sheriff of the Famous City of London," describing how, on a diplomatic mission to Flanders, he met Peter Giles, a town clerk and literate in Antwerp, who introduced him to Raphael Hythloday. It ends with More's plea to know more about Hythloday's adventures, urging that Hythloday tell him and Giles about his extraordinary experiences in Utopia.

Book II is taken up by Hythloday's first-person narrative until, at the very end, More returns, dismissively designating the former's story as being "quite absurd" (1992, 85). What More especially reacts to is Hythloday's favourable reporting on the Utopian ideas of communism and a moneyless society. At the same time, More's final lines come as close to disowning this earlier disclaimer as possible. There, he finishes by saying that, although he could not "agree with everything [Hythloday] said [...] [he] freely confess[es] that there are very many things in the Utopian Commonwealth that in [his] own society [he] would wish rather than expect to see" (More 1992, 85). But More also has Hythloday's description of Utopia *seem* absurd and unreal. Not only is the island paradoxically named Utopia (no land) and the river Anyder, which is Greek for "waterless" (More 1992, 37), but also is its capital called Amaurot. Its Greek name, meaning "shadowy" or "unknown place," has associations with fog and shadow, or Plato's cave. Amaurot is not just the only city that is marked on the map but it is also the only one described in the text. This is explained by Hythloday as self-evident since, while the Utopian cities are all alike (their language, customs and laws are identical and they have a similar size, layout and appearance), Amaurot is the worthiest of all (1992, 41) – yet another paradox. All of this suggests that More does not really want us to believe that Utopia is real. As Wooden and Wall have suggested, More "intends for *Utopia* to become an instrument for seeing that will make possible a dialogue about England because it provides a way of breaking through received assumptions about things-as-they-are [...] that will result in changes being made" (1985, 236). As they point out, "to read *Utopia* is thus to pass through a series of frames, to experience a series of perspectives of the central subject, all the while seeing others 'seeing' *Utopia* from other points of view, other angles" (1985, 244), which ultimately enables readers to 'see' *Utopia* for themselves.

The focus of the 1518 map on these multi-perspectival points of view may also explain the difference between this and the earlier map. Whereas the first map is more concerned with the island's architecture, the second interacts with the narrative in much more intricate ways. More – and Holbein – created Utopia at a time when artists were beginning to experiment with perspective painting. By using so-called anamorphic viewpoints – a Renaissance painting technique that gave two views of an object at once – More forces the viewer to become aware of the problems of perception and perspective, and the question of who controls what is seen.[2] In addition, the story's anamorphic viewpoints are extended diagrammatically to encompass the various narrative positions of the three narrators (Morus, Giles and Hythloday), the map artists and the readers, in order to combine a multitude of perspectives. By putting such a definite emphasis on the act of 'seeing,' their verbal and visual descriptions of Utopia thus function not to portray the ideal state of Utopia, but rather to show England in new ways. As Wooden and Wall point out, these are devices "that force the reader to reexamine conventional ways of seeing and understanding his native landscape" (1985, 254).

It is especially the addition of the prefatory letters which demonstrates the performative power inherent in the later map. As 'nowhere,' Utopia should indeed be 'somewhere' and "give its 'nowhereness' the illusion of a very concrete local habitation and a name" (Wooden and Wall 1985, 255). Whereas the 1516 map is more 'literal,' the 1518 version has a different function, namely that of creating a New World of its own. The map-frame not only matches the story's chiastic structure, which puts the focus on Hythloday's centred narration, but directly interacts with the diverse perspectives of the various narratives. After all, Hythloday is Greek for "nonsense-peddler" and Morus means "foolish" in Latin, which suggests a self-ironic stance on the author's part.

This, I would argue, is what lies behind the strikingly different representations of the island. Hythloday's position, standing at the front edge of the map and pointing in the direction of Utopia, makes him part and parcel of both map and story frame. By contrast, Morus and Giles only belong to the story's *outer* frame. They are thus left out of the Utopian picture. While Morus is not even looking at Utopia but at Hythloday, who is telling him the narrative, Giles, located on the other side of the map frame, has a different perspective on Utopia. At the same time, these multi-perspectival viewpoints are precisely what allows Morus and Giles to adopt cautious and critical positions both on Utopia and on their own governments and societies. More's *Utopia* starts out with a satire on the chaotic contemporary events in England. The narrative then presents the island of Utopia as a radical contrast to the 'island' of England, as a stratagem to suggest alternative ways of thinking. The later map hence extends the iconic function diagrammatically to reflect and enact the text's multiple perspectives in order to act as a potential instrument of change.

In sum, the two maps in the two editions of Sir Thomas More's *Utopia* can be said to serve as an instrument for seeing, designed to call attention to the very act of perception and demonstrating that there are always several points of view. Matching More's elegant strategy of framing fundamental questions about society and government, they both mirror and display the complexity of the narrative organization to criticize, implicitly and ingeniously, political and social wrongs by opening a dialogue between different parties. They show that, by seeing things otherwise, new solutions can be found. At the same time, by locating the island of Utopia at a safe distance far away from England and its institutions, they operate as efficient devices for avoiding censorship as well as royal wrath.[3]

To conclude, the inclusion of the maps in *Utopia* not only emphasizes how the presence of space in language can be made tangible through the spatialization afforded by diagrammatic articulation. It also demonstrates how these abstract relationships make visible the deeply serious intent motivating More's perspicacious work. Combining geography, narrative and imaginaries into an effective visualization that enhances its playful and experimental nature, More's *Utopia* is an outstanding example of spatial modernity.

Notes

1 Magellan did not live to return to Spain since he was killed in the Battle of Mactan in the Philippines in 1521. The circumnavigation was, however, successfully completed by Juan Sebastian Elcano, who took the command after Magellan's death.

2 There are even more fascinating dimensions to the 1518 Utopia map. A recent article by Malcolm Bishop (2005) interprets it as a clever *memento mori*, punning on More's name, in the form of a skull, which was probably commissioned by Erasmus of Rotterdam who, together with Peter Giles, oversaw the publication. To start visualizing this, begin at the ship/teeth to discern the map's skull-like features, with which Ambrosius preceded his brother Hans's placement of an anamorphic skull up front in his famous painting *The Ambassadors* (1533) by fifteen years.

3 Royal wrath actually caught up with More in the end, but for a different reason. He was beheaded in 1535 for refusing to accept Henry VIII as the head of the Church of England, which made him a saint in the Roman Catholic Church.

References

Adams, Robert M. 1992. "The Humanist Circle: Letters." In *Utopia*, translated and edited by Robert M. Adams, 108–133. New York: Norton.

Almagià, Roberto. 2014. "Amerigo Vespucci." Encyclopædia Britannica. March 31, 2014. www.britannica.com/biography/Amerigo-Vespucci.

Bishop, Malcolm. 2005. "Ambrosius Holbein's *Memento Mori* Map for Sir Thomas More's *Utopia*: The Meanings of a Masterpiece of Early Sixteenth Century Graphic Art." *British Dental Journal* 199 (July): 107–112.

Brooks, Peter. 1984. *Reading for the Plot: Design and Intention in Narrative.* New York: Knopf.

Brotton, Jerry. 1998. *Trading Territories: Mapping the Early Modern World.* Ithaca: Cornell University Press.

Chambers, Robert W. 1992. "The Meaning of Utopia." In *Utopia*, by Sir Thomas More, translated and edited by Robert M. Adams, 137–147. New York: Norton.

Conley, Tom. 1996. *The Self-Made Map: Cartographic Writing in Early Modern France.* Minneapolis: University of Minnesota Press.

de Certeau, Michel. 1984. *The Practice of Everyday Life.* Translated by Steven Rendall. Berkeley: University of California Press.

Dodge, Martin, Rob Kitchin, and Chris Perkins. 2009. *Rethinking Maps: New Frontiers in Cartographic Theory.* London: Routledge.

Harwood, Jeremy. 2011. *To the End of the Earth: 100 Maps that Changed the World.* New York: Chartwell.

Ljungberg, Christina. 2012. *Creative Dynamics: Diagrammatic Strategies in Narrative.* Amsterdam: John Benjamins.

———. 2016. "The Diagrammatic Nature of Maps." In *Thinking with Diagrams: The Semiotic Basis of Human Cognition*, edited by Sybille Krämer and Christina Ljungberg, 139–159. Boston: De Gruyter.

Mayer, Robert. 1997. *History and the Early English Novel: Matters of Fact from Bacon to Defoe.* New York: Cambridge University Press.

More, Sir Thomas. 1992. *Utopia.* Second edition. Translated and edited by Robert M. Adams. New York: Norton.

Nöth, Winfried. 2012. "Medieval Maps: Hybrid Ideographic and Geographic Sign Systems." In *Herrschaft Verorten: Politische Kartographie des Mittelalters und der Frühen Neuzeit*, edited by Ingrid Baumgärtner and Martina Stercken, 335–353. Zurich: Chronos.

Wegemer, Gerhard B. 1998. *Thomas More on Statesmanship.* Washington, DC: CUA Press.

Wooden, Warren W., and John N. Wall. 1985. "Thomas More and the Painter's Eye." *Journal of Medieval and Renaissance Studies* 15: 231–263.

3   Of the Novelty of Bird's-Eye Views in Eighteenth-Century Travelling Narratives

Jean-Paul Forster

Views taken from hot-air balloons, drones, helicopters, planes and spacecraft are so common today that we tend to forget that it was not always so. Until the eighteenth century, the main pictorial representations of geographical space were maps for large areas, plans for small ones and profiles or scenic views for landscapes. Like scenic views, bird's-eye views, often called 'prospects,' did exist, but their use was limited to the pictorial representation of proximate spaces like gardens, palaces and towns. On the other hand, they were non-existent in verbal representations of geographical space, whether literary or not. Only recently had they begun to inspire a type of English lyric: the topographical poem. One of the best-known early examples of the genre is John Denham's "Cooper's Hill" (1642), whose much anthologized central passage begins as follows: "My Eye, descending from the Hill, surveys / Where Thames amongst the wanton Valleys strays" (1779, 28). In travel reports, the representation of space took the form of accounts of itineraries and depictions of profiles of landscapes. In fictional kinds of writings, from *Piers Plowman* to *The Pilgrim's Progress* and from *La Chanson de Roland* to *Gargantua* and *Don Quixote*, representations of space were almost exclusively scenic. They presented topographical settings as seen at ground level. Verbal bird's-eye views made their first appearance in 1719 and 1726 in two fictions in which geography was a focus of interest: Daniel Defoe's *Robinson Crusoe* and Jonathan Swift's *Gulliver's Travels*. In these two works, views from above were used at crucial moments in the narrative.

Compared to the other kinds of representations of geographical space, bird's-eye views have never been numerous, and the place they occupy in travelling narratives has always been modest. To deal with them is to focus on a detail of the verbal medium. If they deserve our attention here, it is because they were symptomatic of a change in the way people looked at and lived space and because their occurrence in Defoe's and Swift's narratives is in several respects intriguing.

It is the quasi-didactic clarity with which bird's-eye views are described in *Gulliver's Travels* that draws attention to their novelty. They are beautifully integrated in the framework of the travel account, at the same time as they appraise the geographical usefulness and limitations of such representations. The first bird's-eye view in the satire describes Gulliver's initial impression of Lilliput when he is allowed to rise to his feet. Until then, he had been lying on the ground, bound hand and foot:

> [...] I looked about me, and must confess I never beheld a more entertaining Prospect. The Country round appeared like a continued Garden; and the inclosed Fields, which were generally Forty Foot square, resembled so many Beds of Flowers. These Fields were intermingled with Woods of half a Stang, and the tallest Trees, as I could judge, appeared to be seven Foot high. I viewed the Town on my left Hand, which looked like the painted Scene of a City in a Theatre.
>
> (Swift 1971, 14)

The view from his tall stature is extended. It does not direct the attention to the foreground as in traditional bird's-eye views of geographical space but embraces foreground, middle distance and background. Nor is it scenic in the manner of topographical profiles, which make a view "spring out of the sheet" in engravings or paintings (Nuti 1988, 545). Gulliver's description flattens the topography and geometrizes the landscape, emphasizing forms and measurements: "enclosed fields," "forty foot square," "half a stang" (half a quarter of an acre), "seven foot high."

The second passage goes one step further. Gulliver now stands surrounded by the court of Lilliput and looks down upon them: "The Ladies and Courtiers were all most magnificently clad, so that the Spot they stood upon seemed to resemble a Petticoat spread on the Ground, embroidered with Figures of Gold and Silver" (Swift 1971, 16). This second bird's-eye view shows how, as the angle of observation approaches 90°, the topography of the land looks more and more flat, until the image of reality becomes unintelligible. And the image of the petticoat to represent the Lilliputian courtiers surrounding the giant is in a sense unintelligible. To produce an intelligible picture of the situation, the eighteenth-century geographer would use conventional symbols or pictures and have recourse to "measuring instruments – compasses and scales," as Lucia Nuti puts it (1988, 547); not so the satirist, who relies on figurative language and, what is more, a most fanciful simile as a shortcut to depict the situation. Its depiction is more puzzling than geographically explicit. In the context of the satire, however, the use of the simile pursues a different end. The choice is quite clever. Combining as it does the idea of exaggerated flattening and geometrical pattern (Swift's "Figures") with Gulliver's awareness of the discrepancy between the actual assembly of courtiers and the fanciful character of his simile ("seemed to resemble"), the passage reminds the reader of "the Weakness of [Gulliver's] Eyes"; it brings to mind that what Gulliver sees when he is not wearing his "Pair of Spectacles" (Swift 1971, 23) is a blurred image with bright colours, a clear indication that he is short-sighted. The satirical suggestion is that short-sightedness is a general failing of cartographers as their representations are far too remote from reality.

Swift's next methodological step is to highlight the link between bird's-eye views and visions of a region or country given by maps. This is soon done in and by the fiction. The king of Lilliput orders the "Man Mountain" to "deliver in an exact Survey of the Circumference of [his] Dominions, by a Computation of [the giant's] own Paces round the Coast" (Swift 1971, 30). At the time, this counting of steps was the usual method to calculate distances on land. From the king's request, we can infer that Gulliver is thus the author of the portolan chart prefacing "A Voyage to Lilliput" and, by implication, of all the other maps in the *Travels*.

"A Voyage to Brobdingnag" continues the geographical fiction and discussion of bird's-eye views. In Book II of the *Travels*, Gulliver is made to cut a ridiculous figure. Because he is now too small – a Lilliputian among giants – to get a bird's-eye view of even a small area of the country, we find him pacing a gigantic "Royal Map" of the kingdom (Swift 1971, 104). He relies on this map to give him a general view of Brobdingnag. In this episode, Swift uses the device to draw, once more, attention to the cartographer's lack of concrete hold over geographical reality. By presenting in Book I the fields of Lilliput "like so many Beds of Flowers" (1971, 14) and the Queen's palace like a doll's house (1971, 33), the bird's-eye views give a misleadingly idealized picture of Lilliput. The map of Brobdingnag similarly oversimplifies the picture of the country. Contrasting the smooth geographical representation of a country on paper with Gulliver's chaotic human experience, the voyage becomes the story of the hero's un-deception, a pattern repeated in each voyage. His excessive concern with bird's-eye views and mapping blinds him, at least initially, to the human reality that confronts him in each new situation.

Although "A Voyage to Laputa" makes no reference to geography and mapping, it is nevertheless evident that its spatial representation of the conflict between the flying island of Laputa and its subject island, Balnibarbi, presents another instance of bird's-eye view and cartographic representation. Book III pursues the reflection on their deceptive character. This time, the case does not concern remote countries but neighbours in close contact. The bird's-eye view is that of the inhabitants of the flying island. When they look down from its galleries, what they can see of Balnibarbi are only flat pictures of the land below: images similar to maps or bird's-eye views of one of its areas. The Laputans' habit of living wrapped up in speculation, "one of their Eyes turned inward and the other directly up to the Zenith" (Swift 1971, 155) when their minds are not engrossed in political discussions (1971, 160), does not mitigate their blindness vis-à-vis their subjects below. On the contrary, it adds to their dehumanized view of Balnibarbi. Worse still, this dehumanization opens the door to indiscriminate cruelty and collective violence.

When confronted with opposition, the Laputans do not hesitate to use their bird's-eye view of the subject island to manoeuvre the flying island so as to position it above refractory Balnibarbians and thus "deprive them of the Sun and the Rain" as long as they resist (1971, 170). It is also their bird's-eye view of Balnibarbi that enables them on occasion to "cast great Stones from the lower gallery" of their island to destroy a rebellious town (1971, 170). The Laputans seem unaware that this violence can backfire on them. And the narrative concludes that violence need not spring from a lack of understanding due to different traditions or geographical distances between cultures.

At this point, it is necessary to remember that the map that Swift imagines Gulliver pacing in "A Voyage to Brobdingnag" or the chart that Gulliver draws for the king of Lilliput by walking around his island are different from the highly abstract geometrical patterns of our modern maps. Contemporary maps remained slightly pictorial and, consequently, more similar to bird's-eye views than our modern maps. If rivers and roads were naturally types of lines, hills and mountains were represented as molehills and towns as groups of houses or collections of small black rectangles. There were sometimes pictures of great homes, churches, and trees for forests. Swift himself ridicules this type of maps in his poem "On Poetry: A Rapsody":

> So Geographers in Afric-Maps
> With Savage-Pictures fill their Gaps:
> And o'er uninhabitable Downs
> Place Elephants for want of Towns.

(1967, 574)

If the *geometrica* ratio predominated in representations of space, the *perspectiva ratio* of the stylized bird's-eye view lent some concreteness to the flattening and imperfectly geometrized topography. As seen above, Swift makes full use of the visual possibilities of the *perspectiva ratio*. Gulliver's folk-tale geography is a source of vivid satirical imagery for the author, sometimes humorous, sometimes ferocious as in the above examples. By comparison, Defoe's travel narratives are more sober. To realize this is important for an understanding of their respective treatments of geography.

Swift's practice is of interest for the way he narrativizes the method of geographical observation and its roughly geometrized recording, and Defoe's for the narrativization of geographical space itself. His tales of adventure and exploration fuse geographical and narrative requirements, and his bird's-eye views play a role in this fusion, which in turn influences their nature. They show a character or narrator discovering from an elevated vantage point the space around him. Soon after his arrival on the island on whose shore he has been shipwrecked, Robinson Crusoe climbs up a hill and discovers that it forms part of a ridge stretching "northward" and that the island is "environ'd every Way with the Sea, no Land to be seen, except some Rocks which [lie] a great Way off, and two small Islands less than this, which [lie] about three Leagues to the West" (Defoe 2008b, 96). There is no hint of a scenic effect in the description, only a rough plan of Crusoe's geographical position in his new immediate environment somewhere north of the South American continent. It says simply that his island looks lost in unknown waters and that a ridge seems to form its backbone. The situation suggests that Crusoe has saved his own life but is in a sad predicament. Progressively, the reader discovers that the hero's island is the central piece of a map that extends to other Caribbean islands and the mouth of the Orinoco in South America. The second example is one of several bird's-eye views in another novel by Defoe, *Captain Singleton*. The central part of this novel tells the story of a group of characters who attempt to cross the Southern African continent from East to West. In the following passage, we are told that after travelling "700 miles from the Sea Coast" of the Indian Ocean, the adventurers are confronted with "a high Ridge of Mountains" (Defoe 2008a, 76). They reach the top of the ridge, and what they see is

> a vast-howling Wilderness, not a Tree, a River, or a Green thing to be seen, for as far as the Eye could look; nothing but a scalding Sand, which, as the Wind blew, drove about in Clouds, enough to overwhelm Man and Beast; nor could we see any End of it, either before us, which was our Way, or to the right Hand or left [...].
>
> (2008a, 77)

The emphasis is again on the vastness of a desert. From the top of the mountain, this desert looks hostile to all life and impassable. The adventurers are in a plight that resembles Robinson's.

In these two views from above, both bird's-eye views characteristic of Defoe,[1] the observer does not begin by looking down at what lies below him as in topographical poems or "A Voyage to Lilliput." He looks at the space that opens before him as far as his gaze can see, right up to the horizon, as well as right and left. The observer is a man taking his bearings in expectation or fear, or plotting his next moves. If the horizon is empty or threatening, as in the above examples, his position can even be an image of a man facing the unknown or his destiny. Defoe loves wide perspectives, as much as Swift mistrusts them. Unlike Swift's, his bird's-eye views outline, map out, the surface areas that the travellers are about to cross. What the observer sees anticipates the actual experience. His angle of vision is hardly different from the narrator's as mapper of the characters' itinerary. Nor does the angle of vision change when it comes to the recording of the experience of the next stretch of the route. The following passage shows how the observer-turned-narrator fills in the natural topographical features as these follow each other on the way. He lists them chronologically, much as they would be presented on a ribbon map: an easy stretch, the crossing of a river, the new obstacle of a mountain range in view. The focus of the narrative is the geography because the geography is, to a large extent, the adventure:

> It was the 12th of *October* or thereabouts, that we began to set forward, and having an easy Country to travel in, as well as to supply us with Provisions, tho' still without Inhabitants, we made more Dispatch, travelling some times, as we calculated it 20 or 25 Miles a Day; nor did we halt any where in eleven Days March, one Day excepted, which was to make a Raft to carry us over a small River, which having swelled with the Rains was not yet quite down.
>
> When we were past this River, which by the Way run to the Northward too, we found a great Row of Hills in our Way; we saw indeed the Country open to the Right at a great Distance, but as we kept true to our Course due West, we were not willing to go a great Way out of our Way, only to shun a few Hills; so we advanced [...].
>
> (Defoe 2008a, 95)

Defoe's bird's-eye views make an essentially cartographic contribution to the construction of an imaginary Caribbean island in *Robinson Crusoe* and of an imaginary cross-section of the African continent in *Captain Singleton*. They are typical instances of the author's turn of mind, the turn of mind of a land surveyor who is fond of plans and loves measuring things. Defoe will even, on occasion, tell the reader the size of the skin of a leopard shot by a character (2008a, 68).

Defoe's views from above may be disappointing as bird's-eye views because they lack foregrounds and sometimes even middle distances, but together with indications of distances covered, they function as central articulations of the story: as narrative caesuras[2] between the main stages of the journey. The bird's-eye views usually occur when the characters are confronted with topographical obstacles that make a choice of direction difficult:

> [...] therefore upon every Hill that we came near, we clamber'd up to the highest Part, to see the Country before us, and to make the best Judgment we could which way to go to keep the lowest Grounds, and as near some Stream of Water as we could.
>
> (Defoe 2008a, 73)

The narrative here marks a pause. The important views from above do not only underline the sequence of the stages of the journey, but also the sequencing of the characters' itinerary into segments of distances covered. This is quite striking in *Captain Singleton*. In this way, Defoe points out that the bird's-eye view referred to above comes after a journey of 700 miles and coincides with the end of the second stage and segment of the journey. The end of the first stage and segment comes after 200 miles (2008a, 67), when an impressive cataract, the first great obstacle in the adventurers' crossing of the continent, cuts short their progress, which had been unimpeded up to that point. The second stage and segment begins with a view of the land that the characters will be travelling through: a region peopled by 'savage' tribes and wild beasts (2008a, 67). As for the howling desert that the third stage and segment promises to be, it eventually brings the travellers, after their plodding through "scorching sands" and a cemetery of elephant tusks, to a place 400 miles further and 1,100 miles from their starting point (2008a, 87). The next stage of 400 miles, during which the adventurers follow an uncertain course, leads them to a place about 300 miles from the Atlantic coast. These 300 miles are the last segment of the journey (2008a, 110). The author divides these five long segments into smaller ones that describe stretches of the route between minor natural obstacles, like that of the river that the characters have to cross in the second of the above quotations. In these shorter segments, bird's-eye views also occasionally play a role, orienting the travellers in the track.

This structuring of the journey, to which bird's-eye views draw attention, is interesting because it recalls the method used by explorers to map their progress in unknown lands and record it on a chart or in a report. That Defoe's narrative art was inspired by this practice is confirmed by his own allusion to it in *A New Voyage Round the World* (1725, 223). Henri Bouasse, a French mathematician whose research examines the old ways of mapping new lands, describes the method in the following manner:

> In the absence of precise astronomical coordinates, maps were made [...] by the help of itineraries. The first step was to plan such an itinerary by means of the compass, give it a direction and estimate the total distance to cover or covered.
>
> (1919, 287, my translation)

Henri Bouasse's explanation applies *mutatis mutandis* to the narrative method of *Captain Singleton*. In the novel, the direction of the journey is given by the characters' decision to cross the African continent from Mozambique to either the Congolese Atlantic coast or the Golden Coast further north, and the estimated distance was, according to the knowledge of the time, a little over 1,800 miles (Defoe 2008a, 54, 95–96). The next step, Bouasse explains, was "the sequencing of this total distance into rectilinear segments" (1919, 287, my translation).[3] In the novel, the rectilinearity is ensured by the characters' resolve to follow an east-west route by means of map and compass. Defoe's division of the itinerary into "rectilinear," namely chronological, narrative segments does exactly this when it lays the emphasis on the mileage of the longer segments and on the step-by-step development of the smaller segments usually reckoned in days: "the next Day," "about five Days more," "we march'd three Days full West" (Defoe 2008a, 106, 107). This was also a practice of explorers. Defoe frequently mentions rivers and other topographical features that the adventurers have to cross at right angles. He does so to underline the east-west direction of the expedition, as can again be seen in the second quotation above. It is true that this fictional use of bird's-eye views showing his characters climbing up hills to find the best route compatible with their rectilinear course may look like instances of Gulliverian poring over maps but this is not the case. Narrative and geographical procedures are indebted to what was an agreed method of mapping. In this context, the bird's-eye views can be said to contribute to the vivid description of Defoe's imaginary interior of the African Continent. Introducing as they do the long segments of narrative, they underline the changes of geographical zones from coastal to interior basins, which, in their turn, correspond to changes of terrain posing new problems for the adventurers. The arrival at the "high Ridge of Mountains" (Defoe 2008a, 76) marks the transition from the fertile coastal zone of the Quilloa River to a dry interior plain.[4] For Bouasse, the interesting thing about the old mapping procedure is that it managed to give credible and recognizable topographical pictures, maps, of geographical areas. For the reader of Defoe, the fascinating thing is that the same procedure inspired a narrative method equally capable of producing topographically credible pictures of imaginary continents and islands as scenes of equally credible adventure stories.

Novelists after Defoe and Swift show comparatively little interest in voyages of discovery. Their characters travel on existing road networks around the British Isles and Europe. They usually have precise destinations, which they intend to reach by itineraries that are convenient. If they are not personally familiar with the route, they are at least fully informed about its direction. Bent on their destinations, they pay more attention to the weather and their comfort than to the regions they travel through. The travelling conditions described and the travellers' frame of mind are seldom conducive to the contemplation of landscapes. Occasions for bird's-eye views on the road are not numerous and, in travelling fictions, they are mostly absent. There are a few exceptions. Tobias Smollett's *Humphry Clinker* (1771) is one of these. It is special because its characters are not travelling with a definite purpose in mind. They are touring the main British Isle. In other words, they are travelling for pleasure: the pleasure of enjoying views on and from the road and of visiting places. In one example of a bird's-eye view, Matthew Bramble, travelling from London to Scotland on the great Northern Road, mentions in a letter he writes to his friend Dr Lewis that, from the top of Gateshead Fell, 2.3 miles from the city of Newcastle upon Tyne, he had a splendid view over the countryside. From the road, looking backward, he can see that "the country [around Durham] [...], which extends to

Newcastle, exhibits the highest scene of cultivation that [he] ever beheld" (Smollett 1983, 195). The elevation of 230 feet in an otherwise flat area does indeed offer a pleasant view north over the Tyne River and Newcastle and south towards Durham. Later on, in Scotland, Matthew Bramble is thrilled by the view over the sea from the coast near Inveraray. It "affords," he writes, "one of most ravishing prospects in the whole world [...] the appearance of the Hebrides, or Western islands, to the number of three hundred, scattered as far as the eye can reach, in the most agreeable confusion" (1983, 234). These two bird's-eye views are quite different from those in *Robinson Crusoe* and *Captain Singleton*. They are not intended to situate the observer or the landmarks he is referring to. There is no need to do so, as the region is well known to the writer of the letters as well as to the addressee. There is no geometrizing of the setting as there was in "A Voyage to Lilliput." The purpose is no longer to map and measure a stretch of road. The landmarks mentioned serve to situate an area in order to convey a general impression of its topography. On the other hand, the perspective is wide, as in Defoe. Expressions like "highest scene of cultivation" or "agreeable confusion" are subjective and convey impressions and emotions rather than factual topographical information. What can be said is that, in this novel, the narrativization of space is that of a man of the age of sentiment, a tourist ready to enthuse about impressive landscapes, as poets did in topographic poems. The case is interesting as, in the same period, the taste for topographical verse was waning (Aubin 1936). Should Smollett's very unromantic Matthew Bramble be seen as a forerunner of the Romantics? What is sure is that Romanticism would soon offer fresh illustrations of bird's-eye views in the celebration of authors' walking tours and journeys.

A few words remain to be added on the novelty of bird's-eye views in travelling narratives. Their appearance in Swift's, Defoe's and Smollett's fiction was indeed new but modest in terms of frequency. Far more important in a long-term perspective was the recognition of bird's-eye views outside geographers' circles as a distinct angle of vision on topographical reality. Of this the bird's-eye views in *Gulliver's Travels*, *Robinson Crusoe* and *Captain Singleton* are early manifestations: the satire when it makes bird's-eye views the subject of a critical discussion, and Defoe's two works of fiction when they associate bird's-eye views with the contemporary interest in narratives of exploration. They show that views from above had entered the general consciousness of the age. With Swift's flying monster and Defoe's close link between narrative and mapping, our two writers' bird's-eye views can be said to have given fiction a touch of modernity.

Swift's, Defoe's and a few additional early novelists' use of bird's-eye views is on the whole in line with their general narrative discourse, which turns geography to fictional account, which narrativizes space. But their bird's-eye views as such have been seen to be slightly deficient in so far as they lack foregrounds and sometimes even middle distances. Their views from above lean towards mapping and focus on long-distance perspectives. This departure from the usual practice illustrated by topographical poems is to my mind partly attributable to the predominant eighteenth-century notion of geography as essentially cartographic and its valorization of vast spaces and long distances.

Apart from this singular narrative use, Swift's, Defoe's and other early novelists' bird's-eye views are of course the expression of widely different attitudes to geographical representations of space (Forster 2013). Swift's stands out as particularly severe about an excessive reliance on their reductive and deceptive nature. As seen in "A Voyage to Lilliput," he hints that mappers have as well as produce myopic visions of topographical reality. His strikingly consistent utilization of the 90° angle of vision exposes the dangers of seeing the world too much in cartographic terms. For him, too much mapping has a negative impact on human relationships. Reading "A Voyage to Laputa," one cannot but think of some sinister uses of modern aircraft and drones. Defoe has none of Swift's reservations about cartographic representation. He embraces the advances of the geography of his time with enthusiasm and is even ready to fill in its gaps. As such, he can be said to share Gulliver's blind spots, especially when the cartographic flattening of the topography leads him to minimize natural obstacles. Seas, mountain ranges and deserts are never impassable for his characters. As for the novels of writers of the next generation, their bird's-eye views simply occur, unselfconsciously, as they do on the road or during an outing.

With Swift and Defoe, bird's-eye views made their entrance into literature as a component of the narrativization of geographical space. The German philosopher Georg Simmel once wrote that the development of a straight path between two locations was one of the great exploits of humanity (1957, 2). The utilization of the bird's-eye view in fictional travelling narratives was, I would suggest, an image of the eighteenth-century ambition to multiply such paths and improve world communications. It was also a significant trait of eighteenth-century geography, a geography of travels, not a static geography of ownership and control of land.

Notes

1 For other examples, see *Captain Singleton* (Defoe 2008a, 86, 101–102). See also *A New Voyage Round the World* (2009, 213).
2 Mikhail Bakhtin would speak of mimesis and Roland Barthes of "catalysts" (1966, 9–10).
3 Bouasse's French original reads as follows:

> [...] en dehors de quelques points dont on connaît les coordonnées astronomiques, les cartes se faisaient et se font avec des *itinéraires*. L'itinéraire indique la direction de la route donnée par la boussole, et la distance parcourue évaluée [...]. Le parcours total est divisé en un certain

nombre de parcours rectilignes qu'on transporte sur le papier. Il est remarquable qu'on obtienne ainsi des évaluations relativement exactes.

(1919, 287)

4 Quiloa or Kilwa was not the name of a river but of a once powerful city on the East African coast. Today there are two Kilwa on the Tanzanian coast, both near river mouths. But Quiloa also figured as a river on a map in Defoe's *Atlas Maritimus & Commercialis* (1728): "A Correct Sea Chart of the Whole World According to Wright's commonly called Mercator's Projection."

References

Aubin, Robert Arnold. 1936. *Topographical Poetry in XVIII-Century England.* New York: MLA.

Barthes, Roland. 1966. "Introduction à l'analyse structurale des récits." *Communications* 8: 1–27.

Bouasse, Henri. 1919. *Géographie mathématique.* Paris: Librairie Delagrave.

Defoe, Daniel. 1728. *Atlas Maritimus & Commercialis; or, a General View of the World, so Far as Relates to Trade and Navigation.* London: James and John Knapton.

———. (1720) 2008a. *The Life, Adventures, and Pyracies of the Famous Captain Singleton.* In *The Novels of Daniel Defoe*, Vol. 5, edited by P. N. Furbank. London: Pickering and Chatto.

———. (1719) 2008b. *The Life and Strange Surprising Adventures of Robinson Crusoe.* In *The Novels of Daniel Defoe*, Vol. 1, edited by W. R. Owens. London: Pickering and Chatto.

———. (1725) 2009. *A New Voyage Round the World.* In *The Novels of Daniel Defoe*, Vol. 10, edited by John McVeagh. London: Pickering and Chatto.

Denham, John. 1779. *The Poetical Works of Sir John Denham.* Edinburgh: Apollo Press.

Forster, Jean-Paul. 2013. *Eighteenth-Century Geography and the Representation of Space in English Fiction and Poetry.* Bern: Peter Lang.

Nuti, Lucia. 1988. "The Mapped Views by Georg Hoefnagel: The Merchant's Eye, the Humanist's Eye." *Word & Image* 4 (2): 545–570.

Simmel, Georg. 1957. "Brücke und Tür." In *Brücke und Tür: Essays des Philosophen zur Geschichte, Religion, Kunst und Gesellschaft*, edited by Michael Landmann, 1–7. Stuttgart: K. F. Koehler.

Smollett, Tobias. 1983. *The Expedition of Humphry Clinker.* New York: W. W. Norton.

Swift, Jonathan. 1967. *Poetical Works*, edited by Herbert Davis. London: Oxford University Press.

———. 1971. *Gulliver's Travels*, edited by Paul Turner. Oxford: Oxford University Press.

4 Satellite Vision and Geographical Imagination[*]

David Shim

Introduction

The practice of remote sensing is widespread in contemporary global politics. Literally meaning the acquisition of information about an object, place or phenomenon on the Earth's surface by means of distant observation, remote sensing – or what can also be called 'remote seeing' – is used by a range of actors including governments, militaries, international organizations, civil society groups, companies, scholars, journalists and artists. Images taken from cameras and sensors mounted on balloons, drones, planes and satellites are assumed to provide insights for purposes of, for instance, military surveillance and reconnaissance, environmental analysis and humanitarian operations. While these instruments of observation differ in their applicability, they reveal how the production of knowledge – be it military, geographical or environmental – is connected to, and created by, particular practices of looking. In other words, images taken from overhead devices are not necessarily illustrative, and therefore secondary to knowledge, but actually constitute knowledge in their own right. In this way, they participate in constructing both geographical information and geographical imagination.[1]

One of the most powerful and widespread tools of remote sensing is satellite imagery. Originally produced and used exclusively by nation-states, satellite images are now becoming increasingly available in the public domain. Regularly cited in news media around the world and made popular through, for instance, geospatial information services such as Google Maps and Google Earth, satellite imagery has entered the realm of everyday life. These images are, therefore, both powerful means of engaging the world and an integral part of the processes of how we come to know spaces, places and sites. Satellite images, hence, are cases of what is called here 'visual spatial imaginaries' because they participate in the shaping of our awareness of areas, locations and territories.

A good example of this is the satellite photograph of Earth seen in Figure 4.1. Such images of Earth have not only established a new practice of looking – the view from outer space (cf. Sachs 1994; see also,

Figure 4.1 "The Blue Marble" (2002) – East. Image courtesy of NASA/Earth Observatory.

Cosgrove 1994) – but have also created and sustained the iconography of what is now known as the 'Blue Planet.' Based on visual data obtained by the National Aeronautics and Space Administration (NASA), which began producing and circulating pictures of what it has called the 'Blue Marble' since the 1970s, (satellite) images have been a central part of popular imaginations about the Earth as a fragile place of a unitary biosphere and coherent ecological system (cf. Siemer 2007). It is no coincidence that, according to NASA, the image of the Blue Marble is the most popular and most downloaded item on its website – in contrast to, say, the specific climate- and/or environment-related imagery that forms part of NASA's main scientific portfolio (Keck and Carlowicz 2012). The enormous popularity of the Blue Marble points to the effects that it unfolds. It does not necessarily produce geographical knowledge for people but rather fuels their geographical imaginations about a particular place: the globe.

This chapter is driven by the following core questions: how do people get an idea of the world and its places, and how are our notions or senses of space and place constructed? It will be argued that satellite images are a crucial part of these processes. Furthermore, their spatial authority to 'speak' about places and spaces is arguably greatly enhanced vis-à-vis sites that are deemed secluded, concealed and obscure – none more so than in the case of the Democratic People's Republic of Korea, commonly known as North Korea. The vision provided by a satellite helps us to see and, therefore, to *know* what supposedly obscure places, sites and life 'really' look like on the ground. Against this backdrop, this chapter will discuss one of the image motifs that plays a central role in shaping imaginative geographies of what is commonly known as the most isolated place on Earth: the satellite shot of the Korean peninsula by night (Figure 4.2).

The following section explains what is unique and special about the case presented here. In doing so, it engages with the work of scholars who have addressed questions of spatial politics and the imaginative dimension of the satellite gaze (cf. Dodge and Perkins 2009; see also Aday and Livingston 2009; Crutcher and Zook 2009; Kingsbury and Jones 2009; Parks 2009; Perkins and Dodge 2009). However, the analysis provided here goes beyond their work in that it takes the site of the image more seriously. Put simply, while the aforementioned authors treat satellite images as carriers of the message, this study scrutinizes satellite images as the message itself. It asks what effect the image in question – that is, the night-time representation of the Korean peninsula – has as a

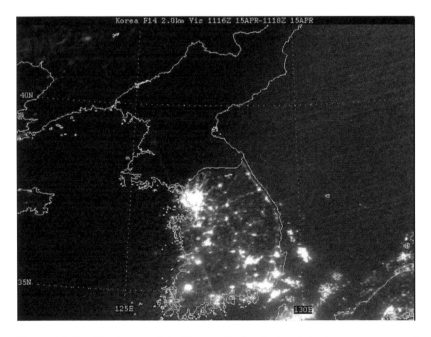

Figure 4.2 Satellite image of the Korean Peninsula by night. Image courtesy of GlobalSecurity.org/John Pike.

result of being portrayed in this way. This has implications, elaborated in the concluding section, for scholars' use of satellite images, as such an approach raises the question of whether these pictures can be incorporated into one's own research as a distinct mode of meaning or whether they are nothing more than supplements, and therefore subordinate, to verbal or written texts. The following part also introduces the methodological criteria for discussing images, which are based on an interpretive analysis of both the image and its accompanying text.

North Korea as Terra Incognita and the Politics of Satellite Vision

There are seemingly few states like North Korea in the contemporary geopolitical order. Often described as a "mystery" (Scalapino 1997), "terra incognita" (Solarz 1999) or "enigma" (Halliday 1981), North Korea captures people's geographical imaginations like no other country in the world. Because North Korea is widely believed to be politically unmapped, economically cut off and culturally secluded, articulations of difference play an important role in describing the spaces and spatialities of what is often called the "black hole" in global affairs. Therefore, North Korea appears to be a terra incognita sui generis; an uncharted land all of its own.

Indeed, North Korea has been labelled a "black hole" on many different occasions and in multiple contexts: it is a "black hole" in terms of communication (Zeller 2006), economy (Noland 2012), energy (Kim 2009) and available intelligence (Sanger and Choe 2013). It is no coincidence, then, that visual references pervade the various actors' approaches to North Korea: it remains unseen and is, moreover, hidden from view.

However, satellites, as Chris Perkins and Martin Dodge (2009) argue, play a central role in lifting the veil of secrecy that covers unknown places, spaces and locations. In this vein, North Korea seems to have been predestined for observation through satellite imagery since the whole entity – and thus not only single sites or facilities at other covert, isolated locations – is believed to be a secret of its own kind. Since satellites are deployed to reveal what would otherwise be invisible, their detecting and exposing of the hidden – or, in other words, practices of looking – relate to a particular power; a power that operates through the visual.

The abovementioned authors provide an apt starting point for the present examination, specifically with the advancement of critical studies of space in mind. It is almost needless to say that the satellite's gaze is neither a neutral nor an objective 'view from nowhere' – it is, of course, always a view from somewhere. In this regard, it is perhaps more accurate to note that it is also a view from someone. For while satellite vision entails a spatial dimension in that the perspective is always deployed from a particular place and captures only particular sites/sights, it is equally important to ask by whom the view from nowhere/somewhere is being exercised. The key question is what the implications are of *whose* view satellites mediate and of *where* sight is directed towards. While these issues relate satellite visuality to questions of spatiality (where/ what) and subjectivity (who), they most explicitly point to the inherent politics of satellite images.

In order to explore the politics of satellite vision it is necessary to turn first and foremost to the site of the image itself. Photographic representations – either in the form of news pictures or satellite images – are widely believed to be mimetic reflections of reality. Through such photographs we are seemingly able to see the world as it is and not as we wish it to be. However, photographs – including satellite images – are characterized by what can be called a 'logic of inclusion and exclusion': some things (are made to) lie within the image's frame of visibility while others (sometimes purposefully) remain outside of its view. No camera shot can capture a setting in its entirety because any attempt to portray the world involves selections and reductions. Satellite images are, hence, always partial representations of space. While the accuracy and sub-stance of such images is not challenged here, it is important to note that (satellite) imaging rests upon an understanding of what is or is not enti-tled to representation, and how. So a satellite image is not simply an inno-cent mode of geographical depiction but rather an interpretive response to what deserves to lie inside *and* outside of the satellite's field of vision.

The case of North Korea provides a good example through which to illustrate the (geo)politics of satellite images. In doing so, it addresses the questions raised above. The inherent logic of inclusion and exclu-sion of the satellite's camera prompts us to ask, for instance, why spe-cific pictures and image motifs are repeatedly accumulated, presented and disseminated to an international audience while others are not. It should be asked, therefore, why daytime pictures of the Korean penin-sula, such as in Figure 4.3, are virtually non-existent while night-time images are common and widely circulated. Why do such photographs of luminosity play no role in geopolitical discourse while the image motif of North Korea in darkness emerges time and again? It could also be asked whose view is being seen in these night-time depictions (e.g. U.S. government agencies) and what the consequences of someone else grant-ing us a (particular kind of) vision are. What follows, then, is the need to be aware that we are only able to know certain things because someone else allows us to see them. Also, the prevalent use of night-time images as particular spatial signifiers for North Korea points to the hegemonic status of such visual practices, which permit only specific perspectives to be taken while excluding others.

Addressing issues of vision – what do we see? – and visuality – how do we see, how are we made to see? – requires one to examine, and take more

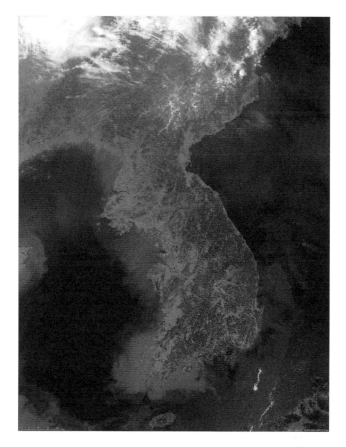

Figure 4.3 Satellite image taken of the Korean Peninsula by day, I. Image
courtesy of NASA/Visible Earth.

seriously, the site of the satellite image itself. In this way, this chapter adopts
what Gillian Rose has called a "critical visual methodology" (2016: 24),
achieved by examining the conditions and effects of seeing. Though
diverging in their conceptual and practical approaches to satellite imagery,
the above-mentioned authors tend to be uniform in their uses of satellite
photos: images merely serve as illustrations for their arguments; the images
themselves are not subject to critical inquiry (see esp. Crutcher and Zook
2009; Kingsbury and Jones 2009). This denotes a hierarchical relationship
between images and texts because the former are meant to serve the latter.

The relationship between images and texts points to the methodological connection between both modes of representation. This methodological approach means not only scrutinizing the composition of the
image – what does it (not) show, what kinds of elements are foregrounded

in the image and how? – but also to examine its relation to other signs –
how does the accompanying text interact with the image and vice versa,
is the image illustrative of the text or is the text illustrative of the image?
In this vein, the empirical part of this chapter not only includes a discussion of the night-time image itself, but also provides an interpretive
analysis of the accompanying text. The written materials to be examined
will consist mainly of official statements of former U.S. Secretary of
Defense (2001–2006) Donald Rumsfeld. As will be outlined in more detail below, Rumsfeld was well known for using the night-time picture of
the Korean peninsula in his standard briefings on North Korea. The use
of this image, which was produced under a satellite program run by the
Defense Department (Figures 4.4 and 4.6), also indicates how satellite
vision speaks to geopolitical and military imaginaries.

Dodge and Perkins (2009) argue that satellite imagery holds decisive
stakes in constructing a kind of truth about familiar places due to its
indexical quality. The following section, in contrast, shows how satellite
imagery unfolds its indexical quality in relation to places which one does
not know. It will be argued that remote sensing implies a greater authority, almost like a form of authorship, enabling certain actors to 'speak'
and 'write' (about) places and sites which are unknown, unmapped and
unexplored – like North Korea.

Satellite Vision and North Korea: The Spatial Imaginary

In contemporary geopolitics, satellite imagery is deeply integrated into
governmental, intelligence and military fact-finding missions and
decision-making processes. Often it provides the main source of information for evaluating the weapons (of mass destruction) programs
and proliferation activities of states like Iran and North Korea. While
satellite images clearly have geopolitical implications – given that they
are invoked to legitimize political and diplomatic actions including
inspections, warnings and sanctions – the following discussion of the
night-time satellite photo of the Korean peninsula will illuminate how
remote sensing also shapes people's geographical imaginations. In order
to engage with the relationship between satellite image and spatial imagination, it makes sense to turn to and examine statements that have been
based on the connection between imaging and imagining. The goal is
thus to reveal what satellite photos are believed – or, to put it differently,
imagined – to signify; in other words, to reveal what sense of place is
imagined when looking at satellite pictures.

During Rumsfeld's tenure, he showcased a photograph in his office
that, according to his own statements, was one of his favourites: a satellite shot of the Korean peninsula by night (Figure 4.4).[2] While it is not
unusual to decorate one's own working environment with pictures that
have particular meaning, it is noteworthy that Rumsfeld assigned this

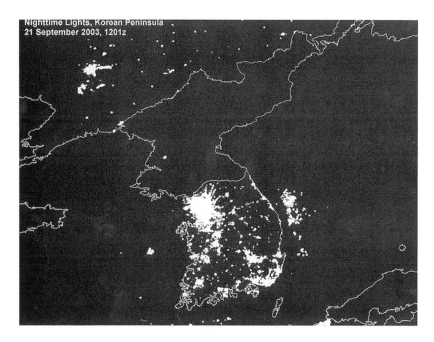

Nighttime Lights, Korean Peninsula
21 September 2003, 1201z

Figure 4.4 Satellite image taken of the Korean Peninsula by night, II. Image
courtesy of GlobalSecurity.org/John Pike.

image a special – that is, a central – place: his desk, the one from where
he managed the United States's geopolitical affairs.

Rumsfeld was well known for showing this image to foreign delegates
and visiting dignitaries including, in 2005, Park Geun-hye, then the
leader of South Korea's largest opposition party and President of the
Republic of Korea between 2013 and 2017. Rumsfeld also explained
to Park that he would always look at the satellite image while working
in his office (Shin 2005). The Secretary of Defense would use and/or
display this picture (motif) on many different occasions: briefings, inter-
views, press conferences, speeches, testimonies and town hall meetings
(Figure 4.5). In all these statements, Rumsfeld related this image to a
greater cause: the sacrifices that had been made by U.S. service members
in the wars in Afghanistan, Iraq and Korea for the sake of freedom, security, democracy and prosperity.

For instance, at the 2004 Munich Conference on Security Policy,
which annually gathers high-ranking policymakers and military officials, Rumsfeld recalled an encounter with a South Korean journalist
who asked him why the South should send troops to Iraq, possibly leading to many (Korean) casualties. While Rumsfeld responded to this question by inverting it (why should the United States have sent troops to the

Figure 4.5 "Rumsfeld on North Korea," October 11, 2006. Image courtesy of
U.S. Department of Defense.

Korean War in the early 1950s?), he explained why military interventions such as in Afghanistan and Iraq were worth the effort:

> The advance of freedom does not come without cost or sacrifice. [...]
> Look out the window. And out that window you could see lights
> and cars and energy and a vibrant economy and a robust democracy
> [...] if you look above the demilitarized zone from satellite pictures
> of the Korean peninsula, above the DMZ is darkness, nothing but
> darkness and a little portion of light where Pyongyang is. The same
> people had the same population, the same resources. And look at
> the difference. There are concentration camps. They're starving. [...]
> Korea was won at a terrible cost of life. [...] And was it worth it? You
> bet. The world is a safer place today because the Coalition liberated
> 50 million people – 25 million in Afghanistan and 25 million in Iraq.
> (US DoD 2004b)

While the night-time satellite image serves here as a visual signifier to
help legitimate and enhance the understanding of the need for military
intervention in foreign countries, indicating how this image is involved
in shaping geopolitical discourse, Rumsfeld's accounts show that it is
not factual information that is meant to be conveyed by such an image
but instead certain geopolitical imaginations; that is, a particular understanding or sense of world affairs that is mediated through and reflected
in the image itself. The satellite photo, hence, becomes an imaginative
site/sight for the geopolitical logic of the United States.

Rumsfeld is not alone in crediting this image motif with a powerful
meaning. It is certainly no exaggeration to assert that no single image

has more decisively shaped popular imaginations about North Korea and its people than this iconic picture. The same photograph, or similar versions of it, have been referred to or reproduced in academic publications (e.g. Harris 2007; Knaus and Lee 2011) and media outlets such as the *New York Times* (Zeller 2006), the *Wall Street Journal* (Gale 2014), the *Washington Post* (Klein 2011) and South Korea's largest newspaper, *Chosun Ilbo* (2010; see also Figures 4.6 and 4.7). Creating a direct nexus between certain kinds of visuality and certain kinds of knowledge, some economists have even used this image to establish a causal link between luminosity and economic growth (see, for example, Henderson et al. 2009; see also Chen and Nordhaus 2011).

It is useful, once again, to turn to Donald Rumsfeld, to show what this picture is believed to mediate about the places and people of North Korea. He presented the image shown in Figure 4.4 during a news briefing held at the U.S. Department of Defense (see Figure 4.5) soon after North Korea had conducted its first nuclear test in October 2006:

> That is my favorite photo. It says it all. There's the south of the Demilitarized Zone, the same people as north, same resources north and south, and the big difference is in the south it's a free political system and a free economic system [...] that dot of light is Pyong-yang. And the people there are starving and their growth is stunted. And it's a shame. It's a tragedy.
>
> (US DoD 2006)

Another example that shows the close relationship between the satellite image and a certain spatial imagination is the critically acclaimed book *Nothing to Envy: Ordinary Lives in North Korea* by well-known *Los Angeles Times* journalist Barbara Demick (2010). Demick, who won the 2010 BBC Samuel Johnson Prize for Non-Fiction for this work, introduces her book with a version of this satellite image:

> If you look at satellite photographs of the Far East by night, you'll see a large splotch curiously lacking in light. This area of darkness is the Democratic People's Republic of Korea. Next to this mysterious black hole, South Korea, Japan, and now China fairly gleam with prosperity. [...] In the middle of it all [there is] an expanse of blackness nearly as large as England. It is baffling how a nation of 23 million people can appear as vacant as the oceans. North Korea is simply a blank [...] a country that has fallen out of the developed world.
>
> (2010, 3–4)

It is important to note that the substance of the satellite photo and the legitimacy of the above-cited readings of it are not questioned here. The aim is not to deny that North Korea appears dark in a night-time satellite

Figure 4.6 Satellite image taken of Northeast Asia by night, I. Image courtesy of GlobalSecurity.org/John Pike.

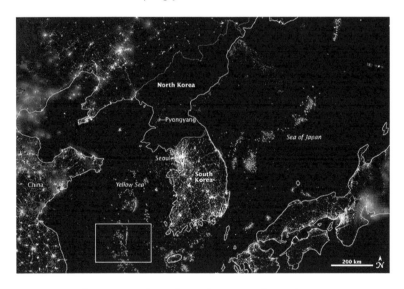

Figure 4.7 Satellite image taken of Northeast Asia by night, II. Image courtesy of NASA/Earth Observatory.

picture of the Korean peninsula, though it can be asserted that what one sees (or not) through remote sensing depends on, in very simplified terms, which lens or sensor is utilized by a satellite. For instance, thermal infrared imagery is not able to generate the visible contrast as seen, for instance, in Figure 4.7, which was produced by the specific low-light imagery sensor of a NASA satellite (Miller et al. 2012). In this vein, the question is not so much whether light is visible or not in such pictures, but, rather, if, how and why such images are *made* visible to us – and with what consequences.

Thus, it can be noted that pictorial references to darkness and colour-lessness in the photograph are used to foreground what can be called the 'otherness' of North Korea (and simultaneously the 'sameness' of South Korea). We are almost never shown daytime images of the country, and are presented instead with extracts from a larger picture and/or close-ups of the Korean peninsula by night. These are demarcated along the North–South axis to facilitate viewing and, consequently, knowing; for to invert the image would alienate familiar viewing/knowing practices. What is interesting about the picture is that it is said to 'speak' by itself of North Korea as a site or place of difference: the image does not need words in order to be meaningful or intelligible, because, as Rumsfeld notes above, "It says it all." In this view, one only has to take a look at the Korean peninsula by night in order to understand what is going on there. So the picture does not communicate any cartographic knowl-edge; rather, it is involved in creating a spatial imaginary of North Korea as a place beyond the realm of comprehension, one which is neither part of our world nor part of our time. It is, according to Demick, "a country that has fallen out of the developed world" (2010, 4).

The image does not serve as a mere illustration to make Rumsfeld's or Demick's point; it *is* the argument itself. This way of reasoning points to the (erroneous) widespread conviction that images are able to speak for themselves; that pictures can only have one specific meaning. While the effects of images depend on a range of discursive practices (such as the interplay of different modes of representation), the photo subject in question – be it North Korea or the world by night – assumes a new meaning when articulated in the context of different discourses. Take, for example, an environmental discourse, which would problematize not the absence of luminosity but, on the contrary, its omnipresence – and the damage that excessive illumination causes to natural ecosystems and physical health. Important to note is that in view of what is sometimes called 'light pollution' by advocacy groups, (excess) illumination does not tell of the modernity, prosperity and security of private and public spaces – such as South Korea as the opposite pole of North Korea – but instead constructs a contrasting imaginary of place that is characterized by concerns about the degradation of the environment, the disruption of ecosystems, the waste of resources and negative health effects.

The above-mentioned references indicate that North Korea's spatial reality is construed in terms of absence, deficiency and scarcity. The picture shows how visuality is linked to questions of knowledge, space and social agency: the way in which we are made to see determines what can be known about, and said to happen, in the various sites of North Korea. The image, hence, serves as a discursive marker of difference, highlighting opposite poles such as freedom/oppression, wealth/pov-erty, development/decline and hope/despair. Therefore, North Korea is imagined as an isolated, empty and mysterious place. However, knowledge derived from this way of seeing is of course flawed since the (in)visibility of light, which is construed by Rumsfeld and Demick to denote the emptiness of North Korea ("vacant," "blank"), cannot serve here as an indicator of human activity – simply because millions of people do live and work in the country. Nevertheless, because North Korea appears to exist in a spatial and temporal void – it is placed outside of the modern world and outside of time – it becomes clear what North Korea cannot be: home.

While the purpose of the night-time image is to 'speak' difference, the recurring use and circulation of this photo subject in academia, politics and media demonstrate its overarching popularity as a hegemonic imaginary: it exceeds spatial and temporal boundaries, as such images find global audiences and appear time and again – for instance in December 2012, when NASA published a whole new series of night-time pictures of the globe and its constituent parts (Figure 4.7). The hegemonic imaginary thus explains the marginalization of daytime pictures in geopolitical discourse as they do not 'speak' the language of difference and otherness.

Conclusion

People come to know the world – and its spaces and places – through visual imagery. It has been my argument here that one of the key ways in which people approach and engage with the world is satellite imagery; it affects how we imagine place. This applies in particular with regard to (allegedly) unknown sites such as North Korea, as satellite vision is one of the principal ways in which we, the outside world, encounter places and people of various terrae incognitae. Because they are a means of mapping, watching, ordering and representing the world, satellite pictures are a pervasive form of geographical knowledge; they make the world *knowable*. Yet, as this chapter has shown, satellite vision not only produces geographical information but also shapes geographical imagination. As such, it contributes to creating particular (visual) spatial imaginaries.

The relationship between (satellite) imaging and (spatial) imagination is complex and mutually reinforcing: images shape and, at the same time, are shaped by imaginations. The satellite picture of NASA's Blue Marble or popular night-time images of the world are cases in point (see Figure 4.1). While the view from outer space forms spatial imaginations of the globe, particular imaginations also (in)form its visual representation. According to one of the creators of the 2002 Blue Marble, Robert Simmon, the Earth was made to look realistic – or, more precisely, as he himself put it, "at least how I *imagined* the Earth would look" (Simmon 2011; emphasis in original).[3]

This nexus points to the manufactured nature of satellite vision. For the realistic appearance of such images – be it the bluish globe or the world at night – is achieved through the application of a range of computer-powered enhancing methods, known as post-processing. Satellite images are compiled out of layers and parcels of shots from different pictures taken at different times, and are corrected so that they can be shown in a meaningful way to audiences. After all, satellite images are based on data; what we see and therefore believe to know through remote sensing is not the capture of physical referents similar to the practice of 'classic' photography where the shutter is triggered, but the result of editing and synthetic imaging processes. The Blue Marble shown in Figure 4.1 is thus a composite view of about 10,000 satellite scenes collected over the course of 100 days. The night-time shot of the Korean peninsula as shown in Figure 4.7 is actually not a photograph but an image consisting of light-sensitive data that conforms more to computer scanners than to simple photo cameras (Simmon, email inquiry 17 June 2013). Moreover, the world is, of course, never entirely dark as is suggested by such night-time imagery, but made to appear dark given that by default one half is always illuminated. While post-processing points to the manufacturing of sight/site, it implies that we see – or are made to see – things and places which actually do not exist as such.

The discussion of the night-time satellite picture has not only shown what sense of place is invoked through satellite's frame of visibility, but it also points to the ambiguous effects of remote sensing. While satellite imagery is usually deployed to reveal hidden sites and secret places, thus representing a way to challenge myths and to dissolve mystery (cf. Perkins and Dodge 2009), the discussion has indicated how it actually does precisely the opposite in this case: North Korea is mystified and constructed as a site of difference, distance and otherness. In this vein, satellite vision is not only involved in creating subjectivities of self/other and us/them but also sets up spatial and temporal notions of home/homelessness, domestic/foreign, here/there as well as of change/stagnation, progressive/backward, developed/undeveloped.

The implications for scholars who work on remote sensing practices mostly concern the way in which they approach the status or the value of satellite imagery. Much critical research has already been conducted on the (misleading) authoritative role of satellite photos, which are believed to impartially document places, spaces and sites (besides the abovementioned authors, see also Campbell 2008; Parks 2005). Similar to their spatial location – watching the Earth from outer space – satellites seem to be capable of what can be called 'extra-discursivity': they are apparently well-positioned to speak freely, operating outside of any sphere of (subjective) influence. As a result, satellites appear to provide objective and transparent reflections of the world. While, as shown above, a logic of inclusion and exclusion – what to scan/show, what not to, how – underlies a satellite's vision (revealing the politics of remote sensing/seeing), it is surprising that despite critical inquiries into the value of the satellite image less analytical attention has been devoted to the site/sight of the image itself – something this paper has strived to begin rectifying.

Conducting one's own inquiry into the question of what the satellite image does by being presented in a particular way means asking, in essence, whether the satellite shot is the messenger or the message itself; is the image used to make a point or is it the point? A discussion of a satellite picture is, then, not so much an interpretation of its meaning but an examination of the work that it is meant to do. In this regard, it is important to pay particular attention to the site of the image itself. Turning to the site of the image also has the benefit of not prioritizing the role of the textual (argument) over the visual (illustration of the argument), and thus avoids the play-off between both modes of representation.

Notes

* This essay is a shortened and updated version of "Remote Sensing Place: Satellite Images as Visual Spatial Imaginaries," reprinted from *Geoforum* 51 (January 2014), 152–160, with permission from Elsevier.
1 The way in which the term 'geographical imagination' is used here not only evokes David Harvey's thinking – thus acknowledging the significance of space and place in the constitution of human life – but also rests on a broader notion which recognizes the processes of how people approach and appraise the world and its spaces (see also Schwartz and Ryan 2003).
2 Other high-ranking officials from different U.S. administrations have also referred to this image in their personal accounts, including U.S. President George W. Bush (2010) and Deputy Secretary of Defense Paul Wolfowitz (US DoD 2004a).
3 Simmon's (2011) account "Crafting the Blue Marble" is insightful. To show what is involved in producing an image of the Earth, it is worth citing a longer passage: "Compositing separate images into a convincing whole is (of course) easier said than done. Even with control of each layer in my image processing software (Photoshop) it took hours of tweaking and re-tweaking transparency, layer masks, hue, saturation, gaussian blur, and curves to get an image that *looked like the picture I had in my head*. [...] Making the clouds appear opaque, while remaining white, rather than gray, was by far the hardest part. It was also tricky trying to get the atmosphere to appear most transparent in the center, and thicker and bluer near the edges" (par. 7; emphasis added). The original Blue Marble is a photograph of the Earth made in 1972 by the crew of Apollo 17. The 2002 Blue Marble was compiled by Reto Stöckli and enhanced by Robert Simmon.

References

Aday, Sean, and Steve Livingston. 2009. "NGOs as Intelligence Agencies: The Empowerment of Transnational Advocacy Networks and the Media by Commercial Remote Sensing in the Case of the Iranian Nuclear Program." *Geoforum* 40 (4): 514–522.

Bush, George W. 2010. *Decision Points*. New York: Crown Publishers.

Campbell, David. 2008. "Tele-vision: Satellite Images and Security." *Source* 56 (Autumn): 16–23.

Chen, Xi, and William Nordhaus. 2011. "Using Luminosity Data as a Proxy for Economic Statistics." *Proceedings of the National Academy of Sciences* 108 (21): 8589–8594.

Chosun Ilbo. 2010. "北, 밤만 되면 어둠속으로...전력사정 어떻기에?" 21 December, 2010. http://news.chosun.com/site/data/html_dir/2010/12/18/2010121800234.html.

Cosgrove, Denis. 1994. "Contested Global Visions: One-World, Whole-Earth, and the Apollo Space Photographs." *Annals of the Association of American Geographers* 84 (2): 270–294.

Crutcher, Michael, and Matthew Zook. 2009. "Placemarks and Waterlines: Racialized Cyberspaces in Post-Katrina Google Earth." *Geoforum* 40 (4): 523–534.

Demick, Barbara. 2010. *Nothing to Envy: Ordinary Lives in North Korea*. New York: Spiegel & Grau.

Dodge, Martin, and Chris Perkins. 2009. "The 'View from Nowhere'? Spatial Politics and Cultural Significance of High-Resolution Satellite Imagery." *Geoforum* 40 (4): 497–501.

Gale, Alastair. 2014. "North Korea Cloaked in Darkness." *The Wall Street Journal*. February 26, 2014. https://blogs.wsj.com/korearealtime/2014/02/26/photo-north-korea-cloaked-in-darkness/.

Halliday, Jon. 1981. "The North Korean Enigma." *New Left Review* I/127: 18–52.

Harris Mark. 2007. *Inside North Korea*. San Francisco: Chronicle Books.

Henderson, J. Vernon, Adam Storeygard, and David N. Weil. 2009. "Measuring Economic Growth from Outer Space." NBER Working Paper Series, Working Paper 15199.

Keck, Aries, and Mike Carlowicz. 2012. "Earth, Behind the Scenes." *NASA Earth Observatory*. February 4, 2012. http://earthobservatory.nasa.gov/IOTD/view.php?id=77085.

Kim, Mikyoung. 2009. "A Black Hole: North Korea's Place in East Asian Energy Debates." *Hiroshima Research News* 11 (3): 3.

Kingsbury, Paul, and John P. Jones. 2009. "Walter Benjamin's Dionysian Adventures on Google Earth." *Geoforum* 40 (4): 502–513.

Klein, Ezra. 2011. "Kim Jong Il's dark legacy." *The Washington Post*. December 20, 2011. www.washingtonpost.com/business/economy/2011/12/19/gIQA-1Fca5O_story.html.

Knaus, John, and Lynn Lee. 2011. "Opening North Korea." *Journal of Democracy* 22 (2): 170–173.

Miller, Steven D., Stephen P. Mills, Christopher D. Elvidge, Daniel T. Lindsey, Thomas S. Lee, and Jeffrey D. Hawkins. 2012. "Suomi Satellite Brings to Light a Unique Frontier of Nighttime Environmental Sensing Capabilities." *Proceedings of the National Academy of Sciences* 109 (39): 15706–15711.

Noland, Marcus. 2012. "The Black Hole of North Korea." *Foreign Policy*. March 7, 2012. www.foreignpolicy.com/articles/2012/03/07/the_black_hole_of_north_korea.

Parks, Lisa. 2005. *Cultures in Orbit: Satellites and the Televisual.* Durham: Duke University Press.

———. 2009. "Digging into Google Earth: An Analysis of 'Crisis in Darfur.'" *Geoforum* 40 (4): 535–545.

Perkins, Chris, and Martin Dodge. 2009. "Satellite Imagery and the Spectacle of Secret Places." *Geoforum* 40 (4): 546–560.

Rose, Gillian. 2016. *Visual Methodologies: An Introduction to the Interpretation of Visual Materials.* London: Sage Publications.

Sachs, Wolfgang. 1994. "Satellitenblick: Die Ikone vom blauen Planeten und ihre Folgen für die Wissenschaft." In *Technik ohne Grenzen*, edited by Ingo Braun and Bernward Joerges, 305–346. Frankfurt am Main: Suhrkamp.

Sanger, David E., and William J. Broad. 2005. "U.S. Cites Signs of Korean Steps to Nuclear Test." *The New York Times.* May 6, 2005. www.nytimes.com/2005/05/06/international/asia/06korea.html.

Sanger, David E., and Sang-hun Choe. 2013. "Intelligence on North Korea, and Its New Leader, Remains Elusive." *The New York Times.* May 6, 2013. www.nytimes.com/2013/05/07/world/asia/intelligence-on-north-korea-still-out-of-reach.html?pagewanted=all&_r=0.

Scalapino, Robert. 1997. "Introduction." In *North Korea After Kim Il Sung*, edited by Dae-sook Suh and Chae-chin Lee, 1–12. London: Lynne Rienner Publishers.

Schwartz, Joan, and James Ryan, eds. 2003. *Picturing Place: Photography and the Geographical Imagination.* London: I. B. Tauris.

Shin, Hyo-sup. 2005. "나는 항상 한국 위성사진 보고 일한다." March 13, 2005. www.chosun.com/politics/news/200503/200503170433.html.

Siemer, Stefan. 2007. "Bildgelehrte Geotechniker: Luftbild und Kartografie um 1900." In *Konstruieren, Kommunizieren, Präsentieren: Bilder von Wissenschaft und Technik*, edited by Alexander Gall, 69–108. München: Wallstein Verlag.

Simmon, Robert. 2011. "Crafting the Blue Marble." *NASA Earth Observatory.* October 6, 2011. http://earthobservatory.nasa.gov/blogs/elegantfigures/2011/10/06/crafting-the-blue-marble/.

Solarz, Stephen J. 1999. "Foreword." In *Kim Il-song's North Korea*, edited by Helen-Louise Hunter, ix–xii. Westport: Praeger.

United States Department of Defense. 2004a. "Africa Center for Strategic Studies Senior Leader Seminar – Remarks by Deputy Secretary of Defense Paul Wolfowitz." U.S. Department of Defense (website). February 9, 2004. www.defense.gov/Speeches/Speech.aspx?SpeechID=98.

———. 2004b. "Secretary Rumsfeld Remarks at the Munich Conference on Security Policy." U.S. Department of Defense (website). February 7, 2004. www.defense.gov/transcripts/transcript.aspx?transcriptid=2033.

———. 2006. "DoD News Briefing with Secretary Rumsfeld and Gen. Casey." U.S. Department of Defense (website). October 11, 2006. www.defense.gov/transcripts/transcript.aspx?transcriptid=3755.

Zeller, Tom. 2006. "The Internet Black Hole That Is North." *The New York Times.* October 23, 2006. www.nytimes.com/2006/10/23/technology/23link.html.

Part II
Island Spaces

5   Crossing the Sand
The Arrival on the Desert Island

Barney Samson

Can movement through space tell us anything about ideology? In what ways can the reactions of fictional protagonists to their surroundings indicate what texts *mean*? I will address these questions in the context of two novels that take place within the tightly constrained environment of the desert island: Daniel Defoe's *The Life and Strange Surprising Adventures of Robinson Crusoe* (1719) and William Golding's *Lord of the Flies. Robinson Crusoe* was a publishing sensation; within six months of publication, there were four editions and a sequel (Rogers 1979, 4–8). Ian Watt tells us that by 1900, "there had appeared at least 700 editions, translations and imitations" (Watt 2001a, 95). Although not an immediate commercial success with first-year sales of 4,662 (Faber & Faber 1955), Golding's novel soon became extremely well-known; by July 1969, UK sales had reached two million (Carey 2009, 324).

Although they share a setting, *Robinson Crusoe* is about a lone adult and is narrated by the protagonist, while *Lord of the Flies*, published almost 250 years later, is narrated in the third person and is about a group of children. Further, they contain different ideological relationships with modernity, which are announced by their protagonists' early movements on the island. My theoretical starting point for this discussion is Michel de Certeau's (1988) discussion of "Spatial Stories" in *The Practice of Everyday Life*, which deals with the ways in which narratives structure space and thereby create meaning. For de Certeau, stories

> traverse and organize places; they select and link them together. [...] By means of a whole panoply of codes, ordered ways of proceeding and constraints, they regulate changes in space [...] in the form of places put in linear or interlaced series.
>
> (1988, 115)

Thus, like a metaphor – de Certeau points out that *metaphorai* is the word modern Greeks use for public transport – a story, through its organization of space, can transport you (1988, 115).

For de Certeau, narratives are made up of different types of citations of places, based on "the itinerary (a discursive series of operations) and the map (a plane projection totalizing observations)" (1988, 119). My contention is that the way Robinson Crusoe moves around his island reveals a map-like understanding of space, while *Lord of the Flies*, in its "manipulations of space," more resembles the itinerary (1988, 119). The reason for this lies in their respective ideological journeys. Robinson in his youth wanted to travel, but we learn that his parents warned him against this and that his leaving them was "to act the rebel to their authority, and the fool to [his] own interest" (34). Thus, if *Robinson Crusoe* can be said to express an overriding ideology, it is that trust should be placed in authority; when stranded far from home, the best way to survive is to recreate its structures, which are modern in their prioritization of individualism and economic behaviours (James 1996, 7). *Lord of the Flies* is more discursive in terms of Ralph's relation to space (in that he wanders and meanders) because he goes on an ideological journey; initially, Ralph is delighted to be away from the constraints of home, but the novel contains a nuanced and complex exploration of the importance of society in regulating human behaviour. Both novels contain lessons about how to behave: in de Certeau's formulation, "stories tell us what one can do in [a space] and make out of it" (122).

Alongside de Certeau's spatial approach, my analysis will reference the sociological work of Zygmunt Bauman, which draws on the writings of Michel Foucault. I will argue that Robinson Crusoe's and Ralph's early movements on the desert island can respectively be seen as evoking and challenging modernity. For Foucault, modernity was characterized by the use of discipline to ensure civic obedience. In order to reconstitute the criminal, it is necessary to discover "the disadvantage whose idea is such that it robs for ever the idea of a crime of any attraction," using punishments that are "as unarbitrary as possible" (Foucault 1995, 104). Robinson Crusoe tells the reader that it was in defiance of authority that he wanted to travel the world (Defoe 2003, 34). His crime, then, is to desire otherness, and his punishment is to be 'imprisoned' in a space of otherness. The crime and the punishment look identical, taking to an extreme Foucault's symbolic resemblance of punishment and crime. Discipline is about the training of the body, as imprisonment becomes the dominant technique of the penal system in the modern era (Foucault 1995, 131). The training of the body relies on what Foucault calls "docile bodies" and "proceeds from the distribution of individuals in space" (1995, 141). In prisons, as well as in schools, barracks and factories, citizens are contained within the cell, "a place heterogeneous to all others and closed in upon itself. It is the protected place of disciplinary monotony" (1995, 141–142). On a desert island, it is clear that the body of the protagonist is spatially restricted. Further, Robinson Crusoe must undertake highly structured (capitalistic) activities in order to survive, conforming to the disciplinary idea of "control of activity" (1995, 149). Robinson teaches Friday English and converts him to Christianity, enacting Foucault's "organization of geneses" (1995, 156), the transfer of knowledge through apprenticeship structures.

The task for individuals in the modern era was, for Bauman, "to use their new freedom to find the appropriate niche and to settle there through conformity: by faithfully following the rules and modes of conduct identified as right and proper for the location" (2006, 7). This describes well the ideological core of *Robinson Crusoe*, in which the protagonist on the desert island attempts to perfect the society he has left behind. "Certainty, orderliness, homogeneity became the orders of the day," writes Bauman regarding the modern era, as "unlicensed difference is the main enemy" (1992, xiv, xvi). Xury is 'licensed' through Crusoe's agreement that his 'friend' be indentured, while Friday is converted, which effaces his otherness. Inversely, it can also be seen that Crusoe's desire to travel made him intolerable to the 'mainland'; there was, in Bauman's terms, "no good reason to tolerate the Other who, by definition, rebelled against the truth. [...] Modernity was not merely the Western Man's thrust for power; it was also his *mission*, proof of moral righteousness and cause of pride" (1992, xiv; emphasis in original). As such, Crusoe is shown by Defoe to *deserve* 'casting away.' The monadic, unitary desert island is an ideal symbolic setting for this project, as "the heterogenous [sic] experiences of the real indicate a number of differences which must be brought to similarity, which must be homogenized into a unitary subject" (Peter De Bolla, quoted in Bauman 1992, xvi).

Lord of the Flies opens after a plane crash leaves a group of British schoolboys on an uninhabited island. Ralph attempts to impose a system of governance based on rules: "Because the rules are the only thing we've got!" (2011, 99). Ultimately, this breaks down as a rival, Jack, convinces the majority of boys to join his hedonistic, violent rejection of Ralph's rules. Several boys have died, and Ralph is running for his life when a British Navy cruiser anchors offshore, and the boys are "taken off" the island (224). Much analysis of *Lord of the Flies* has focused on "Golding's view of man's nature" (McCullen 1978, 204). This derives in part from Golding's own comments: "[Its] theme is an attempt to trace the defects of society back to the defects of human nature. The moral is that the shape of a society must depend on the ethical nature of the individual" (quoted in Epstein 1959, 189). While this may have been Golding's intention, I will argue that the novel has a more contingent and multifaceted moral significance than a doctrine of individual responsibility.

Ted Boyle represents the school of thought arguing that *Lord of the Flies* demonstrates Golding's conviction "that without the restraint of social order the human being will sink below the level of the beast" (1978, 24). For Boyle, Piggy, the rationalist, represents "society as the means of making things work, of keeping the beast at bay" (1978, 25). Likewise, George C. Herndl suggests that the novel is "an implicit tribute to the humanizing power of social institutions" (quoted in McCullen 1978, 215). These readings of *Lord of the Flies* as a modern defence of society fail to recognize that Piggy's rationalism is in vain; society and social order fail to prevent war raging both on the island and in the wider world. Boyle suggests that Ralph refuses to join Jack's hunters to avoid becoming a "savage" (1978, 25). This misses the point that Ralph's steadfast uprightness is ironic; he already contains 'savagery.' As John Whitley puts it, "Golding insists that evil is inherent in man; a terrifying force which he must recognize and control" (1970, 7).

If it is misguided to read *Lord of the Flies* as a defence of rationalism, that is not to say that the novel does not *represent* reason. Piggy, as Claire Rosenfield puts it, "like the father counsels common sense; he alone leavens with a reasonable gravity the constant exuberance of the others for play" (1961, 94). Play represents a challenge to the reason and rules of modernity, but it is not restricted to Jack's followers. Ralph, with whom the reader is encouraged to identify, also 'plays,' as will be shown with regard to his spatial negotiation of the island. He is not simply a modern rationalist, and I will suggest that Golding's novel challenges modernity in two ways. Ralph's playful early movement on the island offers an alternative to the modern understandings of the desert island space found in *Robinson Crusoe*. While this diegetic challenge to modernity lapses back into the importation of discipline to the desert island, the failure of reason to prevent a violent denouement offers an extra-diegetic critique of modernity and its prioritization of reason.

De Certeau likens stories to the ritual *fētiāles* of ancient Rome: a procession before a battle that "opens a space and provides a foundation for the operations of the [people] who dare to cross the frontiers"; a story creates a space "for the actions that will be undertaken" (1988, 124). In desert island narratives, the frontiers of the story are explicit, as the setting is tightly constrained, with a clear physical distinction between home and the space of the other and topological contours that break it into distinct zones: the beach; the interior; the summit. My focus is on the protagonists' arrival and early movements on the desert island. The parts of the narrative I will examine are the time between Robinson Crusoe's abandonment of his ship and his choice of a place to settle (36–48), and Chapter 1 of *Lord of the Flies*, in which Ralph arrives on the island, meets the other castaways and begins to explore (2011, 1–29).

The first significant feature of Robinson's arrival on the island is that it is involuntary. His ship is "driven" and "carry'd" towards the island by storms (Defoe 2003, 35). Abandoning the ship in a small boat, he and his companions row on hopelessly: "[…] we work'd at the oar towards the land, tho' with heavy hearts […] for we all knew, that when the boat came nearer the shore, she would be dash'd in a thousand pieces" (2003, 36). The boat having overturned, a wave "carried me a vast way on towards the shore" (2003, 37). This happens four times, each time leaving Robinson closer to land. All of this movement happens against Robinson's will, which is emphasized by the fact that at one point he is "dash'd [...] against a piece of rock, and that with such force, that it left [him] senseless, and indeed helpless" (38).

The first decisive, voluntary movement that Robinson makes is to cross the shoreline itself: he runs the remaining distance to land and "clamber[s] up the clifts of the shore" (2003, 38). Indeed, Robinson's arrival on the island can be seen as a series of ascents. He is lifted up by the waves and climbs the cliffs (he later goes to sleep in the branches of a tree): "The final arrival is marked by a multiplication of upward movements" (Riquet 2014, 191). Upwards movements, as Johannes Riquet points out, can also be horizontal (2014, 191); both Robinson and Ralph later climb to summits. However, Robinson's early vertical movements, while they may presage such climbs, do not traverse horizontal space; that is, he is moving towards neither the shore nor the interior. From the perspective of an aerial view, a protagonist moving just upwards (such as Robinson climbing the tree) appears static. Thus, Riquet's observation serves to emphasize that Robinson intentionally traverses space only minimally. Robinson's upwards movements might also express a desire to leave the island, to transcend it.

Conversely, *Lord of the Flies* begins with descent: "The boy with fair hair lowered himself down the last few feet of rock and began to pick his way toward the lagoon" (1). This speaks to an engagement with the island, a willingness to exist in a new and unfamiliar place. While he is an involuntary castaway, Ralph's descent enacts his figurative movement towards the idea of being cast away. His reaction to the idea that there are probably no grown-ups around is that "the delight of a realized ambition overcame him. In the middle of the scar he stood on his head and grinned" (Golding 2011, 2). The headstand can be seen as an attempt to get even closer to his new surroundings, while also making explicit that things are figuratively upside down. Ralph's playful and joyous relation to his new environment is emphasized by the verbs used by Golding to describe his movement: he "climbs," "jumps," "dances," "trots," "plunges" and "scrambles," contrasting with Robinson Crusoe, who repeatedly "walks" and in times of heightened danger or emotion "runs." Ralph's joy appears not to be at his survival (nor does he appear to be traumatized by the plane crash); rather, he is simply overjoyed to be there.

Ralph's delight when he arrives on the island evokes Gilles Deleuze's suggestion that "dreaming of islands [...] is dreaming of pulling away, of being already separate, far from any continent, of being lost and alone – or it is dreaming of starting from scratch, recreating, beginning anew" (2004, 10). Ralph has landed in the interior of his island and this fills him with joy. He is eager to explore, curious, so much so that he literally engages with the earth, descending as close as possible to the surface of the island: Ralph "tripped over a branch and came down with a crash"

(Golding 2011, 3). In Deleuzian terms, Ralph seems very happy to be "pulling away, [...] far from any continent" (2004, 10). As such, he represents a challenge to the modern distrust of otherness.

Robinson, on the other hand, is not excited about the idea of "being lost and alone." Like Ralph, he moves without explicit purpose; unlike Ralph, he does so without engaging with his surroundings: "I walk'd about on the shore, lifting up my hands" (Defoe 2003, 38). Robinson's desolation at being shipwrecked illustrates his attachment to the modern (economic, productive) behaviours he may now be forced to abandon. He walks aimlessly; he has no interest in starting from scratch (and he does not). Also unlike Ralph, Robinson is then immobile and contemplative for some time; the older Crusoe narrates that this is the case until a lack of provisions "threw [him] into such terrible agonies of mind, that for a while [he] ran about like a madman" (2003, 39). It can be seen that Robinson repeatedly moves in such a way that he is essentially going nowhere. When he moves voluntarily rather than being driven by waves, he is not exploring but effectively remaining stationary, not walking with purpose but just "walk[ing] about" (2003, 38) and "running about" (2003, 39). The only exception is his actual crossing of the shoreline. Once his immediate survival is assured, Robinson has no interest in becoming of the island but stands on the beach, as close as he can be to home.[1]

Having landed in the interior, Ralph's curious wandering takes him towards the beach: "In a few seconds the fat boy's grunts were behind him and he was hurrying toward the screen that still lay between him and the lagoon. He climbed over a broken trunk and was out of the jungle" (Golding 2011, 4). The frontier between the interior and the beach is marked both by a physical barrier that Ralph must overcome (the trunk) and a flat "screen" (presumably of trees and creepers) that marks the edge. The beach here has a different significance than it does for Robinson, being characterized as a border: "The beach between the palm terrace and the water was a thin stick, endless apparently, for to Ralph's left the perspectives of palm and beach and water drew to a point at infinity" (2011, 4). In this formulation, the beach is not a zone of the island but a boundary. This echoes Greg Dening's conception of beaches that "must be crossed to enter or leave" islands (1980, 3), and which "divide the world between here and there, us and them, good and bad, familiar and strange" (1980, 32).

Robinson, by contrast, seems to conceive of the desert island as a place without borders. He walks inland, but moving from one zone of the island to another appears to have no effect on him; he remarks only that "[he] walk'd about a furlong from the shore, to see if [he] could find any fresh water to drink" (Defoe 2003, 39). Robinson appears oblivious to borders. He does not distinguish between different parts of the island, which as a whole is seen as being only physically (rather than semantically) distinct from what is outside it. That is, Robinson's reaction to being cast away is to treat the island as an extension of 'home,' in other words, to colonize it.[2]

Dening conceives of the beach as a zone in which things take place as well as a border: the nineteenth-century Spanish newcomers to Fatuiva in the Marquesas "had to carve out a new world for themselves. [...] So on the beach they experimented" (1980, 129).[3] In *Lord of the Flies*, Ralph "jumped down from the terrace [...], kicked his shoes off fiercely and ripped off each stocking with its elastic garter in a single movement" (Golding 2011, 4). Again, he is descending and engaging with the island as closely as he can. Enacting Dening's description of the beach as ambiguous, Ralph has now crossed the "screen" and moved onto the beach, transforming it from a boundary into a zone. This demonstrates how, as theorized by de Certeau, narratives create meaning: Ralph's awareness of the broken tree trunk and the jungle "screen" makes him "the mouthpiece of the limit," but his crossing of the barrier "creates communication as well as separation" (de Certeau 1988, 127). De Certeau chimes with Dening in describing the frontier as a "space between" (1988, 127). In this light, then, Ralph's engagement with the border marks him as being an agent of liminality, evocative of the fluidity that Bauman identifies with the breakdown of the modern era.

Ralph moves back into the interior and is at this point constructed as resembling somebody who 'belongs' in this zone. He

> leapt back on the terrace, pulled off his shirt, and stood there among the skull-like coco-nuts with green shadows from the palms and the forest sliding over his skin. [...] He patted the palm trunk softly, and, forced at last to believe in the reality of the island, laughed delightedly again and stood on his head. He turned neatly on to his feet, jumped down to the beach, knelt and swept a double armful of sand into a pile against his chest.
>
> (Golding 2011, 4)

It is in the interior that Ralph removes his shirt (a foreshadowing of the later tension as to whether he will join Jack's group in 'going native') and where the shadows seem to claim him as being of the jungle, camouflaging him against the foliage.[4] The "paradox of the frontier," for de Certeau, is that

> created by contacts, the points of differentiation between two bodies are also their common points. [...] In the story, the frontier functions as a third element. It is an 'in-between' – a 'space between'. [...] The frontier is a sort of void, a narrative sym-bol [sic] of exchanges and encounters.
>
> (1988, 127)

In this light, then, Ralph's engagement with the border marks him as being an in-between character, an agent of in-between-ness. He exists in this site of "exchanges and encounters" and is open to experiencing otherness.

Robinson, by contrast, despite also being on the beach, remains still; he is unwilling or unable to engage with borders because psychologically he remains firmly connected to home. De Certeau discusses how stories about actions delimit spaces: stories "have the function of *spatial legislation* since they determine rights and divide up lands by 'acts' or discourses about actions" (1988, 122; emphasis in original). While Ralph crosses the boundary between the forest and the beach out of sheer exuberance, Robinson crosses only one border (the shoreline) and only in order to retrieve useful goods from his ship (Defoe 2003, 40).[5] As Watt points out, "Crusoe lives in the imagination mainly as a triumph of human achievement and enterprise, and as a favourite example of the elementary processes of political economy" (2001a, 97). In de Certeau's terms, "the bridge is ambiguous everywhere: it alternatively welds together and opposes insularities. It distinguishes them and threatens them" (1988, 128). Robinson has no interest in his 'insularity' being 'threatened' or 'opposed' with the (literal) insularity of the island, and so does not engage with the figurative 'bridges' that might allow him to cross borders. He simply does not notice that this space is not 'home' and in crossing the shore to import tools and provisions from his ship, Robinson colonizes the land as his own. Robinson's border-crossing is not a move into otherness but an incursion of 'home' onto the island, emphasizing the fact that he is essentially static, remaining emotionally and psychologically in England. For Deleuze, castaways "occupy and populate [the island]; but in reality, were they sufficiently separate, sufficiently creative, they would give the island only a dynamic image of itself" (2004, 10). Robinson, by contrast, gives the island only a static image of *himself*.[6] Indeed, writing specifically about *Robinson Crusoe*, Deleuze notes that "the mythical recreation of the world from the deserted island gives way to the restitution of everyday bourgeois life from a reserve of capital. Everything is taken from the ship. Nothing is invented" (2004, 12). Robinson has no desire to embrace otherness; as Watt has observed, the novel is representative of the fact that "modern society is uniquely individualist" (2001b, 60).

Ralph never revisits the crashed plane, and imports nothing physical of home. Indeed, on reaching the beach he divests himself of his clothes, suggesting a figurative rebirth on the island. This is not sustained; Ralph imports democracy and societal ideas from home. After swimming in a pool, Ralph "trotted through the sand, enduring the sun's enmity, crossed the platform and found his scattered clothes. To put on a grey shirt once more was strangely pleasing" (Golding 2011, 9–10). Ralph's pleasure at putting on his school uniform shows him moving back and forth across a figurative border of 'home' and 'the island' (the uniform represents not just home but the disciplinary apparatus of the English public school).

Both Ralph and Robinson climb to the top of a hill in order to survey their surroundings. Robinson "travell'd for discovery up to the top of that hill" and saw that he "was in an island environ'd in every way with the sea" (Defoe 2003, 43). As in his expedition for water, there is no apparent awareness on Robinson's part that he is crossing a border or moving into a different zone of the island. Neither does the landscape appear to have any effect on him; his emotional reaction is not due to his relationship with the environment per se, but with what it means for his chances of survival. Harold Bloom notes that "[a]ll of Defoe's protagonists are pragmatic and prudent, because they have to be; there is no play in the world as they know it" (1988, 2). Again, then, it can be seen that Robinson is concerned not with the island but only its relation to home. Ralph, on the other hand, together with Jack and "vivid, skinny" Simon (Golding 2011, 20), makes a journey that is practical but also motivated by eager curiosity for the island in its own right: "'Come on,' said Jack presently, 'we're explorers'" (2011, 22). The boys face borders and barriers, as the island proves constraining and somewhat impenetrable, with "narrow tracks, winding upwards. [...] Here the roots and stems of creepers were in such tangles that the boys had to thread through them like pliant needles" (2011, 23). Nevertheless, this movement remains satisfying:

> Immured in these tangles, at perhaps their most difficult moment, Ralph turned with shining eyes to the others.
> 'Wacco.'
> 'Wizard.'
> 'Smashing.'
>
> (2011, 23–24)

The boys climb to the summit just as Robinson does, but with explicit enjoyment narrated in vivid detail. Further, their journey is playful, embodying the instability and liminality of this space. Jack spots a rock that moves a little when pushed:

> The assault on the summit must wait while the three boys accepted this challenge. The rock was as large as a small motor car.
> 'Heave!' [...]
> The great rock loitered, poised on one toe, decided not to return, moved through the air, fell, struck, turned over, leapt droning through the air and smashed a deep hole in the canopy of the forest.
>
> (2011, 25)

What is necessary (namely surveying the island) is delayed for what is optional, fun, playful. While the displacement of the boulder could be seen as fulfilling "the ambition of a conquering power" (de Certeau 1988, 128), evoking the colonial associations of islands as the boys disrupt the norms of the island, it can also be read as an attack on the pre-established understanding of islands in which the interior is a space of otherness and threat and the beach is a safer space with more connection to home. This would suggest that the boys' transgression of boundaries and their destructive act in fact represent the destabilization of hegemonic (and colonial) modern perspectives on spaces of supposed otherness.

On the other hand, however, when the boys reach "the square top of the mountain" (Golding 2011, 25) and see the island laid out before them, Ralph declares that "[t]his belongs to us" (2011, 26). The practice and habitation of the island has created ownership, situated at the summit; the protagonist is the thoroughly modern "monarch of all I survey" (Cowper 1782, 305).[7] In moving into the island's interior, Ralph, Jack and Simon transgress the limit that was created by Ralph's jumping between the forest and the beach earlier. In de Certeau's understanding of space, "the primary function [of stories] is to *authorize* the establishment, displacement or transcendence of limits, and as a consequence, to set in opposition within the closed field of discourse, two movements that intersect (setting and transgressing limits)" (1988, 123; emphasis in original). The two intersecting movements here are Ralph's acknowledgement of a border between the forest and the beach, which creates that border, and the later transgression of the same border in returning to the interior. The boys test and challenge the island, with one foot on either side of the figurative border between home and otherness. When the work of surveying is completed, the boys are playful again: "They scrambled down a rock slope, dropped among flowers and made their way under the trees" (28). The boys fluidly alternate between seeming 'of home' and 'of the island,' between evoking and challenging the modern.

With the different spaces of the island set up in this manner, the topography of the rest of the novel can be traced. Progressively, the rejection of rules is located in Jack, while Ralph becomes less playful and more representative of modern discipline. When a ship passes without stopping, Ralph realizes that Jack's hunters have allowed the fire on the mountain to go out; they prioritized hunting in the 'savage' jungle interior over tending the beacon. The link between the hunters and the jungle is emphasized when they kill a sow and leave its head there on a stake. This is explicitly a sacrificial offering to the beast, suggesting that their fear of it has become worship. Later, Ralph and Jack, temporarily in a truce, travel up the mountain together and see what they think might be 'the beast.' The truth is that it is actually a dead parachutist, a reminder that the wider world is at war.

Jack's rejection of Ralph's rule continues on the far side of the island, at Castle Rock, where he builds a fort. Thus, he and his followers physically move away from the main beach with its connotations of home. Here, then, Golding places otherness at a physical distance, on the 'other side' of the island. This expulsion of otherness signals the reintroduction of modern discipline; Jack's savagery takes place in a space that is joined to the main island only by a "neck of land" (114). The implication is that Ralph intended to import democracy and rules (i.e. modern 'discipline') to the island, and has succeeded to some extent in conquering the summit and the beach, the island spaces traditionally most accessible to the European newcomer. The interior remains unknown and threatening, but the savagery of the hunters is successfully restricted to a peninsula. One could also argue that Jack, who now keeps prisoners and rules through fear, is aligned with discipline and the norms of home. This is signalled by the name of Castle Rock, which emphasizes its resemblance to an artificial, 'civilized' building.

It is into this context that Simon returns from the mountain, ready to disseminate the 'truth' that the boys had created the beast themselves. But seeing him come out of the jungle, the hunters mistake him for the beast and attack him, failing to recognize that otherness is within them rather than something external or of the island. Even the most rational, 'civilized' boys want to be in the circle attacking Simon because it offers a protection from fear. Of course, this protection is illusory; "the children first externalize what they fear and hate, and then 'kill' it" (Gregor and Kinkead-Weekes 2002, 31). The children become what they fear, which is signalled by the breaking of the circle: "The beast [Simon] struggled forward, broke the ring and fell over the steep edge of the rock to the sand by the water" (Golding 2011, 169). Here, *Lord of the Flies* can be seen as a critique of desert island narratives such as *Robinson Crusoe* in which otherness is expelled from the mainland to the desert island; it was Crusoe's rebelliousness that led to him being shipwrecked (Defoe 2003, 34). In expelling Simon's perceived otherness *from* the desert island (by killing him), the hunters in *Lord of the Flies* make their island analogous with the modern world that cannot tolerate otherness, and the savagery of all people is laid bare.

The boys' expulsion of the beast can be read as an attempt to rid themselves of evil; from the boys' point of view, they are destroying the source of their fear. From Ralph and Piggy's perspective, the split between them and Jack's followers can be seen in the same light; their (modern) rationalism is set against Jack's savagery. Indeed, Ralph and Jack "are very obviously intended to recall God and the Devil, whose confrontation, in the history of Western religions, establishes the moral basis for all actions" (Rosenfield 1961, 93). Of course, the novel can also be read in terms of the expulsion of all the boys from 'home' onto the desert island. All these rejections of otherness, though, are ultimately undone because the otherness in fact resides not in that which is expelled but in the subject who attempts to expel it. Rosenfield points out that "as Freud reminds us [...], gods and devils are 'nothing other than psychological processes projected into the outer world'" (1961, 93, citing Freud as quoted by Jones).

None of the boys are ever liberated from the fear of the unknown: "The children are already disposed to objectify their inner darkness and expect a Beast who will be other than themselves" (Gregor and Kinkead-Weekes 2002, 23). This applies to Ralph as well as to Jack: when Simon is killed, "Ralph too was fighting to get near, to get a handful of that brown, vulnerable flesh. The desire to squeeze and hurt was overmastering" (Golding 2011, 125). Hynes suggests that "the members of a 'demented society' may create an irrational, external evil, and in its name commit deeds that as rational men they could not tolerate" (1988, 20). What is made clear in *Lord of the Flies* is that this island society is no more "demented" than the world at large. The boys are not murderous because they have 'gone native' but because they are human.

Towards the novel's end, Ralph, Piggy, Sam and Eric see themselves as holding a moral high ground, and put their school uniforms on again to make a 'civilized' appeal to Jack, like missionaries taking the ideology of the beach to Castle Rock. As in the modern era (which, for Foucault and Bauman, is characterized by discipline), "[t]he different – the idiosyncratic and the insouciant – have been thereby dishonourably discharged from the army of order and progress [...] There was really no good reason to tolerate the Other who, by definition, rebelled against the truth" (Bauman 1992, xiv). Ralph and Piggy want to 'civilize' Jack and his 'savage' followers, as, in the modern era, "unlicensed difference is the main enemy" (Bauman 1992, xvi). However, "[c]ommunities are *imagined*: belief in their presence is their only brick and mortar, and imputation of importance their only source of authority" (Bauman 1992, xix; emphasis in original). When the boys gradually decide not to respect Ralph and the conch, they no longer "agree to be bound by the arbitration" imported from 'the world' onto the island (Bauman 1992, xix). In fact, Piggy and Ralph's own colonial mindset is betrayed when Piggy calls Jack and his followers "painted niggers" (Golding 2011, 200). Their mission fails; Piggy is killed and Sam and Eric join the 'savages.'

Initially, both Robinson Crusoe and Ralph move from where they are cast away to the beach. Both begin with some conception of providence, Ralph convinced that his father will rescue him and Robinson believing that God, the ultimate parental authority, will intervene on his behalf. In Deleuzian terms, neither Robinson nor Ralph arrives on the island "sufficiently separate" to leave their old life entirely behind, but it is Ralph who comes closer to doing so, just as it is he who is willing to test the island's physical borders (cf. Deleuze 2004, 10). Robinson is eventually proved right; providence arrives in the shape of a ship that can take him home to England. As such, his choice to remain figuratively on the shore is validated (on its own terms) in that he has survived his time on the island without needing to become like the "savages and cannibals" (Defoe 2003, 129) who, according to the terms of the novel, belong in the island environment. Rather, "Robinson Crusoe embodies a sturdy individualism, the values of the English yeoman. [...] Crusoe illustrates the capitalist idea; of acquiring and producing, and even keeps a store of gold sovereigns" (James 1996, 7). Robinson's faithfulness to the ideologies of modernity means that when he leaves his island, he does so very straightforwardly. Having recognized no borders or limits on the island when he arrived, it is a simple job to step back over the shore – after all, his island is an extension of his home.

For Ralph in *Lord of the Flies*, the return home is more complex and more ideologically nuanced. As chaos reigns, a new source of discipline is imported from home; a naval ship has anchored offshore and an officer is on the beach, where Ralph collapses. It seems that this *deus ex machina* saves Ralph's life, rescuing him from the violence that has been unleashed. From Ralph's point of view, the fantasy space of creation that existed on the island led only to destruction, proving the need for a disciplinary apparatus. This reading posits Ralph and Piggy as emissaries of British 'civilization,' whose reason and intelligence are overturned by the transgression of Jack and his 'savage' physicality; at the close, Ralph weeps for his "true, wise friend called Piggy" (Golding 2011, 225). Such a reading seems to cling onto the rationalism that Piggy embodied, and figures the desert island as ultimately a dangerous place to be subdued by the arrival of rational adults: a very modern ideology. However, Ralph also weeps (we are told by the narrator) "for the end of innocence, the darkness of man's heart" (2011, 225), perhaps mourning the impossibility of rationalism. This would be congruent with an interpretation that considers Jack's savagery analogous to the brutality of (British) adults in so-called civilized society. The savagery on the island is in fact not a result of the boys 'going native,' but is the revelation of part of themselves as projected onto the imaginary beast. The desert island is not a space of otherness, or a space divided into clear zones of otherness and homeliness, but a liminal zone, as signalled by Ralph's initial negotiation of space. As Ralph explains to him what has happened on the island, the navy officer's reaction is to look back across the beach towards home, "allowing his eyes to rest on the trim cruiser in the distance" (2011, 225). The implication is that the violence on the island makes him think of nothing more than the war raging in the outside world, the war that caused the boys to be cast away in the first place. Home is no more civilized than the island, after all, and the father figure has no plausibility as a guiding example.

This revelation challenges modern assumptions that otherness is external and ought not to be tolerated, as described by Bauman (1992, xiv).

Ralph, Jack and the naval officer can all be seen as enacting modernity: on the island, Ralph and Jack both attempt to impose discipline (Jack's rebellion against Ralph is more autocratic than anarchic) while the officer represents the authority of the parent, which is shown to be redundant. These intimations that modernity is failing are presaged by the fact that, on their arrival, the children do not understand or interact with the island as a space that conforms to paradigms resonant with modernity. Ralph's initial movements on the island speak to an engagement with playfulness and liminality: a non-modern willingness to embrace otherness, rather than to colonize or efface it. As such, he negotiates the island in ways that engage with and transform the space, with borders and zones being established, removed, transgressed and reshaped, recalling de Certeau's conception of space understood as an itinerary (1988, 119). Indeed, Ralph's fluidity and fluid understanding of the island are evocative of the 'liquid modern,' Bauman's preferred term for the "present, in many ways novel, phase in the history of modernity" (2006, 2).[8] By way of contrast, Robinson Crusoe's initial spatial practice of his desert island foreshadows the thoroughly modern ideology of his novel. He is largely static, traversing the island only for what is necessary for survival and economic progress. He understands the desert island as a space to be colonized and put to efficient economic use; that is, it is a space in which home can be recreated. Defoe celebrates the disciplinary apparatus of British society, which produces young men who seek to control others and their own otherness. Golding critiques those same tendencies through a protagonist who ultimately imports discipline onto the island but had earlier challenged the norms of modernity by his fluid and playful relationship with space, which complicates and intertwines the ideas of home and other: "The fair boy stopped and jerked his stockings with an automatic gesture that made the jungle seem for a moment like the Home Counties" (2011, 1).

Notes

1 Home can also be a contentious concept, of course. Fallon convincingly argues that Crusoe's home is itself constructed as having a sense of liminality: "Defoe represents England and Englishness not as an isolated or pure 'state' but as a corrupted or hybrid state that is intimately tied to the continent, to the growing slave trade in Africa, and to the 'New World'" (2011, 34).
2 Robinson discusses specific distances between points, so imports a system of measurement; even in his narration he has brought with him the ideals and norms of 'home.'
3 Dening is writing here about an inhabited island, where the beach is the space between the newcomer and the inhabitant. On desert islands (as long as they remain deserted), the whole island may be available as a space of experimentation, especially if it has no zone marked as 'interior.' As Godfrey Baldacchino points out: "Islands, especially small islands, lack hinterlands" (2007, 169).

4 It is also the tactile engagement with the palm tree in the interior that convinces Ralph that the island exists; the retrospective acknowledgement to the reader that he had not previously been certain of this destabilizes both the existence of the island and the reliability of the narrator. The physical engagement with the island (the tree, the sand and the shadows) also speaks to his eagerness to embrace the supposed otherness of the space.

5 Robinson does first walk along the shore to attempt to reach the ship's boat, but unlike Ralph's beach, his is limited; he cannot reach the boat due to "a neck or inlet of water [...] about half a mile broad" (Defoe 2003, 40).

6 Ralph's rival for leadership on the island, Jack, could be seen as sufficiently separate and creative for the island to remain a desert island (on Deleuze's terms) despite his inhabiting it. He rejects the morality of 'home' and bases his savage new society around the idea of the beast that he believes the island to contain. Ultimately, Jack's savagery is revealed to have been imported from 'civilization,' and Deleuze indeed points out that it is never possible in reality to arrive 'separately': people "always encounter [the desert island] from the outside" (2004, 11).

7 The trope of the 'Monarch-of-all-I-survey scene' has been discussed by Mary Louise Pratt (2008, 197) and Rebecca Weaver-Hightower (2007, 1–42).

8 Bauman's designation of the contemporary era as the "liquid modern" recalls the etymology of the word 'island' as "watery land" (Beer 1989, 16).

References

Baldacchino, Godfrey. 2007. "Islands as Novelty Sites." *Geographical Review* 97 (2): 165–174.

Bauman, Zygmunt. 1992. *Intimations of Postmodernity*. London: Routledge.

———. 2006. *Liquid Modernity*. Cambridge: Polity Press.

Beer, Gillian. 1989. "Discourses of the Island." In *Literature and Science as Modes of Expression*, edited by Frederick Amrine, 1–27. Dordrecht: Kluwer Academic.

Bloom, Harold. 1988. "Introduction." In *Daniel Defoe's Robinson Crusoe*, edited by Harold Bloom, 1–4. New York: Chelsea House.

Boyle, Ted E. 1978. "Golding's Existential Vision." In *William Golding: Some Critical Considerations*, edited by Jack I. Biles and Robert O. Evans, 21–38. Lexington: University Press of Kentucky.

Carey, John. 2009. *William Golding: The Man Who Wrote Lord of the Flies: A Life*. London: Faber & Faber.

Cowper, William. 1782. "The Solitude of Alexander Selkirk." In *Poems*, 305–308. London: J. Johnson.

de Certeau, Michel. 1988. *The Practice of Everyday Life*. Translated by Steven Rendall. Berkeley: University of California Press.

Defoe, Daniel. (1719) 2003. *Robinson Crusoe*. Edited by John Richetti. London: Penguin.

Deleuze, Gilles. 2004. "Desert Islands." Translated by Michael Taormina. In *Desert Islands and Other Texts, 1953–1974*, edited by David Lapoujade, 9–14. Los Angeles: Semiotext(e).

Dening, Greg. 1980. *Islands and Beaches: Discourse on a Silent Land: Marquesas, 1774–1880*. Melbourne: Melbourne University Press.

Epstein, Edmund. 1959. "Notes on Lord of the Flies." In *Lord of the Flies*, edited by William Golding, 188–192. New York: Capricorn Books.

Faber & Faber. "*Lord of the Flies*: Sales to September 16." 1955. [Sales note.] Faber Archive, E17/56(A). September 16, 1955.

Fallon, Ann Marie. 2011. *Global Crusoe: Comparative Literature, Postcolonial Theory and Transnational Aesthetics*. Farnham: Ashgate.

Foucault, Michel. 1995. *Discipline and Punish: The Birth of the Prison*. Trans. Alan Sheridan. New York: Vintage Books.

Golding, William. (1954) 2011. *Lord of the Flies*. London: Faber and Faber.

Gregor, Ian, and Mark Kinkead-Weekes. 2002. *William Golding: A Critical Study of the Novels*. London: Faber.

Hynes, Samuel. 1988. "[William Golding's Lord of the Flies]." In *Critical Essays on William Golding*, edited by James R. Baker, 13–21. Boston: G. K. Hall.

James, Louis. 1996. "Unwrapping Crusoe." In *Robinson Crusoe: Myths and Metamorphoses*, edited by Lieve Spaas and Brian Stimpson, 1–12. London: Macmillan.

McCullen, Maurice L. 1978. "Lord of the Flies: The Critical Quest." In *William Golding: Some Critical Considerations*, edited by Jack I. Biles and Robert O. Evans, 203–236. Lexington: University Press of Kentucky.

Pratt, Mary Louise. 2008. *Imperial Eyes: Travel Writing and Transculturation*. Second edition. London: Routledge.

Riquet, Johannes. 2014. *The Aesthetics of Island Space: Perception, Ideology, Geopoetics*. Unpublished doctoral dissertation. University of Zurich.

Rogers, Pat. 1979. *Robinson Crusoe*. London: George Allen & Unwin.

Rosenfield, Claire. 1961. "'Men of a Smaller Growth': A Psychological Analysis of William Golding's Lord of the Flies." *Literature and Psychology* 11 (4): 93–101.

Watt, Ian. (1951) 2001a. "Robinson Crusoe as a Myth." *Essays in Criticism* 1 (2): 95–119.

———. (1957) 2001b. *The Rise of the Novel: Studies in Defoe, Richardson and Fielding*. Berkeley: University of Los Angeles Press.

Weaver-Hightower, Rebecca. 2007. *Empire Islands: Castaways, Cannibals, and Fantasies of Conquest*. Minneapolis: University of Minnesota Press.

Whitley, John S. 1970. *Golding: Lord of the Flies*. London: Edward Arnold.

6 Two Centuries of Spatial 'Island' Assumptions

The Swiss Family Robinson and the Robinson Crusoe Legacy[*]

Britta Hartmann

Island physicality lies at the heart of Johann David Wyss's *The Swiss Family Robinson*, first published between 1812 and 1813: the narrative – as an island castaway story – requires an island setting by its very definition. This aligns it with a myriad of other nineteenth-century castaway stories that tell the tale of families (or groups of children) stranded on islands. These stories – known as Robinsonades[1] – speak back to the imperial urtext of Daniel Defoe's *Robinson Crusoe* (1719), and include Wyss's *The Swiss Family Robinson*, Frederick Marryat's *Masterman Ready* (1841–42) and R. M. Ballantyne's *The Coral Island* (1858). Stories like these need an island setting in order to function: they require a bounded space in which characters can develop into self-sufficient colonists and imperialists (see, for instance, Weaver-Hightower 2007, xi). Castaways require an island on which to be cast away. Moreover, Robinsonades are highly preoccupied with positioning their islands as bounded spaces: this is in line with real-world colonialism for, as Epeli Hau'ofa writes in a Pacific context, "[n]ineteenth century imperialism erected boundaries [...], transforming a once boundless world into the Pacific islands states and territories that we know today" (1993, 10). Key to this imperial mission was turning "a sea of islands" (1993, 8) into "tiny, isolated dots in a vast ocean" (1993, 7): islands became bounded spaces, contained within a border of ocean and set apart from the rest of the world.

However, as this chapter argues, there is in actual fact very little evidence of an island setting in *The Swiss Family Robinson*, bounded or otherwise. The characters of this novel do not fully explore the land on which they have been cast, and readers are never afforded irrefutable evidence of the space's bounded-by-water nature. Nonetheless, characters and readers – including scholars – have assumed an island setting for the novel. This chapter proposes that this blatant spatial assumption has come about as a result of the legacy of Defoe's *Robinson Crusoe* and our broader cultural engagement with fictional island spaces. Martin Green considers *Robinson Crusoe* to be "the mythic fuel of our cultural engine"

(1990, 3), and it is this fuel that has led the Swiss family Robinson to be cast on an assumed island. Consequently, in order to understand the spatial assumptions at play in our discourse surrounding *The Swiss Family Robinson*, it is imperative to understand the broader narrative context in which the story is situated and, more specifically, the foundational constructs at work in Defoe's *Robinson Crusoe*.

Constructing the Island: *Robinson Crusoe* and Robinsonades

Islands have been heavily inscribed over time, leading to island spaces being steeped in a myriad of generalized meanings. As Godfrey Baldacchino highlights,

> [s]tatements and assertions abound about what islands and islanders are [...]. It seems as if the geography is simply too gripping; the island image too powerful to discard; the opportunity to 'play God' on/for an island too tantalizing to resist.
>
> (2005, 247)

Island physicality and stereotypically imperial human attitudes towards these locations become linked: in the context of writing the island from the outside, Western engagement with such spaces often occurs through the geography of terrain and exists within a discourse of power and control. Baldacchino posits that people who are asked to draw an island will often give it a circular shape fitting within a single piece of paper (2005, 247). "Why should this happen?" he asks, before suggesting that "[p]erhaps the answer lies in an obsession to control, to embrace an island as something that is finite, that may be encapsulated by human strategy, design or desire" (2005, 247). Island physicality – in this case, the circular line demarking the border between land and ocean – comes to the forefront in such pictures, as though a space can somehow be controlled through its shape. These circular islands, however, are constructed images: the landforms they represent are not inherently conquerable. Rather, they have been constructed and reshaped to better suit ideologies of power and domination. They have been made into a bounded shape, thereby standing in opposition to Hau'ofa's "sea of islands" stance, which advocates an approach to islands that emphasizes connectivity over boundedness.

Daniel Defoe's *Robinson Crusoe* can be considered the archetypal novel of island conquest. James Joyce views the titular character as "the true prototype of the British colonist" (1964, 24) and Edward W. Said similarly highlights the integral role played by the "colonizing mission" in Crusoe's "[creation of] a new world of his own in the distant reaches of the African, Pacific, and Atlantic wilderness" (1994, 75).

Furthermore, Crusoe and his island are firmly etched into the psyche of Western culture: Michel Tournier[2] goes so far as to say that "Crusoe is one of the basic constituents of the Western soul" (1991, 183), while J. M. Coetzee[3] refers to the story's influential power when he observes that Crusoe "has become a figure in the collective consciousness of the West" (2001, 20). Moreover, Virginia Woolf lends a kind of inevitability to the story's existence: it "resembles one of the anonymous productions of the race rather than the effort of a single mind" (1984, 86). The story has an authorial presence beyond Defoe. In a cyclical manner, it is thus both a product of its culture and a key player in further shaping that cultural consciousness.

It is not only the text itself of which this can be said, for as Green writes,

> the Robinson story is much more than the book Defoe wrote. That story was being – and still is – pirated, adapted, abridged, drama-tised, hundreds of times [...]. But it is above all the independent retellings that convince us that we are dealing with something of a different order from an ordinary book.
>
> (1989, 35)

Elsewhere, he makes the broader point that

> the adventure tales that formed the light reading of Englishmen for two hundred years and more after *Robinson Crusoe* were [...] the energizing myth of English imperialism [...] they charged England's will with the energy to go out into the world and explore, conquer, and rule.
>
> (1980, 1)

The influential power of *Robinson Crusoe* thus extends to the countless narratives that it spawned, both directly through the Robinsonade and indirectly through the broader realm of adventure fiction. The novels that came in the wake of Defoe's text drove generations of people to nurture, and in some cases act upon, ideologies of conquest.

The Robinsonade was particularly prevalent in children's fiction of the nineteenth century. According to Humphrey Carpenter and Mari Prichard, it "became for a time the dominant form in fiction for children and young people" (1984, 458). Crusoe revisions of this era, Rebecca Weaver-Hightower explains, "packaged empire for chil-dren and provided an important vehicle for their enculturation into imperial society" (2007, 38; see also Walcott 1997, 37). Island set-tings played an important role in this process of constructing, teach-ing and endorsing imperial ideologies. Young readers and characters alike were given the space to become what their culture wanted them to be: empire builders. "The island territory," writes Diana Loxley, "provides the ideal mythic space – a fictional parallel of the actual historic and geographic sites of colonial activity – as a laboratory for the propagation and nurturing of a perfect masculinity" (1990, 117). Children's Robinsonades thus rely on their setting to achieve their purpose: these texts need to be anchored to a physical location so as to give their ideologies greater power. Nineteenth-century textual islands acted as colonial sites that existed parallel to reality; they were places of childhood imperialism, stepping-stones en route to real-world empire expansion.

Robinsonades are scripted through *Robinson Crusoe* – characters engage with the castaway experience in relation to their urtext. Crusoe and his island are permanently in the background of these stories: the very definition of a Robinsonade hinges on this relationship. That dynamic creates a firm set of genre expectations, as each new novel harks back to its predecessor and, in many cases, further affirms existing tropes: narrative expectations govern the behaviour of fictional castaways and the representation of their surroundings. In particular, there are certain plot developments that are likely to occur within island castaway stories of the nineteenth century: the characters salvage provisions from the wreck of the ship on which they were travelling, discover (often from the peak of a mountain) that they are on an island, build temporary shelters, find food, explore their surroundings, construct several grand homes and domesticate the terrain. Readers and characters approach their island space through a textual legacy: castaways have a preconceived notion of how they *should* act upon being cast away on an island, and readers come to expect that behaviour.

In this context, islands are usually represented as places to be possessed (often in a figurative sense through abstract symbolization) and places that are possessed, or haunted, by a textual legacy. This possession occurs through the language of spatiality. While more recent rewritings of the *Robinson Crusoe* story have often sought to overturn their urtext, they nonetheless remain firmly rooted to the imperial history of Defoe's novel: islands continue to be considered through notions of possession and being possessed. The fictional islands of the castaway tradition are constructed both as items of property and as spaces inhabited by a kind of haunting spectre.[4] These insular places are possessed by the needs of others: they no longer represent themselves, but instead represent what others want them to represent. They become property, contained pieces of land existing merely for human benefit. They are haunted spaces, stereotypically negotiated through the ideologies and behaviours of Defoe's Robinson Crusoe.

The Swiss Family Robinson

Turning back to *The Swiss Family Robinson*, one can ask: how is it that expectations are able to obscure the reality of a text, and how do scholars and fictional castaways engage with, or respond to, settings that do not fulfil generic expectations? Wyss's *The Swiss Family Robinson* is one of the most overt examples of a Robinsonade built on narrative expectations and assumptions. It was originally published in German, between 1812 and 1813, by the author's son Johann Rudolf Wyss. Like *Robinson Crusoe*, it has been extensively reimagined in a variety of formats: countless editions, translations and expansions exist, most notably by Johann Rudolf Wyss, Isabelle de Montolieu, Mary Jane and William Godwin, and W. H. G. Kingston. Many of these editions differ substantially from one another through the introduction of new characters and adventures. The complexity of the novel's legacy has also been increased through the publication of sequels like Adrien Paul's *Willis the Pilot*, first published in French in 1855, and Jules Verne's *The Castaways of the* Flag, first published in French in 1900. The twentieth and twenty-first centuries have also seen the story translated to the screen through adaptations and continuations like *Swiss Family Robinson* (Walt Disney, Annakin 1960) and *Stranded* (Hallmark Entertainment, Beeson 2002).

The existence of so many versions of the story has fascinating analytical ramifications: it becomes possible to chart the manner in which representations of one island, and one family's castaway experience, have evolved over the centuries. Simultaneously, one can examine how our understanding of *The Swiss Family Robinson* has been shaped by cultural constructs that are inseparable from Western modernity and its obsession with islands (cf. Conley 1996, 167–201; Gillis 2004, 84–85; Kiening 2006, 202–247; Ruddick 1993, 56). Novels like *Robinson Crusoe* and most of the nineteenth-century Robinsonades that followed in its wake provide islands that, like those in Baldacchino's earlier quoted observation, are small, contained and finite. *The Swiss Family Robinson*, however, features an 'island' that is very large and that is not seen in its entirety until later sequels and filmic adaptations. Indeed, its status as an island is highly questionable, thereby raising an issue, namely the definition of an island, that has been given much thought within the field of island studies scholarship (see Fletcher and Crane 2017, xiv–xv). Paradoxically, it is in these later versions of the story that the island, now contained within a more rigid and visible physical boundary, becomes increasingly connected to the outer world.

Examining the 2007 Seelye Edition

John Seelye's 2007 literary edition of *The Swiss Family Robinson* is the closest one can find to an authoritative English version of the original text. According to Seelye, this edition is "the original, the faithful Godwin translation of Wyss's novel, read in English by two generations of children before the Montolieu material was added to it" (2007b, xix). His claim is, in the light of the novel's complicated publishing history, a little contentious: David Blamires offers a detailed examination of the story's publication history, and proposes that the early Godwin translations were in fact more reliant on Montolieu's French translation than Seelye's comment suggests (2009, 82). Nonetheless, the Seelye edition does replicate the events of Wyss's original: the significant plot developments introduced by Johann Rudolf Wyss, Montolieu, Kingston and others are not present in this text. Seelye's edition thus provides access to the story on which the other editions were built.

The Swiss Family Robinson presents its protagonists – an unnamed father and mother, and their four sons Fritz, Ernest, Jack and Francis – as potential colonists from the very beginning of the novel. Though they leave their war-ravaged and economically depleted home of Switzerland to travel to Tahiti for missionary work, their ultimate goal is to travel on to Australia to become "free [settlers]" (Wyss 2007, 7). The ship on which they travel is itself situated in the colonial mission: having been "sent out [from England] as a preparation for the establishment of a colony in the South Seas," it is stocked with "a variety of stores not commonly included in the loading of a ship" such as animals, plants, seeds and tools (2007, 80–81). A violent storm between Java and New Guinea, however, cripples the ship and sees the crew flee; the family construct a raft, escape to a nearby shore and set to work building new lives for themselves. The location fulfils their desires and provides them with the opportunity to turn colonial dreams into a colonial reality far sooner than their initial plans could have.

This colonial reality is anchored in Crusoe's island experiences. The Swiss characters undertake the same kinds of tasks that their predecessor does: they salvage valuable items from the wrecked ship, build a temporary shelter, explore the area, construct permanent shelters, grow crops, domesticate animals and teach themselves new trades like carpentry. The parallel is implicit for most of the novel as Defoe's hero is rarely mentioned in the context of these specific actions. This makes the behaviour of the family seem natural rather than intentionally imitational. Their actions appear to be driven primarily by an inherent attitude towards the situation and location, although readers familiar with *Robinson Crusoe* will notice the parallels. Moreover, by dislocating Crusoe's castaway behaviour from its text, the novel presents his method of survival as *the* method when placed in such a situation. Defoe's central story informs *The Swiss Family Robinson*'s plot and characterization, and supplies it with a structural and narrative foundation. An editorial endnote emphasizes that *Robinson Crusoe* "provided the model for all subsequent castaway stories" (Seelye 2007a, 445)[5]. The figure of Crusoe plays a key role in this process within *The Swiss Family Robinson*. His attitude towards the island is taken up and turned into a generic and largely unspoken stereotype. Indeed, the editorial endnote could easily be adapted to suit a discussion of setting: *Robinson Crusoe* "provided the model for all subsequent castaway" engagements with 'island' spatiality. Wyss's castaways see their 'island' through the eyes of Crusoe, and transform it accordingly.

Overall, Crusoe shapes the experiences of the family as an implicit model dictating their actions at the level of genre (the result of which is the family's unacknowledged imitation of Crusoe's behaviour). To a lesser extent, he also functions as a textual guide within the story itself: there are moments in which explicit, intertextual references to Defoe's hero are made. Most significantly, Fritz discovers a copy of *Robinson Crusoe* among their possessions towards the end of the novel, and announces that

> [h]ere [...] is our best counsellor and model, *Robinson Crusoe*; since Heaven has destined us to a similar fate, whom better can we consult? as far as I remember, he cut himself an habitation out of the solid rock: let us see how he proceeded; we will do the same.
>
> (Wyss 2007, 381)

Robinson Crusoe is given historicity, authenticity and authority; its protagonist becomes a teacher whose lesson can be accessed through text. However, the family's engagement with the story suggests an imperfect knowledge of it: Ernest, for instance, believes Fritz and their father will find coconuts "like Robinson Crusoe" did (Wyss 2007, 40), even though Crusoe's island did not have coconuts (Seelye 2007a, 445). Moreover, no mention is made of the adventures described in *Robinson Crusoe* before and after the hero's island entrapment. Thus, Wyss's characters engage with the text in much the same way as Western culture has over time: the framing narrative is forgotten, and all that remains is the mythic core represented by the island experience.

This dynamic has a profound effect on the setting of *The Swiss Family Robinson*. The 'island' of this novel is quite different to the one found in Defoe's narrative: it is larger and located in the Pacific Ocean (rather than the Atlantic Ocean), and has a far broader, even impossible, range of flora and fauna.[6] However, by superimposing Crusoe's lifestyle onto their location, the family cause the setting to take on certain attributes of Crusoe's island. Wyss's characters construct several habitations and plant a number of agricultural plots across their domain, which creates an aesthetic similarity between the two diegetic spaces. As in *Robinson Crusoe*, the work undertaken by the castaways directly relates to their survival and comfort in their new surroundings. This process predictably changes the terrain: rocks are shattered and dug into, trees are felled, seeds are sown and houses are built. Crusoe's lifestyle is etched into the very topography of the space; his story is carved into the adopted home of the family.

However, it is in the islandness of the space that the repercussions of living as a Crusoe figure most come to the fore. Crusoe's island is understood to be a bounded and contained site. After being shipwrecked, Crusoe climbs a nearby hill to give himself a better view of his surroundings. Once on the hilltop, he tells the reader:

> I saw my Fate to my great Affliction, (*viz.*) that I was in an Island environ'd every Way with the Sea, no Land to be seen, except some Rocks which lay a great Way off, and two small Islands less than this, which lay about three Leagues to the West.
>
> (Defoe 1994, 40)

Surveying the island from the peak, he is able to see it in its entirety: irrefutable proof shows that it is an island. Mountaintop visits, commonly labelled "monarch-of-all-I-survey scenes," occur in most castaway narratives, and are rife with colonial and imperial subtext. Mary Louise Pratt, applying the term to her discussion of non-fictional travel narratives, describes it as "a brand of verbal painting whose highest calling was to produce for the home audience the peak moments at which geographical 'discoveries' were 'won' for England" (2008, 197). Vision and the recounting thereof become integral to the process of acquiring foreign land. Scholars like Richard Phillips (1997) and Weaver-Hightower (2007) have, in turn, applied the term to fictional island stories.[7] Weaver-Hightower writes that such scenes, when used in island narratives, represent a "visual [appropriation]" of island territory (2007, xviii) by "providing the fictional colonist with a fantasy of power over the land he views"; such texts "enable their readers to establish and maintain a fantasy of legitimate ownership over colonized lands symbolized by the fictional island" (2007, 3). Crusoe, standing on the mountaintop, sees the island spread out around him and in so doing claims it as his own. He interprets his vision of the land through a seemingly inherent (and of course highly problematic) right to possession. The island is his: it has, to use Pratt's phraseology, been "'won' for England," won for himself and won for the reader.

A similar monarch-of-all-I-survey scene related in *The Swiss Family Robinson* is far less conclusive. In search of other shipwreck survivors, two of the castaways climb a summit that "would not fail to give us a clear view of all adjacent parts" (Wyss 2007, 50). Once on the peak, they see "a magnificent scene of wild and solitary beauty, comprehending a vast extent of land and water" (2007, 50). The passage gives no evidence that they are viewing a panorama of land entirely surrounded by the sea, nor does it suggest that the hill climb is motivated by a desire to confirm their insular state. It therefore becomes a pseudo monarch-of-all-I-survey island scene: the castaways act in a stereotypical manner by climbing the hill, but the act neither stems from an explicit desire to confirm the islandness of their location nor does it provide them with an all-encompassing view of the land on which they find themselves.

This lack of island evidence continues throughout the novel, and is paradoxically accompanied by the characters exhibiting a firm and unquestioning belief that they have been wrecked on an island. The unfounded nature of this assumption is apparent throughout the story. Several editions of the text contain a map that, although it varies in design, usually illustrates the same content. This map clearly juxtaposes the characters' assumptions against their actual reality: it is entitled "Settlements of the Swiss Pastor & his Family in the Desert Island" (Wyss 2007, xxvi–xxvii) but depicts a peninsular outcrop bordered by ocean and blank territory. The map "reveals," as Seelye observes in his introduction to the text, "that despite several insular allusions in the book, the family has landed on part of a larger land mass" (2007b, xvi). Furthermore, the map has a place within the diegesis of the text: one can presume it to be the "sketch" drawn by one of the castaways and referred to in the novel's fictional "Postscript by the Editor" (Wyss 2007, 433). It thus gives the reader topographical information concerning the setting, and also reflects the contradictory understanding the characters have of their surroundings.

This biased understanding of setting filters through to the exploration of the location. Though the castaways explore their surroundings, they do so with no interest in confirming the overall form of their location. Even the discovery of a long barrier of rocks does not give the family grounds for changing their attitude. Travelling beyond this rock wall is important to the father of the family, but not for the sake of addressing an uncertainty regarding their insular state: as he explains to the reader,

> I had formed a wish to penetrate a little further into the land, and ascertain whether any thing useful would present itself beyond the wall of rocks. I was, besides, desirous to be better acquainted with the extent, form, and general production of our island.
>
> (Wyss 2007, 284)

His desire is thus motivated by the search for resources and the broadening of his knowledge concerning the *island* domain.

Defining that domain as an island is not considered necessary. The father returns to the topic of the unknown space beyond the rocks a little later, explaining that the group wanted to determine "what might be found on the other side of the rocks, for as yet we were ignorant whether they formed a boundary to our island, or divided it into two portions" (320). The possibility that they may have been wrecked on a continental peninsula, and that the rocks might be hiding territory far larger than a "portion" of an island, is never raised. Moreover, when the area beyond the rocks is eventually described, no evidence is given that the overall setting is insular: the father and his accompanying son see a wide-reaching plain and "a chain of gently rising hills, the long green verdure of which was tinged with blue, [that] stretched as far as the eye could discern" (321). The plain is very large: the father explains that, "[b]y stretching our eyes [...] as far as we could see, we thought we perceived at a great distance some specks upon the land" (321). These specks are buffalos that run "beyond the reach of our sight" (325). The novel thus emphasizes the largeness of the space but, simultaneously, refuses to acknowledge that it might be part of a continent. This allows the text to have an island setting without restricting itself to the boundaries imposed on such landforms by Western imperialistic thinking. An acknowledged non-island setting would also undermine the family's control of the space.

The systematic and unfounded representation of the setting as an island is a vital element of the novel that can be read through the lens of genre and narrative tradition. The setting must be represented as an island so as to conform to the narrative expectations that accompany the Robinsonade. As with other castaway narratives, this agenda is met through the characters' engagement with space. Wyss's Swiss family actively imagine their surroundings as an island, and that imagining, in turn, shapes the setting into exactly that: it is an island because the characters – and, by association, the readers – see it as such. The space beyond the rocks is never fully explored in this version of the story. The family members can thus experience the adventure of living on an island – and can continue to define themselves as island castaways – whilst simultaneously benefiting from the expanded space of unknown, unbounded territory. The open nature of the territory, coupled with the presence of the animals, allows it to be seen as a wilderness. According to Lawrence Buell, "wilderness denotes *terra incognita*, typically of large size, the abode of beasts rather than humans: a place where civilized people supposedly do not (yet) dwell" (2005, 149; emphasis in original). The untamed nature of the area gives the family something against which to define themselves: their part of the island is a safe home, and not a vast 'wilderness.'

The "yet" of this definition is particularly important to *The Swiss Family Robinson* – though the area behind the rock is uninhabited space, it could become inhabited place. Y-Fu Tuan posits that "[s]pace lies open; it suggests the future and invites action [...]. It has no fixed pattern of established human meaning; it is like a blank sheet on which meaning may be imposed" (1977, 54). By contrast, he continues, "[e]nclosed and humanized space is place. Compared to space, place is a calm center of established values" (54). A balance between the two is vital, as people "require both space and place. Human lives are a dialectical movement between shelter and venture, attachment and freedom" (54). Wyss's setting is a perfect example of this dynamic. It offers both 'space' and 'place' – the place of the family's habitations, and the uninscribed space beyond the rocks. Crusoe eventually leaves his island and travels into the space and freedom of the outside world; had he remained on the island, he would have stagnated in the shelter and attachment of place. The Swiss family, on the other hand, remain in their adopted home. There are countless more adventures to be had in the space/place of their unbounded 'island,' as is indicated by the complicated publishing legacy of the text.

Lastly, turning to the most authoritative English version of the extended *The Swiss Family Robinson* story (Seelye 1991), one finds that island assumptions continue to overpower textual reality. This version is based on several of the standard nineteenth-century texts that incorporate material from the Montolieu sequels: while Wyss's original story ends after two years on the island, Montolieu's continuation expands the castaway adventure to more than ten years. Though new adventures occasionally take the family beyond the rock wall, there is still no clear moment of island identification. This emphasizes the high degree of assumptions and expectations at play in the mindsets of these characters: they are able to live in a location they deem an island for more than ten years without feeling the need to determine the insular state of their surroundings.

Scholarly and Fictional Responses

Most surprisingly, the lack of evidence regarding the islandness of the setting has been largely ignored by scholarship. Seelye is one of very few scholars, if not the only one, to discuss the non-insular depictions of the castaway location, and he does so in the introductions to the two editions discussed earlier (1991, xiii; 2007b, xvi). Most scholars (including Green, Loxley and Weaver-Hightower) generally take *The Swiss Family Robinson*'s island setting as a given. This is particularly odd given the novel's status as an iconic *island* text. It appears that the assumptions held by characters within the story have carried through to scholarship on the novel. Weaver-Hightower, for instance, reads the hilltop moment as though the castaways have discovered that they are on an island, and uses the scene to illustrate certain points of her theory concerning monarch-of-all-I-survey scenes (2007, 30). The Watermill Press 1980 edition she refers to is an extended version of the story, and thus includes greater exploration than the 2007 Seelye edition. Nonetheless, it does not contain an insular monarch-of-all-I-survey scene. Standing on the mountaintop, the characters see water to one side and an "inland" view to the other (Wyss 1980, 32). As is routinely the case in editions of *The Swiss Family Robinson*, there is no evidence within this passage that the castaways are surrounded by water. Weaver-Hightower's argument thus appears to be informed, to a certain extent, by genre expectations. Such an engagement with the novel is not unique, as explained earlier: most scholars (excluding Seelye) assume, like the Swiss family themselves, that the story's setting is an island. Its insularity is generally, in the academic discourse, neither questioned nor proven: it is just accepted as such.

While the issue is not taken up extensively by scholarship, fictional responses to the novel have been more attentive to the lack of island evidence. Two 'sequels' to Wyss's story, Paul's *Willis the Pilot* and Verne's *The Castaways of the Flag*, acknowledge that *The Swiss Family Robinson*'s castaways do not fully explore or view their surroundings and thus cannot know if they are on an island or a continent. While Paul's novel engages only briefly with the question, Verne's story takes it as a fundamental reason for re-engaging with the text: as the preface of the English translation states, Verne did not consider the original to be complete as "[t]he surface of the island had not been fully explored" (Verne 1924, iii). The issue is so central to the novel that it is raised in the second paragraph of the first chapter: "After eleven years spent upon this land," the reader is told, "it was none too soon to attempt to ascertain whether it was a part of one of the continents laved by the Indian Ocean or whether it must be included by geographers among the islands of those seas" (1924, 1). The story sees several characters, including young Jack, climb a mountain for the express purpose of defining their surroundings. The subsequent monarch-of-all-I-survey scene becomes a crucial point in the island's human history. As Verne writes, "[a]t last, about two o'clock in the afternoon, Jack's ringing voice was heard – the first, no doubt, that had ever resounded from this pinnacle. 'An island! It really is an island'" (1924, 232). Verne's phrasing highlights the significance of the moment: the first voice to speak from this newly reached peak proclaims the bounded and finite nature of the setting. The importance of the island as an island is also emphasized through the inclusion of a map that visually confirms the setting's bounded nature.

Filmic adaptations of the novel, in turn, also take up the question of the setting's topographical form. The 1960 movie *Swiss Family Robinson* (Annakin) sees its characters grapple with the uncertainty of the island/peninsula dilemma: "How do you know it's an island?" asks one character, "Why couldn't it be a peninsula?" A subsequent monarch-of-all-I-survey scene clarifies the location's form: "There's no question about it now," the boy proclaims, "This is an island." The 2002 *Swiss Family Robinson*-inspired televisual film *Stranded* prioritizes the question by providing the audience with a convincing monarch-of-all-I-survey scene scarcely twenty minutes into the three-hour two-part film. This is followed by a dialogue between characters to confirm the find: "We climbed high and looked down. We're on an island," says one of the boys to his father (Beeson 2002). "An island? Are you sure?" asks his father, to which the boy replies "Yes." Moreover, the audience is given a bird's-eye view of the island towards the end of the film, which testifies to the film's continued preoccupation with clearly delineating the setting as an island.

Somewhat surprisingly, it is these versions of the story with their water-bounded settings that offer less isolated islands. Wyss's original castaways are segregated from the rest of the world: they are isolated by definition. As the years have passed, however, their island has been connected to a wider world. Jules Verne's story constructs the space as a promising colonial settlement, and positions exploration and knowledge of the island as integral to the civilizing of the space in preparation for anticipated colonists. Finally, the films present their islands as being firmly enmeshed in a network of local islanders, pirates and traders. The family's island, translated onto the screen, becomes a veritable hub of arrivals and departures.

Setting thus lies at the heart of *The Swiss Family Robinson* and its textual legacy. We have, for more than two centuries, primarily interpreted Wyss's original story as though it were set on an island. The characters need to be on a bounded island in order to grow as stereotypical Robinsonade castaway colonists; our twenty-first-century island assumptions are thus grounded in nineteenth-century imperialism and bespeak a spatial modernity that is tied to an ideology of island geography. Moreover, the characters need to be on an island because they belong to a certain textual tradition. So significant are these requirements within our collective consciousness that scholarship has neglected the text's lack of island evidence. The setting of *The Swiss Family Robinson* has unquestionably become an island in cultural and scholarly discourse: like the family, we have collectively imagined an insular setting into existence.

Notes

* Content from this chapter appeared in the author's doctoral dissertation (Hartmann 2014).
1 The origin of the term Robinsonade is generally attributed to Johann G. Schnabel, the author of a *Robinson Crusoe*-style narrative entitled *Die Insel Felsenburg* (1731–43). See Green for a discussion of this novel and the etymology of the term "Robinsonade" (1990, 14, 43–45, 51).
2 Tournier is the author of a twentieth-century *Robinson Crusoe* rewrite entitled *Friday* (1967).

3 Coetzee is the author of a twentieth-century *Robinson Crusoe* rewrite entitled *Foe* (1986).
4 See Pierre Macherey (2006, 177–277) for an in-depth discussion of textual history, literary production and Jules Verne's engagement with *Robinson Crusoe*.
5 Seelye acknowledges Robert Kosten's help in compiling the editorial endnotes (2007, xxv).
6 For a discussion of "the unreality of [an] island" as "a comment on the unreality of cultural island fantasies" in relation to *The Swiss Family Robinson* and other texts, see Graziadei et al. (2017, 262).
7 It is worth noting that William Cowper used the term "monarch of all I survey" in his 1782 poem entitled "Verses, Supposed to be Written by Alexander Selkirk, During his Solitary Abode in the Island of Juan Fernandez." The opening lines of the poem read "I am monarch of all I survey, / My right there is none to dispute" (1980, 403).

References

Annakin, Ken, dir. 1960. *Swiss Family Robinson*. Walt Disney. DVD.
Baldacchino, Godfrey. 2005. "Islands – Objects of Representation." *Geografiska Annaler* 87B (4): 247–51.
Ballantyne, R. M. (1858) 1990. *The Coral Island: A Tale of the Pacific Ocean*. Edited by J. S. Bratton. Oxford: Oxford University Press.
Beeson, Charles, dir. 2002. *Stranded*. Los Angeles: Hallmark Entertainment. 2002. DVD.
Blamires, David. 2009. *Telling Tales: The Impact of Germany on English Children's Books 1780–1918*. Cambridge: Open Book.
Buell, Lawrence. 2005. *The Future of Environmental Criticism: Environmental Crisis and Literary Imagination*. Malden: Blackwell.
Carpenter, Humphrey, and Mari Prichard. 1984. *The Oxford Companion to Children's Literature*. Oxford: Oxford University Press.
Coetzee, J. M. (1986) 2010. *Foe*. New York: Penguin.
———. 2001. *Stranger Shores: Essays 1986–1999*. London: Secker.
Conley, Tom. 1996. *The Self-Made Map: Cartographic Writing in Early Modern France*. Minneapolis: The University of Minnesota Press.
Cowper, William. (1782) 1980. "Verses, Supposed to be Written by Alexander Selkirk, During His Solitary Abode in the Island of Juan Fernandez." In *The Poems of William Cowper*, edited by John D. Baird and Charles Ryskamp, 403–404, Vol. 1. Oxford: Clarendon.
Defoe, Daniel. (1719) 1994. *Robinson Crusoe*. Edited by Michael Shinagel. Second edition. New York: Norton.
Fletcher, Lisa, and Ralph Crane. 2017. *Island Genres, Genre Islands: Conceptualisation and Representation in Popular Fiction*. London: Rowman and Littlefield.
Gillis, John R. 2004. *Islands of the Mind: How the Human Imagination Created the Atlantic World*. New York: Palgrave Macmillan.
Graziadei, Daniel, Britta Hartmann, Ian Kinane, Johannes Riquet, and Barney Samson. 2017. "Island Metapoetics and Beyond: Introducing Island Poetics, Part II." *Island Studies Journal* 12 (2): 253–266.
Green, Martin. 1980. *Dreams of Adventure, Deeds of Empire*. London: Routledge.

———. 1989. "The Robinson Crusoe Story." In *Imperialism and Juvenile Literature*, edited by Jeffrey Richards, 34–52. Manchester: Manchester University Press.

———. 1990. *The Robinson Crusoe Story*. University Park: Pennsylvania State University Press.

Hartmann, Britta. 2014. *Island Fictions: Castaways and Imperialism*. Unpublished doctoral dissertation. University of Tasmania.

Hau'ofa, Epeli. 1993. "Our Sea of Islands." In *A New Oceania: Rediscovering Our Sea of Islands*, edited by Eric Waddell, Vijay Naidu, and Epeli Hau'ofa, 2–18. Suva: University of the South Pacific.

Joyce, James. 1964. "Daniel Defoe." *Buffalo Studies* 1 (1): 1–27.

Loxley, Diana. 1990. *Problematic Shores: The Literature of Islands*. Houndmills: Macmillan.

Kiening, Christian. 2006. *Das wilde Subjekt. Kleine Poetik der Neuen Welt*. Göttingen: Vandenhoeck & Ruprecht.

Macherey, Pierre. (1966) 2006. *A Theory of Literary Production*. Translated by Geoffrey Wall. Abingdon: Routledge.

Marryat, Frederick. (1841–42) 1970. *Masterman Ready: Or The Wreck of the Pacific*. London: Dent.

[Paul, Adrien]. 1858. *Willis the Pilot, a Sequel to The Swiss Family Robinson: Or, Adventures of an Emigrant Family Wrecked on an Unknown Coast of the Pacific Ocean*. Boston: Mayhew. Translation of *Le pilote Willis, pour faire suite au Robinson suisse*, 1855. Tours: Mame.

Phillips, Richard. 1997. *Mapping Men and Empire: A Geography of Adventure*. London: Routledge.

Pratt, Mary Louise. 2008. *Imperial Eyes: Travel Writing and Transculturation*. Second edition. London: Routledge.

Ruddick, Nicholas. 1993. *Ultimate Island: On the Nature of British Science Fiction*. Westport: Greenwood.

Said, Edward W. 1994. *Culture and Imperialism*. London: Vintage.

Schnabel, Johann G. (1731–43) 1959. *Die Insel Felsenburg*. Stuttgart: Reclam.

Seelye, John. 1991. "Introduction." In *The Swiss Family Robinson*, by Johann D. Wyss, vii–xxiii. Oxford: Oxford University Press.

———. 2007a. "Editorial Notes." In *The Swiss Family Robinson*, by Johann D. Wyss, 435–459. New York: Penguin.

———. 2007b. "Introduction." In *The Swiss Family Robinson*, by Johann D. Wyss, vii–xxi. New York: Penguin.

Tournier, Michel. (1967) 1997. *Friday*. Translated by Norman Denny. Baltimore: John Hopkins University Press. Translation of *Vendredi: Ou les limbes du Pacifique*. Paris: Gallimard.

———. (1977) 1991. *The Wind Spirit*. Translated by Arthur Goldhammer. London: Methuen. Translation of *Le vent paraclet*. Paris: Gallimard.

Tuan, Yi-Fu. 1977. *Space and Place: The Perspective of Experience*. Minneapolis: University of Minnesota Press.

Verne, Jules. (1900) 1924. *The Castaways of the* Flag. Translated by Cranstoun Metcalfe. New York: Grosset. Translation of *Seconde patrie*. Paris: Hetzel.

Walcott, Derek. 1997. "The Figure of Crusoe." In *Critical Perspectives on Derek Walcott*, edited by Robert D. Hamner, 33–40. Boulder: Lynne Rienner.

Weaver-Hightower, Rebecca. 2007. *Empire Islands: Castaways, Cannibals, and Fantasies of Conquest*. Minneapolis: University of Minnesota Press.

Woolf, Virginia. (1925) 1984. *The Common Reader: First Series*. Edited by Andrew McNeillie. San Diego: Harcourt.

Wyss, Johann D. (1812–13) 2007. *The Swiss Family Robinson*. Edited by John Seelye and translated by William Godwin and Mary Godwin. New York: Penguin. Translation first published 1816. Translation of *Der schweizerische Robinson*. Switzerland: Johann R. Wyss.

———. (1812–13) 1991. *The Swiss Family Robinson*. Edited by John Seelye. Oxford: Oxford University Press.

Wyss, Johann. 1980. *The Swiss Family Robinson*. Mahwah: Watermill.

7 Island Stills and Island Movements

Un/freezing the Island in 1920s and 1930s Hollywood Cinema

Johannes Riquet

At the beginning of Frank Capra's screwball comedy *It Happened One Night* (1934), we see a series of still images that show a stereotypical South Sea island landscape of beaches, palm trees and lagoons while the opening credits are displayed. After a final static shot of a sailing yacht in a harbour, the film proper begins with a – now moving – shot of another sailing boat in the ocean, introducing us to the story of an American millionaire's daughter's attempted elopement. The island setting of the credits seems to be entirely unrelated to the story, a mere decorative background. Its significance, however, lies precisely in its status as a static background and its narrative irrelevance. By 1934, images of Pacific islands constituted a cultural backdrop that American audiences would have intuitively recognized: similar images were widely circulated in movie theatres, newspaper articles, travelogues and even trivia such as stamps (*LAT*, 3 March, 1935). This chapter claims that the poetic and (non-)narrative form of island representations in Hollywood films from the 1920s and 1930s – notably their stillness and their position outside the narrative proper – speaks to contemporary anthropological fantasies of place-bound and static premodern cultures, fantasies that are themselves a product of specifically modern visual regimes and spatial orders.

It Happened One Night is not about South Sea islands, but its use of the island backdrop is revealing precisely for this reason. It re-emerges briefly in what is arguably the most important scene of the film, the moment in which the young woman (Ellie) and the journalist with whom she has been travelling (Peter) realize their desire for each other as they are lying in a roadside motel room with a blanket hung up between their beds for propriety. In response to Ellie's question whether he has ever been in love, Peter answers with a vision of island bliss: "I saw an island in the Pacific once," he begins, and goes on to describe an island landscape that recalls the images shown in the opening credits. It is at this point that Ellie crosses over to the other side of the blanket and declares in a dreamy voice: "Take me to your island." Stanley Cavell reads the screen-sized blanket – at which Ellie is gazing intently while listening to

Peter – as a self-reflexive comment on the illusions of cinema and their intersection with personal fantasies (1981, 80–86). For Cavell, the scene also marks the high point of the film's preoccupation with illicit sexuality and censorship at a time when the Hays Code was about to be enforced (1981, 82–83). Yet while Cavell comments on the island reference, his analysis misses its specific cultural context and its place in film history. For him, the island evoked by Peter represents a purely personal fantasy space where home and desire meet (1981, 100), but Pacific geography, however minimally present, is important here. Peter's island, of course, is not located in the real Pacific but belongs to what Paul Lyons (2006) has termed the "American Pacific archive," a textual Pacific made up of words and images. And American cinemas were full of South Sea islands when *It Happened One Night* was made.

It has been convincingly demonstrated that Pacific islands played a crucial role in the formation of anthropology as an academic discipline (see, among others, Geiger 2007 and Shepherd 2012). The accounts of eighteenth-century navigators such as George Robertson and James Cook, as well as the scientists travelling with them (such as Joseph Banks, Johann Reinhold Forster and his son, Georg Forster), offer lengthy descriptions of the islands of Oceania and their inhabitants that anticipate later ethnographic studies like Bronisław Malinowski's work on the Trobriand Islanders in the 1910s and Margaret Mead's 1928 study of adolescent sexuality in Samoa. As K. R. Howe puts it, "[t]he importance of the Pacific islands as a laboratory in the development of geographic and anthropological thought cannot be overstated" (2000, 42).

The eighteenth-century writings developed a set of conventions and practices that shaped the institutionalized forms of ethnography that emerged at the turn of the twentieth century. These include the impulse to classify as well as the use of visual documentation for the purposes of scientific investigation.[1] One recurrent structural feature of these texts is the separation of narrative and descriptive sections. Thus, James Cook's account of his first stay in Tahiti in 1769 begins with a chronological account of events entitled "Remarkable Occurrences, etc., at Georges Island" (1893, 60). The account ends with the departure from the island but is followed by a descriptive 'appendix' (1893, 88–107) with several subsections entitled "Description of King George's Island" (1893, 88), "Of the Produce" (1893, 89), "Person of the Natives" (1893, 91) and "Manners and Customs" (1893, 94). Joseph Banks's *Endeavour* journal is similarly structured: the account of the voyage is punctuated by a number of descriptive sections that are appended to the chronological entries, including a long descriptive section (1896, 127–178) on the "language, manners, and customs" that Banks took "to be general among these seas [i.e. the South Seas]" (1896, 126).

Structurally, the geo- and ethnographic descriptions of Pacific islands and islanders in the journals of Banks and others have the same status as the island vistas at the beginning of *It Happened One Night*: they are static, and they are separated from the narrative itself. This resemblance is a symptom of the persistence of a representational tradition in the Western cultural imaginary, and of its pervasive presence in 1920s and 1930s America. Visuality and spatiality intersect in specific ways in this tradition. Pacific islands and their inhabitants are represented as (passive) objects of an (active) Western gaze, and the islands themselves are portrayed as static while mobility is assigned to the ethnographic subject. This division between mobile and static spatialities, a division that Tim Cresswell sees as constitutive of modernity (2006, 16), is performed by the poetic and structural patterns of the texts in question.

The imaginative investment in the Pacific helped to mask the realities of U.S. imperialism and was part of what Howe describes as a long history of appropriating Oceanic islands to play through Western desires and anxieties (2000, 1–4). In the case of *It Happened One Night*, these preoccupations revolve around sexuality, morality and censorship, and South Sea islands by that time already had a long history of being associated with sexual license. Here, too, anthropology had a role to play. Thus, Margaret Mead's controversial study of Samoan sexual mores in *Coming of Age in Samoa* from 1928 may be more revealing if it is read as a comment on the restriction of sexuality in the United States rather than a reliable account of Samoan culture (see Mead 2001, 3–11). As Lyons points out, the opening lines of Mead's book sound like the romantic effusions of contemporary travelogues (2006, 142; cf. Riquet 2014, 145), and their tone and content resembles the opening shots of *It Happened One Night*: "As the dawn begins to fall among the soft brown roofs and the slender palm trees stand out against a colourless, gleaming sea, lovers slip home from trysts beneath the palm trees or in shadow of beached canoes" (2001, 12). *It Happened One Night* thus inherits a representational tradition from other films and cultural texts, a tradition of which it only retains the form. It is neither *about* islands nor *set on* an island, but its islands are present – literally and figuratively – as a static backdrop against which the American characters' fantasies take shape.

It is thereby significant that Peter himself only "saw an island" in the Pacific rather than having been on one. The island films I will turn to in the second part of this chapter all have opening credits that closely resemble those of *It Happened One Night*; Peter might well have seen his island in one of those films (cf. Riquet 2012, 135). In them, too, the visual prologues freeze islands into static images that are split off from the narrative. However, while the images seem to be outside the film proper, their literal stillness also encapsulates the ways in which the films immobilize their islands in different ways. Conversely, early cinema, in a sense despite itself, arguably produces an excess of movement that runs counter to the static depiction of these islands. This chapter will read the visual regime of Hollywood's imaginary Pacific islands through the lens of spatial theory. After a discussion of the visual and spatial constructions of early anthropology, specifically the opening chapter of Malinowski's *Argonauts of the Western Pacific*, I will use the framework developed in that section to analyze a variety of visual prologues from different island films. In the last part, I will examine MGM's *White Shadows in the South Seas* (1928) in more detail and show that the film ultimately fails to construct a static spatiality, and that its freezing of island space is undercut by various forms of uncontrollable movement, some of which are inadvertently generated by the cinematic apparatus itself.

Anthropology, Visuality and Spatiality

The first American film to show a Pacific island was *Sailor in Philippines*, a short film produced by Kalem in 1908. The 1910s saw the production of numerous films set in the Pacific, mainly in the South Seas, but the genre exploded in the 1920s and 1930s.[2] As Jeffrey Geiger has shown, Hollywood's enthusiastic 'discovery' of South Sea islands in the interwar period served various cultural needs. On the one hand, the time after the First World War was a "time of profound, collective self-interrogation for Europe and the US. In the wake of a brutal war, civilization seemed to signify the opposite of progress" (2007, 69). Rapid social changes and technological developments in increasingly complex urban environments contributed to a general unease about civilization and a nostalgia for a different way of life. On the other hand, the aestheticization of South Sea islands also masked the United States' increasing imperialist presence in the Pacific (Lyons 2006, 27; Kahn 2011, 9–17), which had begun with the economic exploitation of Pacific islands in the nineteenth century (Eperjesi 2005, 25–57) and become more aggressive with the annexation of Hawai'i and the American-Filipino war at the turn of the twentieth century (cf. Eperjesi 2005, 25–57; Lyons 2006, 24–34). Anthropology and the emerging tourist industry were implicated in the perpetuation of static images of Pacific islands. While steamship companies and travel agencies manufactured a fantasy of unspoilt island paradises for tourists, salvage anthropologists "lamented the destructive capacities of 'civilization' and argued the case for leaving the Pacific alone" (Howe 2000, 44).

However anti-colonial in sentiment, this "fatal impact" view (Howe 2000, 44) still perpetuated the dichotomy between a mobile (Western) subject of representation and a passive ('native') object of representation (Geiger 2007, esp. 118–159) that had already structured the eighteenth-century journals. Again, visual documentation played an important role (Geiger 2007, 128–133). Early ethnographers such as Franz Boas, Margaret Mead and Gregory Bateson carried photo and film cameras with them to record indigenous cultures (Jacknis 1984, 1988; MacDougall 1997; Ruby 2000); conversely, the ethnographic films of early documentary film makers turned the filming of indigenous cultures into a visual spectacle (Geiger 2007; Riquet 2014). Thus, Robert Flaherty's *Moana* (1926) was the film of which John Grierson famously said that it had "documentary value" (quoted in Barsam 1992, 42), for the first time applying the word "documentary" to a film. Flaherty took his family to live on the Samoan island of Savai'i from 1923 to 1924 to shoot *Moana*. The film presents a "fictitious idyll of Samoan life" (Barsam 1992, 35), evoking "nostalgia for untouched primitive life amidst natural surroundings" (Geiger 2007, 127). Purporting to give a faithful account of Samoan life, Flaherty staged his own idealized vision that was part reconstruction of customs that had been out of use for a long time, part Flaherty's invention altogether (Barsam 1992, 36, 118).

The ethnographer's cinematic gaze manifests a visual and cartographic logic that also structures Malinowski's *Argonauts of the Western Pacific*, first published in 1922. *Argonauts* provides an account of the *Kula* ring, an archipelagic trade network in the Solomon Sea. While its focus on the islanders' inter-island movements partly challenges early anthropology's tendency to think of islands as bounded and static cultural entities that offer ideal fieldwork conditions (cf. Beer 1989, 22; Edmond and Smith 2003, 2–3), mobility is nonetheless principally assigned to the ethnographer and his readers. The first chapter, "The Country and Inhabitants of the Kula District," begins with a cartographic overview, dividing the area into different zones and classifying their inhabitants – drawing, to cite Epeli Hau'ofa's critique of the colonial spatial organization of Oceania, "imaginary lines across the sea" (1994, 153). The logic of cartography is explicitly evoked: "If we glance at a map and follow the orographical features [...]" (Malinowski 2002, 28). The chapter also features a map that shows, names and numbers Malinowski's divisions, superimposing an abstract geometrical pattern on the region. Text and map correspond to each other as the former takes the reader through the different sections of the latter; by dividing up the region, the cartography of the text constitutes the space as much as it describes it. Michel de Certeau's distinction between "map" and "tour" (or "itinerary") spatialities sheds light on the logic of Malinowski's text:

> [...] description oscillates between the terms of an alternative: either *seeing* (the knowledge of an order of places) or *going* (spatializing actions). Either it presents a *tableau* ('there are...'), or it organizes *movements* ('you enter, you go across, you turn...').
>
> (1984, 119; emphasis in original)

Malinowski begins with a short static overview of the "map" type, which is followed by an imaginary "tour" through the islands, "following the order in which a visitor, travelling from Port Moresby with the Mail boat, would come in contact with these districts, the way indeed in which I received my first impressions of them" (2002, 32). Accordingly, the next section begins as follows: "Let us imagine that we are sailing along the South coast of New Guinea towards its Eastern end" (33).

It would be inaccurate, however, to say that Malinowski's text here simply switches from "map" to "tour" mode. Rather, the chapter now oscillates between the two modes. While the imaginary movement from island to island, aligned with Malinowski and the imagined visitor (a surrogate for the Western reader) organizes space via movement, the ensuing descriptions of the islands and their inhabitants belong to the "map" mode that de Certeau regards as typical of modernity's cartographic spatialities (1984, 121). Indeed, de Certeau emphasizes that the two modes are typically entwined and condition each other (1984, 119–120). In Malinowski's account, it is the mobility of the ethnographic gaze which enables the static description of landscapes, villages and people:

> When, on a hot day, we enter the deep shadow of fruit trees and palms, and find ourselves in the midst of the wonderfully designed and ornamented houses hiding here and there in irregular groups among the green, surrounded by little decorative gardens of shells and flowers [...], it seems as if the visions of a primeval, happy, savage life were suddenly realised, even if only in a fleeting impression.
>
> (2002, 35)

The initial movement leads to a timeless and idealized description of Pacific paradise, a (however fleeting) vision of an eternal present with the ethnographic subject "in the midst." This is what Geiger describes as the visual and spatial fantasy of early ethnography, "at once erecting walls that create cultural monads and then placing oneself at the center – with a panoptic view inside an endlessly signifying and self-contained cultural discourse [...]" (2007, 130). The split between mobile subject and static object extends to a "tour" of the islanders' bodies, which are treated like the landscape:

> When we approach the natives closer and scan their personal appearance, we are struck [...] by the extreme lightness of their skin, their sturdy, even lumpy stature, and a sort of soft, almost effete general impression which their physique produces.
>
> (2002, 36)

In his introductory remarks on the ethnographic method, Malinowski strikingly uses a hunting metaphor: "But the Ethnographer has not only to spread his nets in the right place, and wait for what will fall into them. He must be an active huntsman, and drive his quarry into them" (2002, 8). The ethnographer moves, and his object of study is immobilized.

Malinowski's textual construction of an active ethnographic position that captures nostalgic *tableaux* of island life aligns his vision with the photographic gaze as theorized by Susan Sontag. Sontag argues that photography partly emerged from a nostalgic fantasy of preserving an idealized world in the face of human-induced transformation of the planet: "As photographs give people an imaginary possession of a past that is unreal, they also help people to take possession of space in which they are insecure" (1977, 9). Photography thus functions as an elegiac art as the camera replaces the gun to which it is still metaphorically linked (1977, 14–15). As we have seen, Hollywood, tourism and anthropology were complicit in the visual appropriation of South Sea islands, an appropriation that is epitomized by the photographic gaze: "[...] the most grandiose result of the photographic enterprise is to give us the sense that we can hold the whole world in our heads – as an anthology of images" (1977, 3). For Sontag, "aesthetic distance seems built into the very experience of looking at photographs" (1977, 21), which differ from moving images "because they are a neat slice of time, not a flow" (1977, 17).

Sontag's theory of photography as an art form linked to specifically modern anxieties and fantasies of control resonates with critiques of the organization of space in Western modernity by Doreen Massey and others (cf. introductory chapter). For Massey, the violence of modernity's colonial projects went hand in hand with an understanding of space that suppresses interaction, multiplicity and openness. Instead, "[t]he modern, territorial, conceptualisation of space understands geographical difference as being constituted primarily through isolation and separation" (2005, 68). This form of spatiality ties cultures, societies and nations to specific places rather than seeing them as emerging through interaction (2005, 64; 71). It includes the temporalization of space as "spatial difference [is] convened into temporal sequence" (2005, 68). Non-Western cultures were seen as belonging to earlier stages in the development of humanity, which was understood in terms of a uniform movement towards Western modernity (2005, 68–71). Drawing on the work of Johannes Fabian, Massey maintains that anthropology was complicit in this taming of alterity and multiplicity: "Difference/heterogeneity here is not only neatly packed into its bounded spaces, but also dismissed to the ('our') past" (2005, 69). Fabian argues that modern anthropology produced a "classificatory, tabular space" (1983, 19) in which space and politics converged: "After all, it is not difficult to transpose from physics to politics one of the most ancient rules which states that it is impossible for two bodies to occupy the same space at the same time" (1983, 29). For Fabian as for Massey, then, modernity goes hand in hand with an understanding of space that is based on extension and boundaries and an anthropological construction of alterity as spatially and temporally distant, which simultaneously "has the effect of *decreasing* the actuality (one might say the challenge) of difference" (Massey 2005, 69; emphasis in original). The forced relocation of indigenous populations and early anthropology's fantasies of place-bound, isolated cultures living in premodern harmony are different variants of this type of spatial thought, which assigns single identities to discrete spaces (Massey 2005, 66–67; cf. also Fabian 1983, 29–30 and Wolf 1982). This is exactly the kind of spatiality that photography produces in Sontag's view: "The camera makes reality atomic, manageable, and opaque. It is a view of the world which denies interconnectedness, continuity [...]" (1977, 23). The islands in the films that we will now turn to are cinematic, but their (near) stillness aligns them with photography and with the static spatiality critiqued by Massey and Fabian.

An Anthology of Islands

Like *It Happened One Night*, these films indeed begin with, to use Sontag's phrase, an "anthology of images" of South Sea islands. In each of them, the film proper is preceded by a series of still or almost still island vistas. These generic images of palm trees, beaches and lagoons construct a prelapsarian fantasy of paradise, echoing a long tradition of representing Pacific islands as Arcadian, paradisal or golden-age spaces deeply rooted in Indo-European mythology (Howe 2000, 8–14). The islands in these films have a regenerative function for the American protagonists; they function as a backdrop against which the latter's position in modern Western society is (re-)negotiated. W. S. Van Dyke's *White Shadows in the South Seas* (1928) recounts the destructive impact of the pearl trade on a previously 'unspoilt' South Sea Island. In King Vidor's *Bird of Paradise* (1932), a young American falls in love with the daughter of a Polynesian chief although she has been promised to somebody else. In *Mr. Robinson Crusoe* (A. Edward Sutherland, 1932), protagonist Steve Drexel jumps ship to live on a South Sea island and bets with his friends that he will survive without any difficulties; he enters into a liaison with a girl who has fled from an arranged marriage and names her Saturday. Arthur Greville Collins's *Paradise Isle* (1937) alludes to the South Sea experiences of Paul Gauguin in its story of an artist who has gone blind and is shipwrecked on a Pacific island. He starts a love affair with an island girl, who helps him regain his *joie de vivre*. Finally, James Whale's *Sinners in Paradise* (1938) has an airplane crashing on a Pacific island inhabited by an American who is wanted for murder.[3]

In all of these films, the island vistas at the beginning of the film signal an ideal that cannot unproblematically exist in the narrative proper, whose intrigues and conflicts compromise or threaten the 'purity' that is posited by the former. The static and timeless character of these vistas aligns them with the anthropological visions of bounded and unchanging island realms existing (even if under threat) in some distant space in the writings of Malinowski, Mead and others. Their (almost) photographic quality and their position on the margins of the narrative set them apart from the stories recounted in the films. Their (near) stillness suggests a fixed and immutable space, and their nostalgic construction of a premodern idyll located in some distant past is reinforced by their place in the 'prehistory' of the film itself. In de Certeau's terms, they belong to the fixed order of the map and not to the movements of the itinerary and the temporality of change; those are the domains of narrative.

The static presentation of the island-image manifests itself in different ways in each film. *Paradise Isle* begins with two static (but filmed) shots of palm trees on a beach, with the camera facing the ocean and the promontories of the coast; the credits are displayed over the images. At the end of the film, we see a shot of the artist and the girl walking away from the camera before the image fades to black, signalling the conclusion of the narrative. However, this is followed by a final static shot of a beach on which "THE END" is superimposed in the same letters as the opening credits. This last shot returns us to the beginning: as conflict (and, along with it, movement and narrative) has been banished from the island, the latter is allowed to reassume its ideal state. Implicitly, the protagonists walk into this ideal version of the island, yet the two seconds of blackness before the final image also create a gap between the diegetic island and its non-narrative counterpart.

The opening shots of *Mr. Robinson Crusoe* show us the same combination of beach, palm trees and ocean, but they immobilize the island more completely by using painted images. However, they are not immediately recognizable as paintings. While they are clearly aestheticized, they could also be photographs if it were not for the waves. The credits are made to look as though they were standing on the beach through the use of three-dimensional writing and shadows. This aligns the painted background with the textual space of the letters; in a metapoetic gesture, the island becomes visible as a construction. The intertitles that are shown against the backdrop of the second image explicitly announce a fantasy of prelapsarian bliss: "From the time Adam and Eve were banished from the Garden of Eden, man has vainly sought to find solace, comfort and earthly pleasure in an artificial world of his own creation." It is hard to miss the irony of these words, however inadvertent it may be: set against a visibly painted and strongly aestheticized background, they suggest that the "artificial world" might be that of the island rather than, to cite the following intertitles, "so-called civilization." The film ends in the midst of the latter as we see Saturday dancing for an enraptured audience on Broadway. As in *Paradise Isle*, the film ends with the reunification of the couple after the threat of separation and the suggestion that the cultural spheres of the protagonists are unbridgeable. Yet the reunification of the couples does not bridge the lovers' worlds. Rather, it reinforces their separation: in *Paradise Isle*, the American artist renounces 'civilization' and 'goes native'; conversely, in *Mr. Robinson Crusoe*, Saturday is absorbed by American consumer culture. This film, too, ends with a fade-out and a black screen before a final shot takes us back to the painted island beach of the first image. This final transition from Broadway to the South Seas shows us the island exactly as what it is: a commodified image exported to American (movie) theatres to be consumed by American audiences.

In *Sinners from Paradise*, the island's role as an aesthetic backdrop that exists for the benefit of the American characters and the gratification of American audiences is even more apparent as no islanders are present at all. As in *Mr. Robinson Crusoe*, the opening credits are superimposed on a series of still images. Some of them are clearly painted while others are possibly photographs. The opening shot gives us a realistically painted, hazy view of an island seen from the sea. The foreground is dominated by an airplane flying away from the island. The next three shots show us hazy views of a beach with palm trees and the ocean in the background that could be either overexposed and somewhat blurry photographs or realistic paintings. The initial view of the island from the sea emphasizes its discreteness and distance, in line with the common Western representation of islands as bounded objects that can be visually apprehended at a glance (cf. Létoublon 1996; Baldacchino 2005). While the airplane already signals a disturbance, its direction at the same time emphasizes the island's disconnection from 'civilization.' In the third and fourth images, however, the vapour trail in the background announces the airplane's crash on the island. The opening vistas thus signal an ideal that is under threat, a visual equivalent of the title: *Sinners in Paradise*. In the absence of a local population, however, the function of the island is purely regenerative: as in *It Happened One Night*, the island fantasy is here emptied of its anthropological content. The island is there to restore the 'sinners' to their place in the 'civilized' world.

In both *Mr. Robinson Crusoe* and *Sinners in Paradise*, then, the still images of the island are photographic and perform the nostalgic and possessive functions that Sontag ascribes to photography. Their (sometimes literally) indeterminate status, caught between photographic and painterly modes, further increases the "aesthetic distance" that Sontag sees as characteristic of the "experience of looking at photographs." Nonetheless, their proximity to photography also offers an illusion of verisimilitude. On the one hand, then, the images seem to suggest that the islands they depict *could* exist; on the other hand, they mark their unreality. This aligns them with the visual logic of island representations in contemporary anthropology and its cartographic organization of space. The images signal that the islands of the films are both distant from the modern Western world and subject to its gaze. They are figured as both timeless and fragile; spatial distance translates into cultural separation. Their static spatiality is performed by their position outside the realm of narrative, which is aligned with the mobility of the Western visitors.

At the same time, the obvious artificiality of the images draws attention to their generic quality and makes it possible to read them, against their explicitly stated message, as a self-reflexive comment on the role of film and other visual media in perpetuating such visions. This is particularly evident in *Bird of Paradise*. The film begins with a filmed view of a beach and a second shot showing a lagoon. The second image dissolves into an extravagant shot in which we see the edge of a beach covered in palm trees. The camera tilts downward until all we see is a group of palm trees reflected in the water. As the camera comes to rest, the title and the opening credits are displayed over the image; at the end of the film, the end credits are superimposed on the same image. Here, the island emerges in its insubstantiality as a cinematic illusion, a projected image. On the one hand, this transition from a real Hawaiian beach to an image flickering in water exemplifies the ways in which these films produce their islands as static images and spaces. On the other hand, this production is also self-reflexively foregrounded. Furthermore, the image is not entirely stable: it flickers in the gentle movement of the water. The 'freezing' of the island into an image in these films does not remain unchallenged, and in what follows, I will discuss *White Shadows in the South Seas* (1928) in more detail to explore the tensions between movement and stasis that marks the opening shots, and extends to the entire film.

Unfreezing the Island-Image: *White Shadows in the South Seas*

Directed by W. S. Van Dyke and Robert Flaherty,[4] *White Shadows in the South Seas* was released in 1928. The film opens with a series of island vistas: an island seen from above; another high-angle, but closer shot of the shore of an island; a shot of an islander arriving in his canoe, taken from the beach and framed by a palm tree; finally, an eye-level shot of an island taken from the water. The shots are interrupted by intertitles describing the islands as "for happy centuries the last remnant of an earthly paradise," "Islets 'fresh from the touch of God'" and finally "Memories that lingered from the Morning of Creation." As in the other films, the island here constitutes a pure image in the double sense of being *purely* image and offering an image *of* a pure and immaculate space. It is very clear that the images do *not* depict the (imperfect, colonized) island where the narrative will begin. But the vistas do not exactly represent the same island before the 'fall,' i.e. before the arrival of white traders, either: as the intertitles make clear, they present a timeless, eternal ideal, a generic island that constitutes a backdrop against which the diegetic islands of the ensuing narrative will be measured. The images thereby also stage the act of seeing itself: the first shot begins with a fade-in, opening the field of vision from the centre of the image through the use of an iris diaphragm; after about ten seconds, the image fades out in the same way. The shot thus imitates the opening and closing of a human eye. It comments on cinema as presenting a series of images appearing before the viewer's eye. The iris diaphragm is again used to fade out the last shot. Pure fantasy and ideal form, the island exists as a perceptual event before it becomes a physical location for the film's narrative.

The ideological underpinnings of the opening shots become apparent once they are considered in relation to the overall rhetoric of the film. The intertitles that follow the island vistas state: "But the white man, in his greedy trek across the planet, cast his withering shadow over these islands . . . . and the business of 'civilizing' them to his interests began." After this, we enter a fallen world of sickness, death and debauchery where white pearl traders are ruthlessly exploiting a South Sea island. A disillusioned doctor, Matthew Lloyd, picks a quarrel with a particularly greedy trader, who places him on a schooner full of plague victims to get rid of him. Lloyd is shipwrecked on an island whose inhabitants are still unaware of Western civilization. He lives with the islanders but, in a moment of weakness, makes a fire that attracts the ship of the greedy trader. The central episode of the film, which Geiger interprets as a dream sequence (2007, 176), actualizes the ideal portrayed in the opening vistas. What is initially presented to us as a vanished ideal and abstract idea thus receives a location in the diegesis of the film. The whole history of the West's discovery, exploitation and colonization of the South Seas is repeated and condensed in the discovery and corruption of the second island. At the end of the film, nothing has effectively happened: the narrative cancels itself out and we return to the beginning. Despite its anti-colonial message, the film conveys a problematic ideology that represents islanders as helpless victims, an essentializing "myth of a people frozen in time" (Geiger 2007, 1; cf. Riquet 2012, 144).

Throughout the film, white men are the centre of action, change and transformation. They are solely responsible for narrative impetus. While the disappearance of island culture is lamented, it is also presented as doomed to die out, in line with the "fatal impact" view of salvage anthropologists. The long central episode of the film is essentially without narrative development. The only eruption of narrative occurs when the son of the chief is saved by Lloyd, but this episode attains its narrative dimension only through the intercession of the latter. Lloyd's almost magical resuscitation of the boy not only presents him as an active force, but also smooths the way for his union with the chief's daughter, Fayaway. Otherwise, the episode takes the form of an ethnographic documentary that manifests the same "taxidermic impulse" (2007, 121) Geiger sees at work in Flaherty's *Moana*. Abandoning narrative altogether, the film indulges in close-ups of food preparation, courtship and dancing; in the probing gaze of the ethnographer, the camera tilts and pans, tracks forward and sideways. This ethnographic impulse is particularly evident in a sylvan scene of bare-breasted women bathing under a waterfall. After a moment of voyeuristic hesitation, the camera tracks forward into their midst from behind some ferns. It is decidedly not associated with Lloyd's gaze: only after a minute has passed do we see him emerging from behind a screen of large leaves. Reminiscent of Malinowski's textual construction of an imaginary observer in the midst of static island life, the ethnographic camera here speaks to a collective cultural fantasy validated and perpetuated by the audience.

While the camera is mobile, the islanders are static. At best, they are given a kind of static mobility, repeating the same actions over and over again, as when we see a group of islanders swiftly climbing coconut trees. With this in mind, there is a perverse logic to the renewed corruption of the island paradise: the film requires the unspoilt space of the island to be annihilated in order to make it available for aesthetic consumption again. When, in the final shot of the film, we see a distraught Fayaway, dressed in a Western gown and burying her face on the ground before the image is gradually veiled and then darkened altogether in a visualization of the film's "white shadows," this is a metaphorical rendition of the death of the island culture. But this death is only the logical conclusion to what has been implicit in the film from the opening island vistas: the mythical island and its inhabitants are never more than a static, frozen image.

Unlike photographs, however, these initial images are not *quite* still. Firstly, there is a tension between stasis and movement within the image itself. In the first shot, the stillness of the island is counterbalanced by the movement of the ocean. In the second shot, the movement of the leaves in the wind adds to the movement of the water to the right. And there is one moment of surprise: a wave rears up before arriving on the island, visible for just a split second before the cut. Writing about Lumière films from the 1890s, Dai Vaughan contends that the fascination of early cinema resided in its capacity to record the spontaneity and unpredictability of the world. He argues that "people were startled" by cinema's "ability to portray spontaneities of which the theatre was not capable" (1990, 65). For him, films like *A Boat Leaving Harbour* (1895) "[survive] as a reminder of that moment when the question of spontaneity was posed and not yet found to be insoluble: when cinema seemed free [...] of the threat of its absorption into meanings beyond it" (Vaughan 1990, 66–67). He goes on to argue that "[t]he promise of this film remains untarnished because it is a promise which can never be kept, its every fulfilment is also its betrayal" (67). This "promise" of cinema is antithetical to intention. What interests Vaughan is the potential of cinema to resist the appropriation and absorption of its images into a culturally coded sign system. I would argue that the island-images of *White Shadows* also resist the ideological positions they are made to signify; the island-as-image is fluid on its margins.

Yet the movements *within* the image are only the first, simplest level of this. On repeating viewings, one notices that the image itself moves. It trembles continuously yet unpredictably and thus duplicates the movement of the water within it. Any image in analog cinema trembles slightly, even more so in 1920s cinema when cameras were clunkier and less steady. As such, the apparatus itself participates in working against the smoothness of its images and the fantasies they transport. The more one watches these opening shots, the more one notices that the island-image is disturbed in yet another way. The shots also flicker because of the graininess of the analog image. More than that, the island-image is in constant danger of disappearing. In the first shot, the shadows cast by the leaves of the iris diaphragm never quite disappear: they flicker in and out on the margins. In the second shot, a black triangle hovers in the top left-hand corner; a shadow moves in and out from the left in the third shot. In both cases, it is not quite clear what causes the shadows; in all probability, they were present in the original film, but even this is difficult to determine with absolute certainty.

Yet another process undermines the stability of the island visions: the disintegration of the image itself. This level is furthest removed from intention and control. Just before the end of the fourth shot, a comparatively large black blotch appears for a split second in the water; thin lines striate the images (a particularly nervous one wanders from left to right around the centre of the island in the first shot); a tiny white thread shoots comet-like onto the island in the second shot; stains, white and black spots, specks of dust flicker up everywhere. Once one starts focusing on them, one cannot help noticing their abstract and random play. Most of this visual interference is the effect of time, attacking and corroding the notoriously fragile film stock, although some of the interference is likely to have been present from the beginning. But the point is not that there was initially a 'pure' film which then began to disintegrate. The point is that the image is eroded from the moment of its emergence. The version of the film that has been preserved for us makes visible a process that is at the heart of the analog cinematic image. Largely in spite of itself, and quite beyond self-reflexive play, the film fails to uphold the island as an abstract, frozen and pure idea, making it visible as both illusive and elusive, and the materiality of the film unwittingly plays a part in undermining its island myth.

At the same time, such a reading of the visual prologue of *White Shadows* paves the way for an analysis of the difficulties the film exhibits in establishing the island as a pure space in the main narrative. In terms of narrative logic, the ideal that the initial image aspires to motivates Lloyd's journey to the second island. Intertitles announce "Days in . . . . days out . . . . days of sun and slimy calm . . . . days of hot and savage wind . . . . ." They are followed by a static shot of the silhouette of an island, apparently filmed from another island (we see a palm tree in the foreground). The shot appears curiously out of place. It serves no narrative purpose: there is no indication that it represents an island that Lloyd actually encounters on his journey (in fact, it cannot even represent his perspective). It is in conflict with the intertitles preceding it, which lead us to expect a shot of the endlessly open sea. Nonetheless, it has an important function: it recalls the initial (equally non-narrative) island images, whose aesthetics it repeats. At the same time, it points forward, announcing the island at the end of Lloyd's journey.

Yet Lloyd's arrival is fraught with uncertainty. After the stormy voyage, we see him struggling to swim and staggering through the water as the image fades out. The next shot shows a tiny and tidy island seen from the water, referring back to the series of island vistas that began in the prologue. But Lloyd's rebirth is overshadowed by its messy beginning. As he approaches the beach, he is knocked down by waves several times; when the image fades out, he is still caught in a zone between water and (is)land. For all we know, he never leaves this in-between zone; the ellipsis between this shot and the next also signals that we move into a space of fantasy. The transition cannot be shown because it is an impossible one. In order to establish a clean beginning for Lloyd, the film requires, literally and metaphorically, a fade-out and a cut: the space Lloyd leaves behind has to be eclipsed.

The film solves this problem by letting Lloyd arrive a second time. He discovers a second, larger island, swims across, and now his arrival is clean and unproblematic. This second voyage is preceded by him gazing across to the island, marked by point-of-view shots. Lloyd can thus truly become a discoverer: the aimlessness and passivity of the first voyage is replaced with the purposefulness and agency of the second. As Lloyd steps onto the beach, we see the island on which he first stranded behind him; the shot is an almost exact repetition of the first shot after the storm. The composition visually reinforces the notion that the small island is a foil against whose backdrop – and *only* against it – Lloyd can successfully step onto the larger island. Lloyd has to pass, impossibly, through the island-image itself: the ideal island, as image, fantasy and phantom, is its condition of possibility. The renewed destruction of the island paradise at the end of the film is thereby the logical consequence of the overall development of the narrative. Lloyd dies a martyr's death in the attempt to protect the island from the pearl trader, thereby ultimately seeking to defend the ideal island image announced in the opening shots. Even in Lloyd's protest, however, the film holds on to an ideology that assigns the island and its inhabitants a static spatiality and makes them the objects of a visual fantasy.

And yet, as we have seen, the film's ideological operations are not as smooth as they would be. *White Shadows'* real unsettling power does not reside in its ostensible indictment of colonial violence. It resides in the film's murky zones, in the impurities of its narrative and its island-image.

The most unsettling of the film's shadows are not the carefully fabricated ones as manifest in the veiling of the very last shot, but the shadows the film produces unwittingly, which are present from the first image. Not yet quite fixed, the island-image encourages revision. Framed by the modern machine that is cinema, the island is immobile and belongs to a rigid spatial order. But the machine stutters and trembles, and the imperfect apparatus itself partly unfreezes the island it aims to freeze. Caught between photography and film, between stasis and movement, between ideal and disruption, the modern narratives of premodern paradise in *White Shadows* and other films certainly reinforce imperial boundaries and cartographic abstractions, but they also generate some of the surprises that Massey sees as constitutive of the dynamics of space (2005, 111). In this sense, the imaginary geographies of Hollywood's South Sea islands speak to the contradictions of spatial modernity.

Notes

1 The systematic drawings of Tahitians (and Tahitian flora) by Sydney Parkinson, one of the artists accompanying Cook, are a case in point (cf. Geiger 2007, 32–38).

2 For an overview of Pacific islands film made between 1908 and the 1990s, see Langman (1998). Cf. also Betts (1991) and Man (1991).

3 All of these films were adaptations: *White Shadows in the South Seas* was based on Frederick O'Brien's bestseller travelogue of the same title; *Bird of Paradise* adapted an immensely popular Broadway play that premiered in 1912; the literary model of *Mr. Robinson Crusoe* requires no explanation (although the plot is entirely different from Defoe's novel); *Paradise Isle* was based on a short story by Allan Vaughan Elston entitled "The Belled Palm"; and *Sinners in Paradise* on a story by Harold Buckley ("Halfway to Shanghai").

4 Flaherty left *White Shadows* before completion because of disagreements with Van Dyke (Geiger 2007, 167).

References

Baldacchino, Godfrey. 2005. "Editorial: Islands – Objects of Representation." *Geografiska Annaler* 87 (4): 247–251.

Banks, Joseph. 1896. *Journal of the Right Hon. Sir Joseph Banks during Captain Cook's First Voyage in H.M.S. Endeavour in 1768–1771*. Edited by Sir Joseph D. Hooker. London: Macmillan.

Barsam, Richard M. 1992. *Nonfiction Film: A Critical History*. Revised and expanded edition. Bloomington and Indianapolis: Indiana UP.

Beer, Gillian. 1989. "Discourses of the Island." In *Literature and Science as Modes of Expression*, edited by Frederick Amrine, 1–27. Dordrecht: Kluwer.

Betts, Raymond F. 1991. "The Illusionary Island: Hollywood's Pacific Place." *East-West Film Journal* 5 (2): 30–45.

Capra, Frank, dir. 1934. *It Happened One Night*. Culver City: Sony Pictures, 2008. DVD.

Cavell, Stanley. 1981. *Pursuits of Happiness: The Hollywood Comedy of Remarriage*. Cambridge: Harvard UP.

Cook, James. 1893. *Captain Cook's Journal during His First Voyage Round the World Made in H.M. Bark "Endeavour," 1768–1771*. Edited by Captain W. J. L. Wharton. London: Elliot Stock.

Cresswell, Tim. 2006. *On the Move: Mobility in the Modern Western World*. New York: Routledge.

de Certeau, Michel. 1984. *The Practice of Everyday Life*. Translated by Steven Randall. Berkeley: University of California Press.

Edmond, Rod, and Vanessa Smith. 2003. "Editors' Introduction." In *Islands in History and Representation*, edited by Rod Edmond and Vanessa Smith, 1–18. London: Routledge.

Eperjesi, John R. 2005. *The Imperialist Imaginary: Visions of Asia and the Pacific in American Culture*. Hanover: Dartmouth Press.

"Exotic Stamps from the South Sea Islands." 1935. *Los Angeles Times*. March 3, 1935.

Fabian, Johannes. 1983. *Time and the Other: How Anthropology Makes Its Object*. New York: Columbia UP.

Flaherty, Robert, dir. 1926. *Moana*. New York: Kino Classics, 2015. DVD.

Geiger, Jeffrey. 2007. *Facing the Pacific. Polynesia and the U.S. Imperial Imagination*. Honolulu: University of Hawai'i Press.

Greville Collins, Arthur, dir. 1937. *Paradise Isle*. London: Reel Enterprises, 2007. DVD.

Hau'ofa, Epeli. 1994. "Our Sea of Islands." *The Contemporary Pacific* 6 (1): 147–161.

Howe, K. R. 2000. *Nature, Culture, and History: The "Knowing" of Oceania*. Honolulu: University of Hawai'i Press.

Jacknis, Ira. 1984. "Franz Boas and Photography." *Studies in Visual Communication* 10 (1): 2–60.

———. 1988. "Margaret Mead and Gregory Bateson in Bali: Their Use of Photography and Film." *Cultural Anthropology* 3 (2): 160–177.

Kahn, Miriam. 2011. *Tahiti beyond the Postcard: Power, Place, and Everyday Life*. Seattle and London: University of Washington Press.

Langman, Larry. 1998. *Return to Paradise: A Guide to South Sea Island Films*. Lanham: Scarecrow Press.

Létoublon, Françoise, Paola Ceccarelli, and Jean Sgard. 1996. "Qu'est-ce qu'une île?" In *Impressions d'îles*, edited by Françoise Létoublon, 9–27. Toulouse: Presses Universitaires du Mirail.

Lyons, Paul. 2006. *American Pacificism: Oceania in the U.S. Imagination*. New York: Routledge.

MacDougall, David. 1997. "The Visual in Anthropology." In *Rethinking Visual Anthropology*, edited by Marcus Banks and Howard Morphy, 276–295. New Haven: Yale UP.

Malinowski, Bronislaw. (1922) 2002. *Argonauts of the Western Pacific*. Collected Works, Volume 2. London: Routledge.

Man, Glenn K. S. 1991. "Hollywood Images of the Pacific." *East-West Film Journal* 5 (2): 16–29.

Massey, Doreen. 2005. *For Space*. London: SAGE.

Mead, Margaret. (1928) 2001. *Coming of Age in Samoa.* New York: Harper Perennial.

Riquet, Johannes. 2014. "Killing King Kong: The Camera at the Borders of the Tropical Island, 1767–1937." *Nordlit* 31: 133–149.

Ruby, Jay. 2000. *Picturing Culture: Explorations of Film & Anthropology.* Chicago: The University of Chicago Press.

Shepherd, Robert. 2012. *Partners in Paradise: Tourism Practices, Heritage Policies, and Anthropological Sites.* New York: Peter Lang.

Sontag, Susan. 1977. *On Photography.* New York: Farrar, Straus and Giroux.

Sutherland, A. Edward, dir. 1932. *Mr. Robinson Crusoe.* Los Angeles: Cobra Entertainment, 2011. DVD.

Van Dyke, W. S., and Robert Flaherty (uncredited), dirs. 1928. *White Shadows in the South Seas.* Burbank: Warner Bros., 2010. DVD.

Vaughan, Dai. 1990. "Let There Be Lumière." In *Early Cinema: Space, Frame, Narrative,* edited by Thomas Elsaesser and Adam Barker, 63–67. London: British Film Institute.

Vidor, King, dir. 1932. *Bird of Paradise.* Hayesville: Roan Group Archival Entertainment, 1999. DVD.

Whale, James, dir. 1938. *Sinners in Paradise.* Narberth: Alpha Home Entertainment, 2007. DVD.

Wolf, Eric R. 1982. *Europe and the People without History:* Berkeley: University of California Press.

Part III
Shorelines/Borderlines

8 Words and Images of Flight

Representations of the Seashore in the Texts about the Overseas Flight of Estonians during the Autumn of 1944

Maarja Ojamaa

In the centre of this chapter lie three artworks that mediate the historical event of the overseas flight of Estonians escaping the Second World War. For the sake of an analytical focus, the image (or motif) of the seashore is chosen for a closer reading because the ways of representing seashores in each of these works also reflect the meaning-making dominants of the artistic wholes. The existence of these three texts[1] realized in different media, but mediating one historical episode, is approached as an example of cultural polyglotism.

Polyglotism is, according to Yuri Lotman – the founder of the Tartu-Moscow school of cultural semiotics[2] – one of the defining characteristics of culture (Lotman 2009, 2). The idea of proficiency in a plurality of languages refers to the different sign systems used for communicating in any culture, including verbal, visual and acoustic modes and media. An important characteristic of these languages is their mutual untranslatability. When, for example, transferring a verbal message into a visual one and then back again, we will never get exactly the same message as the original due to the structural incompatibilities of the two languages. This means that between the elements of the sign systems based on words and those based on images there are no exact equivalents, but "the discrete and precisely demarcated semantic unit of one text is, in the other, a kind of semantic blur with indistinct boundaries and gradual shadings into other meanings" (Lotman 2001, 37).

Nevertheless, the mechanism of imprecise translation is one of the main sources of creativity in culture (2001, 37). Thereby, mediating a story in different languages, e.g. in the form of a novel and a movie, opens up new meaningful layers and thus enriches it. All the medial versions of a story, in turn, merge in a mental whole both in individual human memories and in cultural memory. At the same time, the chronological sequence of the subparts of this whole might lose its importance. Later texts influence the interpretation of earlier ones; sometimes earlier texts are (albeit mistakenly) remembered and interpreted as later texts and vice versa. The mental whole is kept in cultural memory as an invariant that is occasionally actualized via medial variations but still maintains its identity. From this point of view, it is important to acknowledge not only the differences between sign systems, but also their similarities. All sign systems and artistic languages are always necessarily interrelated in culture, making literature not only a separate field of art, but simultaneously a part of the painting and the music of the same culture within a given period.

Remembering all this is perhaps especially relevant when talking about texts mediating historical events on which cultural identity depends. In the process of remembering these events, fictional and non-fictional representations are complementary. For most members of culture, works of art are no less important a source for understanding history than textbooks, memoirs or documentary films, let alone scientific papers and monographs. All these sources do not exist separately as discrete units in culture but necessarily form interrelated intertextual and intermedial systems, while from the viewpoint of cultural self-understanding, it is important that there is some coherence between these polyglot versions.

A tool for analyzing the formation and functioning of narrative textual systems originating in multiple languages can be found in the field of transmedial narratology (Herman 2004). This approach implies, firstly, explicating a mental invariant that is shared by all the versions of mediating a given story and, secondly, explaining the variations caused by the differences of sign systems. This way it provides a deeper understanding of the given story itself as well as of the narrative potential and means of mediating the story in different cultural languages.

The Context of the Variations of the Seashore

A glance at a map of Estonia reveals that the country's coastal line is proportionally quite long: the Baltic Sea bounds the land from two sides and, in addition, its territory includes 2,222 islands and islets surrounded by the sea.[3] Thus, the shore seems an evident landmark in the nation's self-descriptions. With some risk of overgeneralizing, one could claim that before the Second World War, the shore was associated with openness and with contact and dialogue with other cultures. During the Soviet occupation that followed the war, however, the shore acquired a diametrically different identity, appearing as a space of disruption, a closed and prohibited border zone. The breaking point between these two epochs was the flight before the closing of the boundary. The overseas escapes began a couple of years earlier but peaked at the end of September 1944. Altogether about 75,000–80,000 people fled the country[4] during the Second World War and the estimated number of those who went by sea (to Sweden, Finland and Germany) is around 30,000 people.

Many more had considered going but were left behind for one reason or another. A major part of the artists who had been creatively active in the independent Republic of Estonia left in fear of persecution. Writer August Gailit and painter Eerik Haamer, the authors of two of the artworks discussed in this paper, were among them. Considering the impact the flight had on Estonian culture, the country's coast seems to correspond not only for geographical, but also historical reasons to what Anthony Smith has conceptualized as ethnoscapes, defining them as "landscapes endowed with poetic ethnic meaning through the historicization of nature and the territorialization of ethnic memories" (1999, 16). Even though ethnoscapes have mostly been described in the framework of creating a nation, the concept seems applicable also in other pivotal contexts.

The following transmedial analysis does not consider all of the texts that retell the story of the flight, but the three that have been chosen are the ones that arguably hold the most prominent place in the cultural memory: a novel by August Gailit (*Across the Restless Sea Üle rahutu vee*, 1951), a film by Sulev Keedus (*Somnambulance Somnambuul*, 2003), and an oil painting by Eerik Haamer (*A Family in Water/Perekond vees*, 1941). Although each of these comprises a limited number of characters, all of the texts have been regarded in Estonian culture as generalizations of the story of the whole nation.

The seashore is first of all obviously the place where the flights started and where many of them also ended, but in none of the three texts is it a central or dominant motif at first sight. However, at a closer look, devices and means used for portraying the seashore also mediate the central meaningful core of these texts. In other words, by modelling the time-space of the seashore, the texts simultaneously model its core non-spatial meanings. Already intuitively, the motif possesses strong semantic and poetic potential as a borderland, a liminal space that both separates and unites the land and the sea, self and other, past and future, hope and despair. Thus, the shore is both a narrative space where people depart from or stay at and a symbolic space of boundaries.

A closely related concept originates from Bakhtin's explanations on the functioning of chronotopes or time-spaces. Although Bakhtin discusses it with regard to novels, the concept of the chronotope is also perfectly applicable to narrative texts in other media. More specifically, the chronotope of the threshold, being "always metaphorical and symbolic, sometimes openly but more often implicitly" (Bakhtin 2004, 248), is an almost exact equivalent of that of the seashore within these texts. Bakhtin associates this chronotope with the time-space of crisis and break in life. This in turn is also compatible with the concept of the boundary – another central notion within the cultural theory of Lotman. The boundary of a semiotic system functions as a buffer mechanism that belongs "simultaneously to both the internal and external space"

(Lotman 2005 [1984], 208), which means that it not only divides, but also unites separate spheres of semiosis. Boundaries are the semiotically most active areas where the birth of new information, i.e. the creation of meaning, takes place (215).

A Literary Variation of the Seashore: August Gailit's *Across the Restless Sea* (1951)

In Estonian literary history, the works of August Gailit (1891–1960) are mostly remembered for their romantic-symbolist language and their characteristically bittersweet humour. *Across the Restless Sea*, which is based on the letters of a fellow refugee, is the author's last novel and very different from his previous works and style. Even though the rhythm and syntax of sentences are recognizably Gailitean, and even though the composition is based on separate short stories, the overall tone is uncharacteristically very gloomy.

The novel was written in 1947 in Sweden, but as its pessimistic viewpoint was difficult to accept for expatriate Estonians, it was not published until four years later. Gailit portrayed the expatriates not as the ones who keep the light of freedom alive overseas, as was the assumed heroizing norm, but as rootless and non-heroic traitors. His overarching belief was that without the homeland one could never be free.

The core events in the novel span a couple of days at sea, until the boat that is destined to sink reaches the ship of the Swedish coastguard and those who have survived the journey are rescued. The text is written as a series of short stories, most of them concentrating on the story of one person from the diverse gallery of characters on the boat. The overall organization of time and the structure of the text are implicitly governed by seashores, while different atmospheres dominate each of the four subparts: (1) the shores of the homeland are still visible; (2) no shores are around, but the thoughts of everyone on the boat are still on the land, either longing for the home left behind or justifying their escape; (3) visionary or illusionary shores that the characters believe they are seeing; (4) the ship of the Swedish coastguard as a guarantee of finally reaching the shore of the destination.

The novel begins *in medias res* on the shore and already the first sentences include semantically active phrases for describing the boat's departure: it "tore itself away" and "tore off the coast" (Gailit 2009, 5; translation here and afterwards mine). Gailit seemingly mediates different sensory impressions, including visible (descriptions of darkness, the fields of water, the seashore of the homeland), audible (boat motor, voices of people), tactile (the feeling of cold and of the boat shaking) and olfactory (the smell of poisoned air) forms of perception. However, this multisensory description does not result in a mimetic seashore that could be a geographically recognizable place on the Estonian coast. It is clearly a metaphorical space, an image of a boundary implying binary oppositions. As mentioned above, the boundary of semiotic systems constitutes a duality of disruption and consolidation where opposite meanings can appear simultaneously divided and united. Mankind's highest aspirations appear fused with the lowest desires on Gailit's seashore and orientation is lost in this fusion. Adding to the psychological struggle of the refugees is their confusing perception of the homeland. It is captured and destroyed by the enemy, turned into a place of the other, but at the same time, the pines, the coastal stones and even some chambers remain exactly as they used to be.

At the background of the human turmoil, Gailit establishes a structurally clear distinction between the connotations of the land and the sea. He associates the land with continuity, stability and responsibility. The homeland is "sanctified a thousand times" (Gailit 2009, 192) through the labour and blood of the ancestors and therefore encompasses everything that is truly valuable. Farmer Alandi, one of the characters on the boat, likens the farmstead to the sun in space and to the heart in an organism, the silencing of which is followed by instant death. The sea, on the other hand, is represented as unpredictable and frightening, as a stranger even to the coastal folk, exactly because one never knows when this provider of food and bridge to faraway people and places might all of a sudden turn into a wet grave, closing one off from all that is safe and valuable. This unstable nature of the sea metaphorically tears the human being naked, as is evident from the way the little boy Mika describes a fellow refugee: "On the beach, standing on his own feet he appears a human, but when on the boat, he turns right into an animal" (2009, 145). The sea offers no support for pretence, and everything ugly about humans seems to surface. This is why some of the characters acquire almost grotesque forms of the traits of narrow-mindedness, heartlessness and brutality during the escape.

The usage of figurative speech for describing the seashore is a dominant characteristic of (Estonian) literary texts portraying the life and soul of coastal folk, along with depicting their life events through comparisons with natural phenomena such as winds, currents and waves, as well as with sinking, swimming and other activities related to the sea. The usage of a language rich in metaphors is intrinsic to Gailit's work as well, exemplified for instance by personifications of nature, like in the cases of describing "the lungs of the homeland" or "the indifference of the sea" (2009, 40). However, in most places, Gailit's images originate in a textual background and, more specifically, in the Bible. Biblical and other metaphors related to Christianity add a generalizing layer to the story, rendering the journey of a small group of Estonians into a story of the human condition. The novel is a psychological and philosophical portrait of a refugee who has lost or betrayed his or her homeland by choosing the wrong side of the seashore.

A Cinematic Variation of the Seashore: Sulev Keedus's *Somnambulance* (2003)

Sulev Keedus (born 1957) is a prominent author of what could be described as Estonian art house cinema. *Somnambulance*, his second full-length fiction film, has an interesting genesis from the viewpoint of cultural polyglotism. The filmmakers found inspiration in the very sound of the word "somnambuul" rather than in its semantics, signifying an illness or a person who walks around in sleep (see Torop 2003). In Estonian, the word could be described as more or less onomatopoetically related to the sound that a drowning or suffocating person makes. With this background in mind, it is perhaps important to stress that the film can be read and interpreted in other ways than exclusively as a historical film even though the historical layer is strongly marked by the film's frame, which indicates the year of the events at the beginning and provides the viewer with additional historical information at the end.

Keedus himself was born more than a decade after the flight happened and thus has a distant perspective on the event, even though writer Madis Kõiv (1929–2014), with whom the script was co-written, had personal memories of it. However, repeatedly mediating and thereby also (re)constructing one's past in different sign systems is a natural auto-communicative act of any culture, and especially important for young cultures like that of Estonia. Keedus does not refer to Gailit's novel and his filmic ways of mediating the event are different, not least for focusing on the people who were left behind. Nevertheless, in cultural memory, these two texts mediating a shared object are juxtaposed.

Somnambulance tells the story of a young woman named Eetla who at the last minute decides not to board the last boat leaving, and stays with her father, the lighthouse keeper Gottfried. Initially, the two seem to be totally separated from the rest of the world in their lonely cottage. Then some Soviet soldiers arrive to guard the area. As was the case historically, the coast has been declared a forbidden zone and the local inhabitants have been deprived of their boats as well as of their freedom to spend time on the shore at their will, especially after sunset. Eetla is constantly oscillating between health and sickness, confusing reality and dream, past, present and future. She simultaneously provokes rape by the soldiers and has an overwhelming fear of it. The multi-layered question of balance related to the characters' physical and psychological existence, to their identities etc. is mediated not only in visual, but also verbal and auditive languages.

The film is structured as a trilogy of seasons: autumn-winter-spring. One might expect such a structure to mediate the processes of death and rebirth reflected in the portrayal of the clearly distinct and even contrasting seasons of this latitude. Instead, the viewer experiences a linear, continuous flow, one deepening state. *Somnambulance* is a significantly slow movie, characterized by thoroughly composed long takes and 'swimming' camerawork. Tones of grey dominate almost all the frames, suggesting a constant feeling of cold. Even though the viewer is shown a reference to an actually existing place, Matsalu, the surroundings of the lighthouse feel like the end of the world, torn away from everything else, an area of empty houses and desolate atmosphere.

The seashore at the location of filming is unquestionably very pictur-esque, but despite that, the authors avoided separate beautiful frames of the sea and every shot of the seashore also includes a human being engaged in some sort of activity, usually struggling to do something. Furthermore, every time they do so, they either fall or slip, i.e. lose their balance in one way or another, just like the whole nation did that same autumn of 1944. The way the seashore is mediated in the film is also characterized by a certain visual indefiniteness in terms of framing. Namely, the frames of *Somnambulance* are often composed in a way that renders the line between the sea and the land unclear. Instead of a single visible boundary, the sea and land cut into each other in several instances due to shallower places reaching out of the surface of the water or small peninsular strips of sand and stones stretching into the sea.

The indefiniteness mediated by the visual devices is complemented by the film's soundtrack. In fact, Keedus has described how the cinematic space was built primarily as an acoustic space as "[t]he atmosphere in cinema is, after all, created by what we hear, because we see only the surface" (Torop 2003). The music, composed by Helena Tulve, an artist perhaps most known for her detailed interest in the primary forms of sound, does not appear as a separate layer commenting on the visible, which is arguably the case in most films. Instead, the sounds seem to grow out of and flow back into the represented landscape. At most in-stances, the rhythmless music resembles a transition of one tone uttered by a single instrument (a flute or some strings) as if looking for bal-ance in time. Besides the music, the other dominant feature of the film's soundscape is the noise of radio waves that often blend into the roaring of sea waves. Mediating similar indefiniteness, these constitute an acous-tic parallel to the visual seashore. Gottfried and Kasper, a doctor who hides at the lighthouse, hope to catch some messages from Sweden via radio. However, all that actually comes through the strange, undecipher-able signals are the time of Moscow and the announcement that the war is over. Thus, the acoustic landscape of the film, defined by the charac-teristics of vagueness and uncertainty, also underlines the inescapable separation from the free world.

In conclusion, Keedus's representation of the seashore does not con-stitute a strong internal articulation between water and land as is the case with Gailit's novel. Here the dominant lies rather in the elusiveness of the boundary between the two. This consciously indefinite amalgam repeated in different sign systems, including the sound, the actress's voice, her costumes and the framing of shots, is also directly related to the motif of losing one's balance. The occupation of the homeland by the other rendered it even more alien than a foreign land would have been. Throughout its 129 minutes, the film conveys the impact of this spatio-temporal experience on individual human beings in its atmosphere.

A Painted Variation of the Seashore: Eerik Haamer's *A Family in Water* (1941)

The existence and interpretation of Haamer's work in Estonian culture is an example of the jumbling of chronological sequences that sometimes characterizes the nonlinear functioning of cultural memory. *A Family in Water* was painted about three years before the main wave of escapes in the autumn of 1944. Its later associations with the event are the result of rereading the text, which was informed by Haamer's own exile and by the influence that the flight of so many people had on Estonian culture. This has mainly happened during the period of regained independence since 1991. From the distance of half a century and more, the first years of the 1940s with all the different events that took place then have evidently blended into a much more uniform – even homonymous – whole compared to how they were perceived at the time or in the immediately following years.

Eerik Haamer (1908–1994) has mostly been characterized as a neorealist painter who, in the earlier years of his long and fruitful career, created emphatic portraits filled with the poetics of everyday life. The large canvases often give the scenes depicted an epic dimension. Haamer's colours are earthy and his motifs originate in his home landscapes of Saaremaa island[5] and the life of its coastal folk.

The first thing that strikes the eye in the portrait are the four expressively depicted figures standing in water near the seashore and a certain vulnerability reflected in their faces and postures. The mother is painted as the centre of the group, the gaze of the father and the son are directed at her. Her unbuttoned shirt and raised skirt could be interpreted as a reference to rape, but her stance communicates stamina and enduring, a refusal to give in to despair. Compositionally, the family is as if pressed into the frame of the painting, which simultaneously portrays them as being forced into a situation and as sticking together. The frontal close-up viewpoint from the sea – and not the land – in turn underlines the deadlock of their condition. They are facing the sea as a wall, having nowhere to proceed nor a place to return to. Thus, they are most definitely facing exile, whether a directly physical or a metaphorically mental one. The author himself has commented on the painting: "It was the beginning of the tragedy of our republic: when our people did not know anymore where to be, what to do or which way to go" (quoted in Uuskyla 1997, 4; translation mine).

The central meanings of the work are also reflected in the painting's brownish and greenish colours and in the way the horizon is depicted. The colours have mostly rather dark tones, the only exceptions being those used for the land behind the people, the mother's shirt and the skin of the figures crossed with the horizontal coast. While Haamer's horizons have commonly been painted rather high, in this case there is only an extremely small strip of sky visible, rendering the horizon as almost closed off. A comparison of the way Haamer paints the seashore to the ways Gailit and Keedus depict it reveals that Haamer's shore does not constitute a binary structure, nor does it stress the elusiveness of the boundary between water and land. In fact, there is no distinct boundary there at all, only dark sea. The proximity of land is indicated rather by the knee-high depth of the water than by its barely visible form in the background.

All of the above renders the painting as a moment into which the helplessness and vulnerability of a small nation is symbolically concentrated. The premonition that the painting contains, the fact that a couple of years later many Estonians stood face to face with the same situation as the depicted family, has led to this painting serving a symbolical function on several recent occasions. Among others, it has represented Estonian culture at the exhibition dedicated to the fiftieth anniversary of the Treaty of Rome (the Treaty establishing the European Economic Community, TEEC) in Rome in 2007, and it also stood for the whole cataclysmic year of 1941 at the exhibition organized for the Presidential reception dedicated to the ninetieth anniversary of the Estonian Republic in 2008.

The Invariant Seashore

We have examined three texts that were created at different times in different cultural and socio-political contexts by different authors in their own style and media, but nevertheless appear to have several meaningful elements in common. The latter are not explained only by the mutual subject per se, but also stem from the artistic treatment of the subject. The first invariant element is the lack of air for breathing, which is something counterintuitive to what one would expect from representations of seashore. Gailit describes the poisoned smell of the air; in the film one hears the characters talking about their inability to breathe and sees the father drowning; and the painting seems to lack air for its compositional choices. Secondly, all three authors associate the seashore with loss of identity and balance. In Gailit's novel, this appears in the characters' monologues and inner speech as well as in the author's attitude towards exile as a betrayal of identity. In the film, there are visual depictions of both Eetla and Gottfried literally falling down and balancing themselves on the edge of the lighthouse. The painting suggests the loss of identity by depicting the people facing the sea, which stresses their hopeless condition of being driven from home and having practically no road to continue on.

The way nature, especially the sea, is portrayed in the three works has an appearance of indifference or apathy to human suffering in common. Gailit likens the way the sea throws the boat to the way "a careless child would be throwing a ball around" (2009, 228). The film shows the beauty and power of the roaring waves in strong winds, which, however, make the survival of human beings a struggle. Haamer's sea around the family is dark and heavy, offering no support and no answers to the Estonian people. Another – even if admittedly disputable – common aspect of the artworks is the depiction of a woman on the seashore as the decider over the destiny of the nation. Stability emerges as a masculine trait that has already been broken, while elusiveness and liminality are conceived as feminine principles.

These three fictional artistic texts are a part of the possibly endless series of medial variations of the mental text of the escape from the Second World War in Estonian cultural memory. Their differences in origin and in the artistic means or affordances of each sign system underlines the polyglotism of remembering, which could also be conceptualized as the transmedial mechanism of cultural memory. On the one hand, this mechanism preserves the past in living memory and thereby strengthens and maintains the coherence of cultural identity. On the other hand, the process of such representations is principally inexhaustible and the reservoir of meaning-creation appears unfathomable. However, the more media and discourses there are in which a historical event has been and could potentially be represented, the deeper the culture's understanding of it will be.

Notes

1 In accordance with the Tartu-Moscow semiotic school's line of thought, the notion of text hereby denotes any structure that "possess[es] a certain integral meaning and fulfill[s] a common function" (Lotman et al. 2013, 58).
2 For an overview of the background and history of the school, see Chernov (1988) and Grzybek (1998).
3 However, only 318 of these are larger than a hectare in size.
4 The general population was around 1,000,000 people.
5 Saaremaa, situated in the West Estonian Archipelago, is the largest of Estonian islands. It measures 2,673 square kilometres and is inhabited by almost 31,000 people.

References

Bakhtin, Mikhail. 2004. "Forms of Time and of the Chronotope in the Novel: Notes toward a Historical Poetics." In *The Dialogic Imagination: Four Essays*, edited by M. Holquist, 84–258. Austin: University of Texas Press.

Chernov, Igor. 1988. "Historical Survey of Tartu-Moscow Semiotic School." In *Semiotics of Culture*. Proceedings of the 25th Symposium of the Tartu-Moscow School of Semiotics, Imatra, Finland 27th–29th July, 1987, edited by Henri Broms and Rebecca Kaufmann, 7–16. Helsinki: Arator.

Gailit, August. (1951) 2009. *Üle rahutu vee*. Tallinn: Eesti Päevaleht; Akadeemia.

Grzybek, Peter. 1998. "Moscow-Tartu School." In *Encyclopedia of Semiotics*, edited by P. Bouissac, 422–425. New York: Oxford University Press.

Haamer, Eerik. 1941. *Perekond vees*. Art Museum of Estonia, EKM M 1716.

Herman, David. 2004. "Toward a Transmedial Narratology." In *Narrative across Media: The Languages of Storytelling*, edited by M.-L. Ryan, 47–75. Lincoln: University of Nebraska Press.

Keedus, Sulev, dir. 2003. *Somnambuul*. Estonia: F-Seitse.

Lotman, Yuri M. 2001. *Universe of the Mind: A Semiotic Theory of Culture*. London: I. B. Tauris.

———. 2005. "On the Semiosphere." *Sign Systems Studies* 33 (1): 205–229.

———. 2009. *Culture and Explosion*. Berlin: Mouton de Gruyter.

Lotman, Yuri M., Vjacheslav V. Ivanov, Aleksandr M. Pjatigorskij, Vladimir N. Toporov, and Boris A. Uspenskij. 2013. "Theses on the Semiotic Study of Cultures (as Applied to Slavic Texts)." In *Beginnings of the Semiotics of Culture*, edited by Silvi Salupere, Peeter Torop, and Kalevi Kull, 51–77. Tartu: University of Tartu Press.

Smith, Anthony. 1999. *Myths and Memories of the Nation*. New York: Oxford University Press.

Torop, Peeter. 2003. "Interview with Sulev Keedus." *Estonian Culture* 2: 28–33.

Uuskyla, Wello. 1997. "Eerik Haamer ja tema poliitiline protestimaal." *Eesti Päevaleht = Estinska Dagbladet*. April 3, 1997.

9 The Literary Channel
Identity and Liminal Space in Island Fictions

Ina Habermann

This chapter focuses on the English Channel as a liminal space, an Anglo-French in-between space that has crucially shaped British national identity. Dividing Britain/England and the mainland, the Channel has given rise in Britain to a prominent narrative of exceptionalism and isolationism. However, a focus on the Channel also shows that the British 'island story' is by no means the whole story: crucially, the Channel serves as a cultural contact zone, a space of exchange where English and French fortunes have been woven together, quite literally in the Bayeux Tapestry, from the time of the Norman Conquest.[1] Many works of literature evoke the historical scenes of contact and exchange, and in what follows, I will discuss some prominent examples. In terms of method, I take my cue from Emily Apter, who also foregrounds the spatial or geocritical approach (Westphal 2007; Tally 2011) in an afterword to the collection *The Literary Channel* (2002):

> The present collection's emphasis on the Channel rather than on the discretely bounded territory of the nation-state shifts the focus away from influence studies and toward a paradigm of 'Anglo-Euro' cultural topography that questions the very ground of cross-cultural comparison. The fluid space of the Channel becomes a metaphor for a zone of mutual refraction where Britain defines itself through its incongruent reflection of Frenchness, and vice versa.
>
> (Apter 2002, 286)

The Channel's significance for constructions of British national identity, I would argue, can hardly be overestimated. As Dominique Rainsford points out, the Channel was often seen as the natural obstacle that saved Britain from invasion and also helped the British to remain independent ideologically. Rainsford sees the Channel and the coast as "an exiguous zone, the antithesis of the cultural density that characterises cities" (Rainsford 2002, 133). Many works of literature are set in this zone and explore its potential for identity formation. As Rainsford observes, the writer Julian Barnes "uses the literary Channel crossing to figure the emotional states and transitions of his characters, and in doing so participates in the tradition [...] of literary uses of the Channel as a space of tension, crisis and change" (2002, 137).

The opening of the Eurotunnel in 1994 moved Britain, at least psychologically, closer to the Continent (see also Darian-Smith 1999 and Wilson 1994). The literary representation of this move, according to Apter, is the "narrative Chunnel," which

> picks up where the literary channel leaves off in suggesting a focus on the relationship between Anglophone and Francophone literary history in the New Europe. [...] Chunnel literature points to a state of postnational borderlessness that sublates regionalist and minority claims in the future history of the novel.
>
> (2002, 287)

For Apter, "best-selling Euro-Fiction may strike readers as being situated in a historical as well as geographical and political vacuum" (2002, 289). The Chunnel becomes a symbol of "Euro-existentialism," as in Michel Houellebecq's novel *Extension du domaine de la lutte* (1994), which "paints a portrait of the modern European citizen as a subject nationally adrift on the infobahns of the EU" (2002, 291). Focusing on such work, Apter appears to foresee a gloomy future for literature about 'Europe.' However, contrasting the 'Chunnel' vision with actual Channel literature, it appears that literature remains a place from which the overly abstract conception of Europe can be both criticized and remedied. As Rainsford remarks, in a discussion of Jonathan Raban's travel book *Coasting* (1986), the Channel "speaks of a Europe that is much more than the sum of the nations that are included within it, [...] a patchwork of identities, but one with habitable rips" (2002, 154). He suggests that Europe should be seen neither as homogenous nor as modular, where "each nation fits to its neighbours with an airtight seal" (2002, 158). Instead, in-between zones such as the Channel, or other topological features such as the Pyrenees or the Alps, serve to relieve its "claustrophobia and potential complacency" (2002, 158) as they become the setting for narratives of people's lives not primarily determined by national(ist) discourse.

Eric Prieto argues that the spatial approach to literary negotiations of identity leads

> away from the individual author and work and toward a more general kind of knowledge, one that breaks through the aesthetic frame that sets works of literature off from the world and seeks to use the study of literature as a way to better think about the world around us.
>
> (2011, 25)

My focus is therefore on works that are set in the Channel region, such as Barnes's above-mentioned *Cross Channel* (1998). In this collection of short stories, Barnes explores the reasons why Englishmen have crossed the Channel over the centuries, choosing various means of transport. The final story, entitled "Tunnel," is set in the future, in 2015, describing how an elderly English writer, a persona of the author, takes the train to Paris from King's Cross, reflecting

> on the surprising banality that within his lifetime Paris had become closer than Glasgow, Brussels than Edinburgh. He could leave his house in north London and barely three hours later be heading down the mild decline of the boulevard de Magenta without even a flap of his passport.
>
> (Barnes 2009, 191)

Still, the crossing has to be done, and in transition, the Channel emerges first and foremost as a memory space. The writer thinks of the many ways in which he has negotiated this divide over the years. Musing upon the points of connection between England and France, he begins to dream up the stories that make up the volume the reader has just read. The entrance into the tunnel becomes the door to the writer's past, and to history:

> The Shuttle terminal at Cheriton slipped by; the train manager announced that they were approaching the Channel. Fences, unsullied concrete, an inappreciable descent, then suave blackness. He closed his eyes, and in the tunnel of memory heard the echo of rhythmic shouting.
>
> (2009, 199)

Barnes depicts the Channel in terms of a chronotope, to use Mikhail Bakhtin's term (1981), where narratives of the past, historical time and the Channel space are inextricably entangled. Reflecting upon English history while in transit, the Englishman realizes the need for the other country, France, as a significant other, a space of projection that throws into relief one's own concerns in a way that is not too immediate and pressing, providing an idealized space or, as he puts it, a "version of pastoral" (2009, 208). This prompts the image of his French counterpart, travelling on the train in the opposite direction:

> an old man in a Shetland pullover entranced by marmalade, whisky, bacon and eggs, Marks and Spencer, le *fair-play*, le *phlegme*, and le *self-control*; by Devonshire cream teas, shortbread biscuits, fog, bowler hats, cathedral choirs, Xeroxed houses, double-decker buses, Crazy Horse girls, black cabs and Cotswold villages. Old fart. French old fart.
>
> (2009, 208)

The story thus imagines the crossing as a kind of time travel that compresses a series of historical and cultural encounters into a space whose negotiation begs the question of the traveller's identity – an identity constantly re-formed in contact with the other, with or without mutual understanding. In the stories that make up the volume, crossing the gap between England and France is seen historically as perilous, transgressive, often violent but also inevitable, since the geographical proximity makes for a common destiny. This is not to deny the existence of distinctive national identities, but to argue that they only make sense in relation, and in contrast with each other (cf. Bradford 2011, Childs 2011, Guignery 2006).

Although, topo-logically speaking, the Channel provides a link that both connects and divides, it is also a geographical expanse, made up – beyond the water that carries boats and covers the tunnel – of islands, and islands have played a significant role in literary negotiations of identity (Billig 2010, Edmond and Smith 2003). Again, Julian Barnes provides a crucial text with his novel *England, England* (1998), set on the Isle of Wight. In this dystopian tale, the island serves as an artificial miniature version of England, with England reconstructed as a kind of heritage theme park. Legitimated by a warped version of postmodern philosophy, this process of compression and displacement foregrounds issues of national identity, memory, the relation of space and place, and notions of authenticity. In his bid to attract "Top Dollar and Long Yen," as he puts it, by offering "Quality Leisure," Sir Jack Pitman wants to recreate England as a tourist attraction. Arguing in a travesty of postmodern reasoning that there is nothing natural anyway, but that any landscape is subject to change and shaped by culture, he wants to go beyond creating a mere theme park or heritage centre: "We are not talking Disneyland, World's Fair, Festival of Britain, Legoland or Parc Asterix. Colonial Williamsburg?" (Barnes 1998, 59). Because of this explicit rejection of the theme park motif, I disagree with Gregory Rubinson's reading, which argues that Barnes's novel offers a straightforward critique of postmodern notions of the simulacrum as developed by Jean Baudrillard (1981). Rubinson reads Barnes as suggesting, by contrasting the fate of Old England/Albion with the development of the heritage park England, England, that "truth cannot be abandoned, despite all the postmodern theories of the death of authenticity or the real" (Rubinson 2009, 49). What, however, is 'truth'? What is 'the real'?

Sir Jack insists that he wants to create "the thing itself" (Barnes 1998, 61; emphasis in original), an island that in time will become an enhanced version of England, made more real by the very energy that has gone into shaping it. Crucially, however, and this has been overlooked, he needs the right geographical and topographical basis for this process of recreation:

'Therefore, if we are serious, if we are seeking to offer *the thing itself*, we in turn must go in search of a precious whatsit set in a silver doodah.' They peered at the map as if cartography was a dubious new invention.

(1998, 61; emphasis in original)

Looking for the right kind of island, with the Scillies judged as too far and the Channel Islands as too French, they hit on the Isle of Wight, which, due to its diamond shape, answers the Shakespearean notion of the "precious stone set in the silver sea" (*The Tragedy of King Richard the Second*, 1997, 2.1.46) as evoked by John of Gaunt. Apart from its location, the Isle of Wight is also perfect in that it does not carry too many historical and cultural associations that would prevent the process of projecting England onto the island space. Its cultural topography does not offer undue resistance to Sir Jack's act of appropriation, or, in other words, it is perceived to have more territory than history. Market research and historical enquiry suggest the items that need to be put into England, England to make it convincing. Gradually, as the stereotypical features of Englishness, including the royal family, are transferred onto the island, the original England loses its former character: renamed Albion, it becomes increasingly isolated and regresses into a rural subsistence economy.

It is crucial for the success of the enterprise, however, that certain elements of the English experience must be real and authentic, even though people are assumed to prefer the replica to the original. While it is acceptable to employ actors to impersonate historical figures such as Dr Johnson or Robin Hood, because the historically real people, where they existed at all, are no longer around, it is impossible to leave the real royal family in Old England. Since the dynasty metonymically represents or embodies the nation, it has to relocate. It is "'*just not the same*,'" says Sir Jack, "'We're *strapped* without Buck House, and don't they know it'" (Barnes 1998, 145; emphasis in original). Eventually, the royals are bribed to move to England, England. Interestingly, however, they become much reduced in authority and dignity in their new miniature kingdom; cut off from the realm ruled by their ancestors, they come across as sleazy and stupid, and in fact, they are often impersonated by actors. So it gradually transpires that the real reason for their relocation is not their presence in England, England, but the need to remove them from their original home. It appears that the really important issue is not one of truth or lie, authenticity or forgery, but of an intrinsic connection between time and space, history and territory. When Martha Cochrane, Sir Jack's "appointed cynic," makes one of her PR speeches about the advantages of the England, England experience, she argues that Michelangelo's statue of David on the Piazza della Signoria in Florence was replaced by a copy a long time ago, and that the copy proved just as popular as the original in a museum (1998, 181). This chopped logic, however, does not prove that there is no difference between the original and the replica, or, conversely, that inauthenticity can be unmasked by a critique of post-modernism. The example, in fact, only serves to suggest that the statue's proper *place* is on the Piazza, and that people may wish to see the work of art in its original context, as it was conceived by the artist. The setting is more important to most people than the authentic statue, which does exist and can be admired in a nearby museum.

History and territory belong together as two sides of the same coin. So Sir Jack is quite right about the way he sees the landscape evolving:

> The hill was an Iron Age burial mound, the undulating field a vestige of Saxon agriculture, the copse was a copse only because a thousand other trees had been cut down, the river was a canal and the pheasant had been hand-reared by a gamekeeper.
>
> (1998, 60)

Similarly, transplanting historical events from the place where they happened is to rob them of part of their meaning. Thus, the really evil move of the England, England project is to transform England into a myth of the everyday in the sense of Roland Barthes, as developed in his book *Mythologies* (first published in 1957). Mythmaking according to Barthes is a process of naturalization and commodification in which signs are emptied of most of their connotations in order to carry an ideological message, a mythic signification. As Sir Jack offers "convenience" to his customers, "following the logic of the market" (1998, 182), as Martha puts it, England is pressed into service as a money-making machine. Since the original country is too complex for this move, it has to be compressed, reduced in size and emptied of a large part of its historical and cultural resonances in order to fit seamlessly into a capitalist narrative, commodified and detachable.

Tellingly, the novel ends with a scene in which Martha Cochrane, who has grown old and settled in Albion, takes a walk and observes a rabbit, "fearless and quietly confident of its territory" (1998, 266); "confident of its territory" as human beings no longer are. This is not a question of 'roots,' but if history is made up of narratives, they have to be set somewhere, and the location is part of their meaning. It is a clever and quite radical move on Barnes's part to set his novel on the Isle of Wight in the English Channel rather than on some fantasy island, tapping into the rich tradition of more exotic island fictions that would have been available to him. As it is, the slight territorial shift throws into relief political and economic challenges that Britain was facing in the late 1990s as Thatcherism was followed by New Labour. It thus becomes possible to critique the neo-liberal and in many ways hypocritical discourse that had taken hold of the country, diminishing its stature through cant. Incidentally, the necessary congruence between history and territory is neatly put in a nutshell by the title of a film released in

1964 and directed by Kevin Brownlow and Andrew Mollo: *It Happened Here*. This counterfactual narrative imagines an alternative history for Britain, a worst-case scenario so to speak, where Nazi Germany has actually seized British territory and occupied the United Kingdom during the Second World War. The film's title neatly encapsulates the chronotopic nexus between history and territory that I have emphasized, gaining its threatening quality from the claim that this event really 'took place' close to home.

In fact, the invasion did not happen in the United Kingdom, but it did take place in the Channel Islands (cf. Bunting 1995, Cruickshank 1988, Forty 1999, Moore 2005, Sanders 2005, Thornton 2012). During the Second World War, the Channel Islands' strategic geopolitical position and, hence, their place in Hitler's invasion plans (Briggs 1995) led to a rather disproportionate presence of German soldiers on the islands. The occupation has a very prominent place in the islands' cultural memory, and there is a wealth of popular historiography about the occupation, as well as middlebrow fiction such as Tim Binding's *Island Madness* (1998) or G. B. Edwards's *The Book of Ebenezer Le Page* (1981), which I will discuss below. There is also plenty of popular fiction, often in a romantic vein, which makes the most of local women's fraternization with the enemy. Considering the history and literature of Guernsey in particular, I would argue that it occupies the opposite position to the Isle of Wight, not only geographically, but also culturally: looking back to centuries of cultural negotiation, at once isolated and in the thick of Anglo-French interactions, it has become a model of idiosyncrasy and hybridity. Unlike the Isle of Wight, which is so unselfconsciously English that it can be used as a blank space, or projection screen, Guernsey must almost inevitably be seen in terms of the chronotope – a territory both shaped by history and shaping history through its presence. One character in *The Book of Ebenezer Le Page* relates that "England and France was once at war for a hundred years and Guernsey was in-between, so got it from both sides" (Edwards 1981, 54; cf. also Goodall 2007, 2008). With characteristic shrewdness, the islanders learnt to profit from the situation: when

> they became smugglers, they smuggled both ways, from France to England and from England to France. When smuggling was made illegal in Guernsey and they took to privateering to be respectable, they captured French ships for the English and English ships for the French.
>
> (1981, 179)

The character of the island is epitomized, and embodied, by Ebenezer Le Page, the fictional author of the memoirs and the chronicle of the island in the twentieth century that make up the book. Le Page comes from one of the old Guernsey families who fetishize the possession of land and money; he is fiercely proud of his island, which he has never left but for a one-day trip to Jersey. He is a shrewd and independent character who negotiates religion, family quarrels and love tangles in his own inscrutable manner, making his living in an approved Guernsey way by growing tomatoes in greenhouses. Crucially, he looks down both on the English and the French. He has learned from his mother to eat well, proper Guernsey beef and golden Guernsey butter, rather than the sickly white stuff the English have (cf. Edwards 1981, 15, 17). While the Le Pages do not want to put English food into their mouths, they speak the island patois, which is a mixture of English and French. Le Page thinks of the English as arrogant and bloodless, and of the French as dirty: "I didn't like the French, and I think most Guernsey people felt the same. I thought they was dirty" (1981, 90). But this does not mean that there is a separate Channel Islands identity. The mistrust of the big, and great, nations divided by the Channel is matched by a deep suspicion of the immediate neighbours: "I am glad I am not a Jerseyman. I would rather be a black man than a Jerseyman. A black man is a black man but a Jerseyman is a Jerseyman" (1981, 45). When archaeological excavations are undertaken on the island and the question of precedence arises, Le Page is pleased that there may have been people on Guernsey first, even before Jersey came into existence, "because in those days [Jersey] was joined to France and wasn't a place at all" (1981, 218). Significantly, although Le Page is an excellent observer, there is very little description of landscape and the natural beauties of Guernsey in the memoir, which shows that Le Page does not think of his island in aesthetic terms such as the picturesque or the beautiful; it is just the place where he lives. Increasingly, in the second half of the century after the German Occupation, this place is the scene of an epic battle against those who want to sell the island to foreign tourists. Even though Ebenezer Le Page makes a little money by taking care of some ancient monuments, significant as tourist attractions, he resists the pull of easy money, insisting that the island is not available to those who want to turn it into a myth.

In this context, his name gains resonance – in the First Book of Samuel, Ebenezer (which means "stone of help" in Hebrew) denotes both the battlefield where the Israelites fought the Philistines and the monument that was erected after the final victory of the Israelites. So on the one hand, Ebenezer Le Page embodies the rock, the island, "Sarnia Chérie, Gem of the Sea," as the anthem of the Bailiwick of Guernsey (quoted at the beginning of *The Book of Ebenezer Le Page*) has it, which will withstand the Philistines. On the other hand, his surname (Le Page) suggests the textual nature of his existence, a fiction created by G. B. Edwards as he looked onto the Isle of Portland from Weymouth, conjuring up his lost home Guernsey. Considering the intertextuality of Edwards's spiritual autobiography, there are strong echoes both of Victor Hugo's

Les travailleurs de la mer (1866), which the French novelist famously composed while in exile on Guernsey, and of Daniel Defoe's *Robinson Crusoe* (1719), the iconic story of a lone man on his island who seeks to construct a meaningful existence, not least with the help of the Bible, a text that forms the bedrock of his culture and identity. So Guernsey is made up both of stones and of words, of the interaction between them, and the island comes to life powerfully in the narrative of a man who is certainly not a "future grateful employee" (Barnes 2009, 63), as Sir Jack imagines the population of the Isle of Wight. Currently, Guernsey is using its historically and geographically liminal situation as a self-governing British Crown possession off the coast of Normandy to act as an offshore finance centre, a global player in the world of finance like other small islands. Whether this move has turned Guernseymen into Philistines is open to debate. In any case, this role as a hotspot of trade has a beautiful logic for an island that embodies exchange and hybridity. Ironically, Guernsey Finance now seeks to style the island as "a 'Safe Haven' amid Brexit Uncertainty" (2016), turning its quaint idiosyncrasy into a promise of stability.

Notes

1 For these historical and cultural entanglements between England and France, see Cambiaghi (2005), Caws and Wright (2000), Collier and Mackenzie (1992), Crossley and Small (1988), Moseley (2011), Norris (2004), Ogée (2005), Radford and Reid (2012), Scott (2002), Sharp and Stone (2000), Simmons (2000), Thomson and Dziembowski (2010), and Tombs and Tombs (2006).

References

Apter, Emily. 2002. "Afterword: From Literary Channel to Narrative Chunnel." In *The Literary Channel: The Inter-National Invention of the Novel*, edited by Margaret Cohen and Carolyn Dever, 286–293. Princeton: Princeton University Press.

Bakhtin, Mikhail. 1981. *The Dialogic Imagination: Four Essays*. Translated by Caryl Emerson and Michael Holquist. Austin: University of Texas Press.

Barnes, Julian. (1996) 2009. *Cross Channel*. London: Vintage.

———. (1998) 1999. *England, England*. London: Picador.

Barthes, Roland. (1957) 1972. *Mythologies*. Translated by Annette Lavers. London: Paladin.

Baudrillard, Jean. 1981. *Simulacra and Simulation*. Translated by Sheila Faria Glaser. Ann Arbor: The University of Michigan Press.

Billig, Volkmar. 2010. *Inseln: Geschichte einer Faszination*. Berlin: Matthes & Scitz.

Binding, Tim. 1999. *Island Madness*. London: Pan Macmillan.

Bradford, Richard. 2011. "Julian Barnes's *England, England* and Englishness." In *Julian Barnes: Contemporary Critical Perspectives*, edited by Sebastian Groes and Peter Childs, 92–102. London: Continuum.

Briggs, Asa. 1995. *The Channel Islands: Occupation and Liberation, 1940–1945*. London: B. T. Batsford.

Bunting, Madeleine. 1995. *The Model Occupation: The Channel Islands under German Rule 1940–1945*. London: HarperCollins.

Cambiaghi, Mara. 2005. "'Moving Times – New Words': The Sixties on Both Sides of the Channel." In *Time Refigured: Myths, Foundation Texts and Imagined Communities*, edited by Martin Prochazka and Ondrej Pilny, 296–314. Prague: Litteraria Pragensia Books.

Caws, Mary Ann, and Sarah Bird Wright. 2000. *Bloomsbury and France: Art and Friends*. Oxford: Oxford University Press.

Childs, Peter. 2011. *Julian Barnes*, Manchester: Manchester University Press.

Collier, Caroline, and Julia Mackenzie, eds. 1992. *The Dieppe Connection: The Town and Its Artists from Turner to Braque*. London: Herbert Press.

Crossley, Ceri, and Ian Small, eds. 1988. *Studies in Anglo-French Cultural Relations: Imagining France*. London: Macmillan.

Cruickshank, Charles. 1988. *The German Occupation of the Channel Islands*. Channel Islands: Guernsey Press.

Darian-Smith, Eve. 1999. *Bridging Divides: The Channel Tunnel and English Legal Identity*. Berkeley: University of California Press.

Edmond, Rod, and Vanessa Smith, eds. 2003. *Islands in History and Representation*. London and New York: Routledge.

Edwards, Gerald B. 1981. *The Book of Ebenezer Le Page*. New York: New York Review of Books.

Forty, George. 1999. *Channel Islands at War: A German Perspective*. Shepperton: Ian Allan.

Goodall, Peter. 2007. "'The Spell of Sarnia': Fictional Representations of the Island of Guernsey." *Shima: The International Journal of Research into Island Cultures* 1 (2): 59–69.

———. 2008. "'The rock whence ye are hewn': *The Book of Ebenezer Le Page* and Guernsey Literature and History." *Modern Language Review* 103 (1): 22–34.

"Guernsey a 'Safe Haven' Amid Brexit Uncertainty." 2016. *We Are Guernsey (website)*. Guernsey Finance. June 30, 2016. www.weareguernsey.com/news/2016/guernsey-a-safe-haven-amid-brexit-uncertainty.

Guignery, Vanessa. 2006. *The Fiction of Julian Barnes*. New York: Palgrave Macmillan.

Moore, David W. 2005. *The Other British Isles: A History of Shetland, Orkney, the Hebrides, Isle of Man, Anglesey, Scilly, Isle of Wight, and the Channel Islands*. Jefferson: McFarland & Co.

Moseley, Merritt. 2011. "Crossing the Channel: Europe and the Three Uses of France in Julian Barnes's Talking It Over." In *Julian Barnes: Contemporary Critical Perspectives*, edited by Sebastian Groes and Peter Childs, 69–80. London: Continuum.

Norris, Christopher. 2004. "'Fog over Channel, Continent Isolated': Theory, Philosophy and the Great Divide." In *Critical Studies: Post-Theory, Culture, Criticism*, edited by Ivan Callus and Stefan Herbrechter, 113–137. Amsterdam: Rodopi.

Ogée, Frédéric, ed. 2005. *'Better in France?': The Circulation of Ideas across the Channel in the Eighteenth Century*. Lewisburg: Bucknell University Press.

Prieto, Eric. 2011. "Geocriticism, Geopoetics, Geophilosophy, and Beyond." In *Geocritical Explorations: Space, Place, and Mapping in Literary and Cultural Studies*, edited by Robert T. Tally Jr., 13–27. New York: Palgrave Macmillan.

Radford, Andrew, and Victoria Reid, eds. 2012. *Franco-British Cultural Exchanges, 1880–1940: Channel Packets*. Basingstoke: Palgrave Macmillan.

Rainsford, Dominic. 2002. *Literature, Identity and the English Channel: Narrow Seas Expanded*. London: Palgrave.

Rubinson, Gregory J. 2009. "Truth Takes a Holiday: Julian Barnes's *England, England* and the Theme Park as Literary Genre." *American, British and Canadian Studies*, special issue *Worlds within Words: Twenty-first Century Visions on the Work of Julian Barnes* 13 (2): 39–49.

Sanders, Paul. 2005. *The British Channel Islands under German Occupation: 1940–1945*. St. Helier: Société Jersiaise.

Scott, Clive. 2002. *Channel Crossings: French and English Poetry in Dialogue, 1550–2000*. Oxford: Legenda.

Shakespeare, William. 1997. *The Tragedy of King Richard the Third*. In *The Norton Shakespeare*, edited by Stephen Greenblatt et al., Volume 1, second edition, 547–628. New York: Norton.

Sharp, Alan, and Glyn Stone. 2000. *Anglo-French Relations in the Twentieth Century: Rivalry and Cooperation*. London: Routledge.

Simmons, Clare. 2000. *Eyes Across the Channel: French Revolutions, Party History and English Writing, 1830–1882*. Amsterdam: Harwood.

Tally, Robert T., Jr., ed. 2011. *Geocritical Explorations: Space, Place, and Mapping in Literary and Cultural Studies*. Basingstoke: Palgrave Macmillan.

Thomson, Ann, Simon Burrows, and Edmond Dziembowski, eds. 2010. *Cultural Transfers: France and Britain in the Long Eighteenth Century*. London: Voltaire Society.

Thornton, Tim. 2012. *The Channel Islands, 1370–1640: Between England and Normandy*. Woodbridge: The Boydell Press.

Tombs, Robert, and Isabelle Tombs. 2006. *That Sweet Enemy: The French and the British from the Sun King to the Present*. London: Heinemann.

Westphal, Bertrand. 2007. *La géocritique: Réel, fiction, espace*. Paris: Minuit.

Wilson, Keith. 1994. *Channel Tunnel Visions, 1850–1945: Dreams and Nightmares*. London: Hambledon Press.

Part IV
Modernity on the Move

10 Montaigne
Travel and Travail

Tom Conley

From a variety of standpoints and methods, the contributors to this collection of essays take *travelling narratives* to mean accounts whose form engages displacement and passage in space and time. Some of the narratives are specific, and so, too, are many of the itineraries taken. A logbook or an assemblage of a traveller's notes registers the day-to-day experience of travel; a collection of poems (say, Petrarch's *Rime sparse* or Du Bellay's *Regrets*) can be a mosaic tale of exile. Mystics tell of their spiritual voyages into unknown realms, beyond belief, from which they return in an altered state (de Certeau, 2014). Others, like Rabelais's Alcofrybas, tell of his adventures in the mouth and belly of Pantagruel, the gentle giant for whom he serves as scribe and historian, who meets familiar things in unfamiliar places. It may be that, from the *Odyssey* to Jack Kerouac's *On the Road* (1957), or from Edgar G. Ulmer's *Detour* (1945) to James Cameron's *Avatar* (2009), from Marco Polo to Jules Verne, any work of writing – musical, pictorial, cartographic, cinematic, novelistic or other – can be taken as a travelling narrative. In the same breath, in their imagination viewers, readers and listeners are 'transported' into areas other than where they are, often getting lost before finding their bearings.

In what follows, the aim is to see how the informal essay, an intermediate or amphibious genre born of the early modern era, can be construed to be a travelling narrative. Touching on philosophy (it inquires of the nature of things), on literature (lacking a pre-existing model, it refuses to conform to codes that dictate how a genre is shaped), on visual rhetoric (its powers of description veer away from pre-given models of narration), on music (its uses assonance and dissonance to suggest harmonic variation), on cinema (it plays on both language and space, and the mix of aural and visual matter), on cartography (charted and plotted, it furnishes readers with what they need to fuel their fantasies of displacement), autobiography (with which its authors create the illusion that their lives are voyages) and so on, the informal essay remains forever a mixed, motley and ever-inventive creation.

In the paragraphs below, it will be argued that the *Essais* of Montaigne, a work that literary historians often consider to be at the

origins of the genre, could be a point of reference for what Johannes
Riquet calls the travelling narrative in the introduction to this volume.
First launched in Bordeaux in 1580, in two modest volumes by local
printer Simon Millanges, the *Essais* were reprinted in 1582 and slightly
expanded to include notes from Montaigne's recent voyage to Italy between September 1580 and the same month in 1581. In 1588, Parisian
editor Abel Langelier published a fourth and further revised edition *in
quarto* that included the first two volumes and, no less, a substantial
third volume. Comprising thirteen essays (in contrast to the shorter essays of the first two, the material of 1588 includes three fairly copious
and lengthy chapters that stand in contrast to the measure of most of
the others in the first two volumes (except for the monstrous "Apologie
de Raimond Sebond," a sort of 'anti-essay' that goes against the grain
of all the others). Like the design of books one and two, the third is
rigorously 'compassed.' Comprising fifty-seven chapters, the essays of
book one set themselves in relation to a mobile centre marked, first, by
the twenty-eighth essay, a reflection on the intimacy of friendship and
on the memory of Étienne de la Boétie, the author's recently deceased
fellow traveller; and then, the aptly numbered twenty-ninth, under
whose title "Vingt et neuf sonnets d'Estienne de la Boëtie, à Madame
de de Grammont, Comtesse de Guissen," in a sort of fearful symmetry,
are printed twenty-nine sonnets that his friend had purportedly written. In conjunction with perspective in painting, Chapter 29 becomes
a vanishing point in a composition where equal units of twenty-eight
chapters on either side of the twenty-ninth serve as a surround or a
frame for the poems that would be encrypted in the centre.[1] Likewise,
composed of thirty-seven chapters, the second book places at its axis
the nineteenth, "De la liberté de conscience" [On the liberty of Con-
science], an essay that treads delicately, going backwards and forwards
over a contested topic among embattled Protestants and Catholics in
the Wars of Religion that officially lasted from 1562 to 1598. As the
Essais evolve, they become longer. The first volume (fifty-seven) gives
way to the next of thirty-seven, and then to the third of only thirteen.
Like that of the books of 1580 and 1582, the numerical pattern of
the material in 1588 suggests that a design of an ever-moving centre
and circumference prevails: the seventh and minuscule chapter, "De
l'incommodité de la grandeur" [Of the Incommodity of Grandeur],
considers the precarious equilibrium of the site and seat (or *siège*) on
which a king is required to sit and rule, an essay in which the author
remarks that his ethic of moderation – and his sense of the spatial
design of his work – has brought him to the middle of things: "Je suis
duit à un estage moyen, comme par mon sort, aussi par mon goust"
[I'm accustomed (duit) to a median level both by my fate and by my
taste].[2] He has come or been led to a middle, buttressed on either side
by two sets of six chapters.

The tessellated play of the essays' numbers, titles and placement of their topics calls for navigational readings. Plot points, recurring markers, image signs, verbal wind roses and coyly placed (and often strategically altered) citations, as well as what Montaigne calls *emblesmes supernumeraires* [supernumerary emblems], punctuate the discourse to imply that it can be read over and across itself. Having to move and shift with the currents of the discourse, the reader is invited to engage a mode of reading that roams and wanders, that oscillates between active and passive or even conscious and unconscious registers. Along the way, the essays reflect on their process and on how they move with the ever-changing nature of their author. "Je n'ay pas plus faict mon livre que mon livre m'a faict, livre consubstantiel à son auteur, d'une occupation propre, membre de ma vie" (1950, 750) [I have no more made my book than my book has made me, a book consubstantial with its author, of its own occupation, a member of my life].[3]

Dealing with a variety of topics, "De la vanité" [Of Vanity], the ninth chapter of the third book, is perhaps the richest and, from the angle of legions of readers, one of the most difficult of all the essays. Infinite rumination on the experience and the art of travel blends with speculations on the author's own life and times and on his own mortality. In this essay, many of the impressions that had been recently registered in the journal of his voyage to and from Rome in 1580–1581 are distilled and transformed into a poetics of displacement across time, space and culture.[4] The design of the incipit and the tenor of the opening sentences suggest how and why:

Chapitre IX.

De la vanité

Il n'en est à l'avanture aucune plus expresse que d'en escrire si vainement. Ce que la divinité nous en a si divinement exprimé devroit estre soingneusement et continuellement medité par les gens d'entendement. Qui ne voit que j'ay pris une route par laquelle, sans cesse et sans travail, j'iray autant qu'il y aura d'ancre et de papier au monde?

(1950, 1057)

[None is peradventure so express than to write of it so vainly. What divinity has so divinely expressed ought to be meditated carefully and continually among knowledgeable people. Who would fail to see that I've taken a road by which, ceaselessly and without travail, I'll go as long as there are ink and paper in the world?]

The beginning literally arches back to the title, a point of departure that becomes a compass-point or polestar for the meander and divagation to follow. We need, he asserts vigorously and vaingloriously, to study vanity meticulously, patiently, deliberately, with diligence and, above all (tongue-in-cheek), *seriously*, so closely that the title becomes an emblem of travel: not merely of "vanity" as it echoes from *Ecclesiastes* (Oh vanity! Vanities of vanities, etc.), but of the movement of writing that arches forwards, that moves ahead, *avant*, that can venture about diligently and heedlessly, *à l'avanture*, going wherever it takes the writer – as what would be a revealing misprision of a careless reader, upon glossing *à l'avanture* who sees and hears an echo of a forwardness, a "l'avanité" in what otherwise would be the unconscious dimension of the title. The force of writing, *travail*, is akin to travel, and what it 'expresses' become dejections squeezed from the writer's mental sphincter and congealed in the printed ink before the reader's eyes. To express, to read and then to contemplate the remainders, the residue or the traces of his expression: thus Montaigne picks through the evidence of a life travelled. Preferring not to be a sedentary stick-in-the-mud, he implies that his writing moves, and that what we read can be grasped in motion and, as a whole, taken to be a sort of viaticum. Given that in a truly material (and hence Marxian) sense the conditions of possibility of writing are ink and paper, Montaigne can travel wherever and whenever he wishes, and all the better without being encumbered with luggage. Writing becomes a more appealing mode of transit than a horse or a coach. When noting that he goes along his path *sans cesse et sans travail*, he suggests that travel, which would connote passage and movement, paradoxically derives from a condition of *travail*, of torture and suffering. In his *Dictionarie of the French & English Tongues* (1611), published in London twenty-three years after Montaigne's first rendering of "De la vanité," Randle Cotgrave registers:

TRAVAIL: *m. Trauell, toyle, teene, labour, businesse, painstaking; trouble, molestation, care; also, the frame whereinto Farriers put various horses when they shooe, or dresse them.* Un homme de grand travail. *A verie painfull man.*

TRAVAILLANT: *Laborious, painefull, industrious, diligent.*

TRAVAILLÉ: *Travelled, toyled, labored, mush busied, or exercised in; troubled, molested, vexed, or wearied with.*

JOYE TRISTE COEUR TRAVAILLÉ: Pro. *Th'aggrieved heart makes heavie cheere.*

TRAVAILLEMENT: m. *A travelling, toyling, moiling, swinking, laboring; molesting, barrying, troubling.*

TRAVAILLER: *To travel, swinke, labour, toyle, moyle, take paines, or busie himselfe in; also, to excercise, hold occupied, set on worke; barrie, wearie, vex, trouble, turmoyle, disquiet, infest.*

TRAVAILLER EN BOURDICAN: *Looke* Bourdican.

TANT TRAVAILLE, & TRACASSE L'HOMME QU'IL SE ROMPE, OU SOMME:
  Prov. *So long a man toyles, and trots up and downe, that at the length he bursts, or falls flat downe.*

To travel means to toil. Displacement carries the annoyance of hiring a team of helpers, packing bags, shoeing horses and gathering provisions. A *via rupta*, the itinerary the traveller sets out to take is by nature broken, dashed, discontinuous, crossed by stopovers, stations, obstacles, or gets looped in detour and deviation. It may be that when considering that the essay – an essay on travel – is a log or register, in moving ahead, in the following sentence the reflection stumbles and then bifurcates at the very mention of *registre*: "Je ne puis tenir registre de ma vie par mes actions: fortune les met trop bas; je le tiens par mes fantasies" (1950, 1057) [I cannot keep an account of my life by my actions: fortune puts them too far down; I do so through my fantasies]. The train of thought shifts from action to fantasy. In the clearly Freudian 'register,' in the sentences that follow, the writing deviates from the existential reality of human action to reflect on how anality and self-study are of the same order.[5] It can be wondered if the "Gentleman" whom Montaigne once knew, who found untold pleasure in his chamber pots, would have been the double of the writer himself. Here he was, arching over his receptacles (that putatively could be the essays), "qui ne communiquoit sa vie, que par les operations de son ventre; vous voyez chez luy, en montre, un ordre de bassins de sept ou huict jours. C'estoit son estude, son discours; tout autre propos, luy puoit" (1950, 1057) [who arranged his life only by the operation of his belly: in his home you see on display an order of basins of seven or eight days. It was his study, his discourse. For him other matters just stank]. His excretions inspire analogy with the measure and matter of the writing, performed at daily intervals, distributed (in the third book) into thirteen container-chapters. Hardly contrary to the exemplary Gentleman (majuscule G in the text of 1588), a *curieux* implied to have routinely stuck his nose into the basins as if he had been sniffing a delicate wine, the writer is he who travels by way of accounting for his bodily movement. "Ce sont icy, un peu plus civilement, des excremens d'un vieil esprit, dur tantost, tantost lache, & tousjours indigeste" (1950, 1057) [These are here, a little more civilly, the excrements of an old mind, sometimes hard, soft sometimes, and always undigeste]. Mental remainders of a man's aging wit (*esprit*) are marked in the Latin *mens* embedded in the excretions, which become, as the essayist noted in the first sentence of the essay, the matter of meditation.[6]

Time and again, whether for the ends of anthropology or purely puerile pleasure, legions of dedicated readers of the *Essais* return to these sentences. What Montaigne makes of excretion has to do with the labours of creativity. Given how much of the essay is about displacement,

economy and ecology, it can be asked if, for its own sake of secrecy, the
essay promotes an art of obliquity – a diagonal, even anamorphic slant
onto what it states; and, at the same time, a tendency to bring the printed
matter into the arena of reflection. The narrative travels when it moves to
and from what it 'expresses' and, both inwardly and outwardly, points
at or *signifies* in its own form. In the context of the 'world' or open-
ended totality of the essay itself, it can be asked if the essay draws the
meridians and latitudes of a broader geographical network in which, as
it advances, the writing frays an ever-bifurcating itinerary along which
it indulges in an art of getting lost.[7]

From its beginning, "De la vanité" becomes an adventure in which the
most innocuous locutions and 'signifiers' belong to the webbing of the
world in which the writer moves: "Il n'en est à l'avanture aucune plus
expresse […]." Meaning "perchance," "perhaps," "peradventure," and
so on, on one level *à l'avanture* seems to temper the assertion and to em-
body the enterprise of the essay itself.[8] In "On Vanity," the formula can
be read crosswise, as what gives onto doubt or creative pause, a state of
reflection in passing, which Cotgrave (1611) registers under "Aventure.
as Adventure; à l'avent: cela n'est point. *I doubt, or tis a question,
whether that be; or perhaps that is not*" but also, in the same breath,
as "Adventure: f. *An adventure, chaunce, hap, lucke, fortune, hazard.*"
Acknowledging that the essay is a display of his own vanity, the essayist
prides himself – *se vante* – in 'venturing' to write of vanity. Thus, he
sets onto – what else – a voyage that could be at once regressive, moving
backwards in time and memory, into a fecal realm, and projective, looking to an uncertain future that as far as the aging author is concerned,
could be close to the end of time. Insofar as adventure connotes risk
staked on the negotiation of material things and ends, by setting travel
into the economy of writing the essay engages the nature of speculation.[9]
In this respect, at the foot of the letter, manifest in the printed substance
of the essay, the reader finds folded into *à l'avanture* some of the characters of the title, as noted above, suggesting that *la vanité* connotes both
what goes ahead, *à l'avant*, in recounting elements of the author's trip
to Rome in 1580–1581 and backwards, to times *avant*, notably to the
Rome he had known through his command of the classical canon.

Spurring the drive to encounter "choses nouvelles et inconnues"
(1950, 1060) [new and unknown things], his will to travel, he avows, includes a nagging desire to be free and done with household affairs. "Je respons ordinairement à ceux qui me demandent raison de mes voyages: que
je sçay bien ce que je fuis, mais non pas ce que je cherche" (1950, 1085)
[Ordinarily I respond to those who ask me why I travel: that I know well
what I'm escaping but not what I'm seeking]. At this moment the essay
makes it clear that it is vectored according to three points of reference,
compass roses as it were, that beg for a spatial reading of its content and,
despite or by dint of much of its obscurity (avowed in the fact that the

author takes pride in its enigmatic character), give it the attributes of a map. Toponyms become points of reference in a meditation owing to mediation, which implies triangulation.[10] Co-present, each of the places that figure prominently – the home or self in Aquitaine, Paris to the north, and Rome to the south and east – also becomes a vantage point that looks onto the others, which include the limits of Christendom. Taken together, along with the eye of the reader following the words of the travelling narrative in which they are noted, the three points of reference establish what might be a Baroque perspective that includes variation and change.

> Entre la variation et le point de vue il y a un rapport nécessaire: non pas simplement en raison de la variété des points de vue [...], mais en premier lieu *parce ce que tout point de vue est un point de vue d'une variation.*
> [Between variation and point of view there holds a necessary relation: not simply for reason of the variety of points of view [...], but because every point of view is a point of view on a variation]
> (Deleuze 1988, 27; translation and emphasis mine).[11]

Variation begins presumably at the site where the essay is written, the tower of the author's chateau. Montaigne takes leave of his house and home, his "maison," which connotes the cultural baggage of his heritage and family and a battery of domestic chores and annoyances. The harried homeowner avows, "Je me destourne volontiers du gouvernement de ma maison" (1950, 1060) [I willingly balk at governing my home]. He laments the hassle of fixing a barn, settling with indigent labourers, or even fixing and cleaning his buildings' gutters: "*Stillicidi casus lapidem cavat.* / Ces ordinaires goutieres me mangent. (c) Les inconvenients ordinaires ne sont jamais legiers. Ils sont continuels et irreparables, nomément quand ils naissent des membres du mesnage, continuels et inseparables" (1950, 1063) [*The drop of falling water cuts through stone* (Lucretius, *De rerum natura*, I, 314). These ordinary gutters eat me away. (c) Ordinary annoyances are never light. They are continual and irreparable, namely when they are born of the parts of the house, continual and inseparable]. When travelling, Montaigne allows himself, first, to be rid of his property and, second, as the reference to his ailing gutters suggests, to take a distance from the internal discord of the Wars of Religion, "la disconvenance aux meurs presentes de nostre estat" (1950, 1069) [the dispute within the current ways of our state], so thoroughly, good bourgeois noble that he is, that on the road he worries only about his pocket book and the effects he carries with him. As noted above: "Je respons ordinairement à ceux qui me demandent raison de mes voyages: que je sçay bien ce que je fuis, mais non pas ce que je cherche" (1950, 1088) [I ordinarily respond to those who beg me to tell them why I travel: that I am well aware of what I flee but not at all of what I am looking for].

In an often nebulous mental zone 'between' home and the indiscernible destination of his voyages – be they for reasons of xenophilia, of a desire to "see and visit" (*voir et visiter*) the world at large, or to contemplate travel to Persia, maybe to puncture the cultural bubble (*bulle*) in which he lives, he thinks of Paris, a cardinal reference for the mobile point of view the essay embraces. A sudden and unforeseen description of the city erupts in the midst of his reflections on current civil strife as if it were a childhood memory of familial affection. Despite its politics of praise, the description of the city is viscerally heartwarming. As many readers have noted over and again with pleasure,

> [j]e ne veux pas oublier cecy, que je ne me mutine jamais tant contre la France que je ne regarde Paris de bon œil : elle a mon cueur des mon enfance. Et m'en est advenu comme des choses excellentes : plus j'ay veu dépuis d'autres villes belles, plus la beauté de cette-cy peut et gaigne sur mon affection. Je l'ayme par elle mesme, et plus en son estre seul que rechargée de pompe estrangiere. Je l'ayme tendrement, jusques à ses verrues et à ses taches. Je ne suis françois que par cette grande cité: grande en peuples, grande en felicité de son assiette, mais sur tout grande et incomparable en varieté et diversité de commoditez, la gloire de la France, et l'un des plus nobles ornemens du monde.
>
> (1950, 1089)

> [I don't want to forget this, that I am never so much in mutiny against France than I gaze upon Paris with delight: since childhood it has captured my heart. And it's come to me like so many excellent things: and ever since, the more I've seen other comely cities, the more its beauty gains on my affection. I love it for itself, and more in its sole being than stuffed with foreign pomp. I love it tenderly, even its warts and blemishes. I am French only because of this great city: great in peoples, great in the beauty of its plan and site, especially great and incomparable in the variety and diversity of things, the glory of France and one of the noblest ornaments of the world.]

Portraying himself as a foreigner to France but a native to its capital, Montaigne sets in place a "point of view on a variation."

The brief encomium that draws attention to the plan or aspect, the *assiette* of the beloved city (in which the essay has been published), anticipates the more complex description of Rome in which its icon as an eternal city is called in question. The loosely tessellated narrative of travel in time and space leads to and then away from Rome, the site where the essay stages another childhood memory of Freudian resonance. Having touched again on household management, on the state of the world in the time of war, whether in Rome or elsewhere, on economy and management, he realizes that he is at home only when uprooted, apart from himself, in a condition of displacement. In the words of Ovid (*Tristes*, III, iv, l. 57), *"Ante oculos errat domus, errat forma locorum"* (1950, 1093) [My house and its surroundings float before my eyes]. Further, separation from a place, a site or being of nourishing origin, or a beloved person, such as the recent passing of his friend Étienne de la Boétie, inspires further rumination on chance, hazard and the fortuitous adventure of writing that wanders. "(c) Mon stile et mon esprit vont vagabondant de mesmes" (1950, 1116) [My style and my mind go wandering together] and, as he notes, the unbound and unconscious character of the writing moves it in every direction, "(c) [j]oint qu'à l'adventure ay-je quelque obligation particuliere à ne dire qu'à demy, à dire confusément, à dire discordamment" (1950, 1117) [added that by chance I have some particular obligation to speak underhandedly, to speak confusedly, to speak discordantly], and thus to valorise vanity and stupidity for the sake of pleasure and of uncontrolled inclination that he would prefer not to monitor.

In this context of errant reflection, Rome comes forward as if in counterpoint to the earlier memory-images of his home and of his beloved city of Paris. In one of the most psychically dense and richest passages of the *Essais*, he recalls:

> J'ay veu ailleurs des maisons ruynées, et des statues, et du ciel, et de la terre : ce sont tousjours des hommes. Tout cela est vray; et si pourtant ne sçauroy revoir si souvent le tombeau de cette ville, si grande et si puissante, que je ne l'admire et revere. Le soing des morts nous est en recommandation. Or j'ay esté nourry dés mon enfance avec ceux-icy; j'ay eu connoissance des affaires de Romme, long temps avant que je l'aye eue de ceux de ma maison; je sçavois le Capitole et son plant avant que je sceusse le Louvre, et le Tibre avant la Seine. J'ay eu plus en teste les conditions et fortunes de Lucullus, Metellus et Scipion, que je n'ay d'aucuns hommes des nostres. Ils sont trespassés. Si est bien mon pere, aussi entierement qu'eux, et s'est esloigné de moy et de la vie autant en dixhuict ans que ceux-là ont faict en seize cens; duquel pourtant je ne laisse pas d'embrasser et practiquer la memoire, l'amitié et la societé, d'une parfaicte union et tres-vive.
>
> (1950, 1117–1118)

[Elsewhere I've seen ruined homes, and statues, and sky, and earth: these are always men [hommes]. All that's for sure; and yet, I cannot fail to see the tomb of this city, so great and so powerful, without being in admiration and reverence. It is praiseworthy for us to care for the dead. Now, since childhood I've been nourished by those here; I had knowledge of the affairs of Rome long before [avant] that of those there: I knew the Capitol and its position before [avant] I had known the Louvre, and the Tiber before [avant] the Seine. I had in my head more of the conditions and fortunes of Lucullus, Metellus and Scipio than I've had of some of the men [hommes] of ours. They're dead. So also is my father, as entirely as they, and he remains as far from me and of life in eighteen years as those others have been in sixteen hundred; nonetheless I never fail to embrace and practice the memory, friendship and society of a perfect and ever-lively union.]

The pages immediately preceding this passage deal with the effects of poetry that bubble out of the speaker's mouth like water from the gargoyle of a fountain. In the splash and froth escape "des choses de diverse couleur, de contraire substance et d'un cours rompu" (1950, 1116) [things of diverse colour, of contrary substance and of a broken flow]. Uttered without rumination or deliberation, poetry, he recalls from philosophy and theology, is "the original language of the Gods" (1950, 1116). His ruminations on the nature of poetry serve as a reader's guide to the construction of his memory of Rome, shards of which could perhaps be recalled from the time he spent in the city between November 30, 1580 and April 7, 1581, or also from a variety of topographies of the 'map,' layout or *plant* of the Eternal City in ancient and modern times, available to tourists and visitors.[12] But Rome had been in his head, he asserts in words of baffling lucidity, long before he became aware of his own country's capitol, and surely before he first entered the city at the age of forty-seven. *Avant, avant, avant*: in the "beforeness," the *avan-ité* of retrospection in which he is moving, the essayist finds himself in two places at once. When *nourished* by the Romans in his infancy, he suckles the breast of Rome, which could be the crown of the Capitol. Setting *sçavoir* in the imperfect past ("je sçavois le Capitole et son plant") adjacent to the verb in the imperfect subjunctive ("avant que je sceusse le Louvre"), and the Roman monument contiguous to its modern counterpart in Paris, he regresses or returns to a primitive scene, a *scène originaire* of being separated *into* the world at large that in the end is indifferent to his presence. In *je sceusse* is scripted *je suce* (I suckle), and in *le Louvre* nestle memory-images both of the palace in scaffolding and repair under the aegis of Catherine de Medici and of the she-wolf, *la louve*, that nourished Romulus and Remus. Frequently illustrated in cosmographies and stamped on coins, the image of the founders of Rome melds with that of essayist in his infancy.[13] In remarking that memories of Lucullus, Metellus and Scipio have been more in his head ("plus en teste") than the notable men of his time, Montaigne mixes images of French and Roman coins, the latter embossed with portraits of the three rulers and the former recalling the *teston*, a piece of money struck during the reign of Francis I. Yet "teste" invokes the image of a teat or nipple a baby would suckle: "*a teat, pap, dug*" (Cotgrave 1611); "*Teter, Premere mammam,*

Lactere, Alimentum maternum trahere, Ubera sugere" (Nicot 1606). Coins appear to belong to an oral fantasy conjoined with those of infantile anality that had opened the chapter.

Along this path, Montaigne's narrative of his travels to Rome regresses, goes back, *en avant,* to Rome to fashion a childhood memory, while venturing forward in the very writing of the essay. Time and space collapse such that in the mortuary realm at the end of the essay Rome becomes a tomb, and soon after, the reader discovers, so does the essay itself. A crypt that holds relics of the past, the ninth chapter is a mass of souvenirs taken *en route,* like the "bulle authentique de bourgeoisie Romaine" that he inflates in reproducing it *verbatim.* Like a dejection (1950, 1121–1122), the document attesting to the fact that Montaigne has been awarded (or has purchased) the sign of eternal citizenship has the aspect of a vainglorious bubble (see McKinley 1995, 62–63). After the originary scene and description of subsequent displacement in the city that had long been cherished in his imagination, the chapter practically avows that it cannot end.

By way of conclusion, and without looping into Montaigne's text's variations upon itself, it can be said that no travelling narrative in the Western canon is of similar facture or consequence. Unlike a narrative of travel, "De la vanité" is a piece of writing that travels within and through its own articulation. In its quasi-autobiographical form, its embrace of voyage and of displacement turns it into a journey not only into the subject or the specious entity we call the 'self,' but into the sensation of birth and often disquieting displacement into the world in which, it becomes apparent, in the midst of accumulated memories and souvenirs, none of us really belongs.

Notes

1 In his *Essais sur les 'Essais'* (Paris: Gallimard, 1968), Michel Butor, the late and regretted novelist, art critic and master of the travelling narrative (for which his *La modification* is a model, see Caroline Rabourdin's contribution in this book), noted the spatial and second-person novel in this volume. The essays, he argued, move towards and away from the axes of each of the volumes.

2 In this context, the use of *duire* [from *ducere,* to draw or to lead] suggests that the author is led or driven to a centre of both ethical and spatial import.

3 I have chosen this edition because its compact size and volume make it fitting as a viaticum. Readers can also consult the Villey-Saulnier edition found at the website for the Montaigne Project (University of Chicago): www.lib.uchicago.edu/efts/ARTFL/projects/montaigne/.

4 Discovered in the eighteenth century among Montaigne's effects, the *Journal de voyage* is composed of notes dictated to his scribe, written in Italian and in French, which register impressions of different people and things seen along the way. A document of early modern anthropology in which Montaigne notes in detail the habits and ways of living in Germany, Switzerland

and Italy, the journal is a pellucid account of the author's curiosity and, because he undertook the voyage to assuage the pain of his bladder stones, it is also a telling account of the pains he suffered along the way. See François Rigolot's splendid edition of the *Journal de voyage* and literature on the work found in *Montaigne Studies*, the *Bulletin de la Société des Amis de Montaigne* and other journals.

5 In a paramount reading of the essay, Gisèle Mathieu-Castellani remarks that writing is fraught with anal phantasms, and that the chapter exudes in the pleasure of *coprophilia,* in *Montaigne: De l'écriture à l'œuvre* (1992).

6 An analyst would wonder if the continence of the Gentleman Montaigne had known would have been the envy of the essayist. The *Journal de voyage* is a register of Montaigne's travels to Italy in which much of the writing is devoted to recording the author's painful secretion of bladder stones.

7 An art for which Rebecca Solnit has written *A Field Guide to Getting Lost* (2005), a book reminiscent of Montaigne's way of writing and travelling. I am grateful to Becca Voelker for having brought this work to my attention.

8 In "Des boyteux" [Of Cripples], in the delicate and risky context of passing judgment in heresy and witchcraft trials, he remarks in an aside, "[j]'ayme ces mots, qui amollissent et moderent la temerité de nos propositions: *A l'Avanture, Aucunement, Quelque, On dict, Je pense,* et semblables" (1155–1156; emphasis in original) [I like these words that tend to mollify and moderate the temerity of our assertions: *Perchance, Somewhat, Some, They say, I think,* and others of the same kind].

9 In *Abenteuer, oder das verlorene Selbstverständnis der Moderne* (1997) and in *The Ideology of Adventure: Studies in Modern Consciousness, 1150–1750* (1987) Michael Nerlich notes that already in Chrétien de Troyes's courtly novels the knightly and chivalric aspect of "setting forth" on a road to save damsels in distress and destroy monsters is freighted with a sense of enterprise and profiteering.

10 In *À fleur de page: Voir et lire le texte de la Renaissance* (2015, 157-162), I have tried to show how Montaigne offers virtual triangles in the ciphers and prose of the essay "De trois commerces" (*Essais,* III, iii).

11 In the essay, the implicit sense of triangulation indicates that, in the words of geographer Franco Farinelli, the triangle "is not only the model of a form, but the model of a productive process. Exactly as shown by the nature of triangulation," in *De la raison cartographique* (2009, 39; my translation).

12 Seen in Sebastian Münster's *Cosmographia universalis* (1565 edition) that Montaigne owned and, at the outset of the *Journal de voyage,* regretted having forgotten to take with him. The cosmography includes copies of maps of contemporary Paris. Current in Rome were maps of the city in time both past and present, those of Pirro Ligorio included in Braun and Hogenberg's *Civitates orbis terrarum* (Cologne, 1572).

13 In *Les plus excellents bastiments de la France* (Paris, 1576), archeologist and architect Jacques Androuet du Cerceau describes the imperfect condition of the Louvre that Montaigne would have known, while in *La Cosmographie universelle,* in François de Belleforest's French edition of Münster, the entry on the history of Rome includes Bernard Salomon's woodcut of the she-wolf nourishing the two infant brothers. The scene figures on the reverse of many coins, notably those bearing images of Lucullus, Metellus and Scipio, which are invoked in the sentence that follows. Here I am retracing the lines of a reading of the same passage in *À fleur de page* (see note 10) 163–166.

References

Certeau, Michel de. 2014. *La fable mystique: XVie-XVIIe siècle*. Volume 2. Edited by Luce Giard. Paris: Éditions Gallimard.

Conley, Tom. 2015. *À fleur de page: Voir et lire le texte de la Renaissance*. Paris: Éditions Classiques Garnier.

Cotgrave, Randle. 1611. *A Dictionarie of the French & English Tongues*. London: Adam Islip.

Deleuze, Gilles. 1988. *Le Pli: Leibniz et le baroque*. Paris: Éditions de Minuit.

Farinelli, Franco. 2009. *De la raison cartographique*. Translated by Katia Bienvenue and Brice Gruet. Paris: CHTS.

Mathieu-Castellani, Gisèle. 1992. *Montaigne: De l'écriture à l'œuvre*. Paris: Presses Universitaires de France.

McKinley, Mary B. 1995. "La Présence du 'Ciceronianus' dans 'De la vanité.'" In *Montaigne et la rhétorique*, edited by John O'Brien, Malcolm Quainton, and James Supple. Paris: Éditions Champion.

Montaigne, Michel de. 1950. *Essais*. Edited by Albert Thibaudet and Maurice Rat. Paris: Éditions Gallimard/Pléiade.

Nerlich, Michael. 1987. *The Ideology of Adventure: Studies in Modern Consciousness, 1150–1750*. Volume 1. Translated by Ruth Crowley. Minneapolis: University of Minnesota Press.

———. 1997. *Abenteuer, oder das verlorene Selbstverständnis der Moderne*. Munich: Gerling Akademie.

Nicot, Jean. 1606. *Thresor de la langue françoyse, tant ancienne que moderne*. Paris: David Douceur.

Rigolot, François, ed. 1992. *Journal de voyage de Michel de Montaigne*. Paris: Presses Universitaires de France.

Solnit, Rebecca. 2005. *A Field Guide to Getting Lost*. London: Penguin Books.

11 The Expanding Space of the Train Carriage

A Phenomenological Reading of Michel Butor's *La Modification*

Caroline Rabourdin

Michel Butor, besides being one of the key early figures of the *Nouveau Roman*, was a keen traveller who enjoyed the privilege of free rail travel granted to family members of SNCF employees in France. For his third novel, *La modification*, he chose a train journey to measure the distance between two cities, Paris and Rome, through the narration of the protagonist's relationship with two women: his wife in Paris and his mistress in Rome. Butor is not only interested in the *genius loci* of a place – he wrote a series of descriptions of seven cities under the title *Le génie du lieu* (1958b) – but also in its relations to other places. Having lived in many different countries, he writes from experience and measures both the distances and the links between things. Visited locations are inscribed in a complex literary trajectory made of moments past, present and future. The novel is punctuated by the succession of train stations along the journey, and Butor makes interesting use of the physical or geographical distances separating them in order to test what Maurice Merleau-Ponty refers to as *lived* space.

In his essay "Le voyage et l'écriture," Butor proposes a new science to study human travel and literature which he astutely names *itérologie*. The word itself is a sort of displacement; from the Latin *iter* or passage, it connotes the notion of iteration or repetition of the travels through the medium of literature. If the essay touches upon something that permeates his works, it remains strangely detached from his fiction and does not attempt to analyse it explicitly. Instead, Butor sets out to list various forms of travel here and various forms of literature there, like an *inventaire à la Prévert*. But perhaps one of the prime realizations of the essay is that for him, *travelling is writing and writing is travelling*, and so, by extension, *reading is travelling and travelling is reading*.

Gare de Lyon, Fontainebleau, Montereau, Saint-Julien-du-Sault, Joigny, Laroche-Migennes, Laumes-Alésia, Darcey, Dijon, Chevrey-Chambertin, Fontaines-Mercurey, Varennes-le-Grand, Senozan, Pont-de-Veyle, Polliat, Bourg… the train itinerary is referred to many times throughout the novel and has subsequently been published as a timetable by Françoise

Van Rossum-Guyon in *Critique du roman* (1970). There she lists more than forty train stations and some twenty-one hours of travel, which unfold over the 236 pages of the novel. If the itinerary covers a territory that is measurable, the narration is not limited to the visited train stations and projects us far beyond. Butor uses words – and the many surfaces of the train carriage – to *project* the reader onto other worlds, and his novel performs and epitomizes what Merleau-Ponty (1969) considers to be the very virtue of language, which is to *project* us to what it signifies. He invites the readers to take their place in the train, and in the following pages, we will see how the main protagonist's body – and by extension that of the reader – is put in the centre of the narrative and is a requisite to our spatial literary experience, as it is through the body that lived distances as well as our sense of movement are understood. Butor's novel starts with these words:

> Vous avez mis le pied gauche sur la rainure de cuivre, et de votre épaule droite vous essayez en vain de pousser un peu plus le panneau coulissant. Vous vous introduisez par l'étroite ouverture en vous frottant contre ses bords, puis, votre valise couverte de granuleux cuir sombre couleur d'épaisse bouteille, votre valise assez petite d'homme habitué aux longs voyages, vous l'arrachez par sa poignée collante, avec vos doigts qui se sont échauffés, si peu lourde qu'elle soit, de l'avoir portée jusqu'ici, vous la soulevez et vous sentez vos muscles et vos tendons se dessiner non seulement dans vos phalanges, dans votre paume, votre poignet et votre bras, mais dans votre épaule aussi, dans toute la moitié du dos et dans vos vertèbres depuis votre cou jusqu'aux reins.
>
> (1957, 7)

> [Standing with your left foot on the grooved brass sill, you try in vain with your right shoulder to push the sliding door a little wider open. You edge your way in through the narrow opening, then you lift up your suitcase of bottle-green grained leather, the smallish suitcase of a man used to making long journeys, grasping the sticky handle with fingers that are hot from having carried even so light a weight so far, and you feel the muscles and tendons tense not only in your finger-joints, the palm of your hand, your wrist and your arm, but in your shoulder too, all down one side of your back along your vertebrae from neck to loins.]
>
> (Butor 1958a, 9)

Butor's phenomenological approach to writing and reading was first brought to light by Lois Oppenheim in 1980, in her book *Intentionality and Intersubjectivity: A Phenomenological Study of Butor's La Modification*. There she reveals, having corresponded with the author about the project, that, unsurprisingly perhaps, Butor had been the pupil of both Merleau-Ponty and Gaston Bachelard and also studied Martin Heidegger and Edmund Husserl's writings "with so much passion" (Oppenheim 1980, 8).

About the use of the second person plural pronoun in *La modification*, Oppenheim writes that it "assumes the presence of the reader," who becomes not only "the accomplice in the action of the novel, but in a sense, is named as the protagonist as well" (Oppenheim 1980, 31). But this *vous*, entering the train, is not just the main protagonist; he is an *embodied* protagonist. In these first few lines, Butor refers to your left foot, your right shoulder, your fingers, muscles, tendons, phalanxes, your palm, wrist and arm, shoulder again, half your back, vertebrae, neck and kidneys, bringing awareness to the reader's entire body by enumerating every part of it from foot to neck. This body, our body, is essential to the understanding of space, and, as Merleau-Ponty puts it, "there would be no space at all for me if I had no body" (1962, 102), and despite evincing a lifelong fascination for Descartes's work on optics and geometry, he writes:

> L'espace n'est plus celui dont parle la Dioptrique, réseau de relations entre objets, tel que le verrait un tiers témoin de ma vision, ou un géomètre qui la reconstruit et la survole, c'est un espace compté à partir de moi comme point zéro de la spatialité. Je ne le vois pas selon son enveloppe extérieure, je le vis du dedans, j'y suis englobé. Après tout, le monde est autour de moi, non devant moi.
>
> (Merleau-Ponty 1964a, 59)

> [Space is no longer what it was in the Dioptric, a network of relations between objects such as would be seen by a witness to my vision or by a geometer looking over it and reconstructing it from outside. It is, rather, a space reckoned starting from me as the zero point or degree zero of spatiality. I do not see it according to its exterior envelope; I live in it from the inside; I am immersed in it. After all, the world is all around me, not in front of me.]
>
> (Merleau-Ponty 1964b, 178)

So if space is assessed from the body as point zero, in the opening sentence of *La modification*, Butor puts the reader of the novel himself in the zero position by dint of the first word "vous," and its recurrence "vous vous" at the start of the second sentence. Thus, the reader's body becomes the point zero of reference for the ensuing spatial experience that the novel unfolds.

L'espace du roman, an essay published seven years after *La modification*, in 1964, is instrumental in articulating Butor's conception of space. For him, the space of the novel is also a lived space that starts from, and extends to, the space of reading. Thus, the sofa in your living room, the chair in the library or the seat in the train where you might be reading the novel become points of departure for the space of the novel. In Butor's work, the reader's body is this point of departure. It is the point from which all distances are measured, as I will show in the first part of this chapter, as well as the place where movement is felt, or 'lived.'

Additionally it is worth noting a number of significant geographical specificities: firstly, the French rail network spreads over the country radially from Paris, with all trains departing from the capital city and, secondly, all distances to and from Paris on road signs and maps are measured from a specific point on the Parvis de Notre Dame on the Ile de la Cité, called the *point zéro des routes de France*, or *point kilomètrique zéro* (point zero of the road system in France or the kilometric point zero). Butor's novel starts with the body as point zero of the spatial experience, departing from the geographical point zero in France.

The first few pages of *La modification* are about settling into the train compartment at the Gare de Lyon, then checking the time on the platform clock and correcting it on your watch, then seeing the neighbouring train set off, and finally feeling the departure of your own train through a jolt of your own rather strained back (Butor 1957, 12).

The movement of the train is not viewed from the outside, it is not simply observed like that of the neighbouring train, but the stress is, once more, put onto the protagonist's and the reader's own body. The jolt that we feel tells us that we are moving; we are not calling on any muscular effort to set our body in motion like we would for walking, yet we are *in motion* on the train. The movement is a relative movement of displacement, which, although it does not call for any particular muscular effort, the author insists is felt through our body. This distinction is important and we will see later how being *in movement* and actually *moving* relate to a form of *literary* movement.

Butor wrote *La modification* in Switzerland, where he was teaching French Literature, but also History and Geography, subjects he was not familiar with at the time, to secondary school students in Geneva. He spent some time preparing for this new assignment, which might explain why the novel is imbued with numerous descriptions of key buildings and monuments, complete with precise historical and geographical details. Butor's interest in and fascination for cities is obvious but he could only write about one city when he had distanced himself from it: he would write about a city from another one.

> J'étais fasciné par les villes, je le suis toujours, mais j'ai pris un recul différent. Pour mieux voir et réfléchir, j'avais besoin de parler d'une ville depuis une autre. Ainsi j'ai écrit *Passage de Milan*, étude sur Paris, quand j'étais en Angleterre. *L'Emploi du temps*, qui se déroule en *Angleterre*, a été écrit à Paris et en Grèce.
>
> (Butor 2006, 58)

[I was fascinated by cities, and still am, but have a different out-
look now. In order to see better and understand, I needed to talk
about a city from another one. Thus, I wrote *Passage de Milan*, a
study of Paris, when I was in England. *L'Emploi du temps*, which is
set in England, was written in Paris and in Greece. (my translation)]

Butor travelled and lived in many different countries and eventually
settled in Lucinges, Haute Savoie, not very far from Geneva, in a house
he named *A l'écart*, meaning "away from," as if to put some distance
between himself and the rest of the world.

We have seen that Butor in *La modification* makes use of explicit physical
distances throughout the train journey as listed by Van Rossum-Guyon –
although here the emphasis is on time when the distance between cities
could also be expressed in kilometres. However, Butor, if he mentions the
various train stations in the course of the narration, really uses those geographical distances in order to test the *lived* distances by Merleau-Ponty
(Figure 11.1):

> Outre la distance physique ou géométrique qui existe entre moi et
> toutes choses, une distance vécue me relie aux choses qui comptent
> et existent pour moi et les relie entre elles.

(1945, 338)

Figure 11.1 Engraving by Albrecht Dürer in *Underweysung der Messung*
(Nuremberg 1525).

[Besides the physical and geometrical distance which stands between myself and all things, a 'lived' distance binds me to things which count and exist for me, and links them to each other.]

(1962, 333)

If we see a village in the distance, consisting of a church spire and a few houses, we can approximately tell the distance that separates us from the village, as well as the distance between the church and the other houses, yet we cannot deduce this distance from what we see alone. The image captured by our eyes is very much like that of a screen, and the distances can only be assessed because of our previous experience of movement. Because we are able to experience distances, i.e. move from one side of the room to the other, we are able to appreciate distances between ourselves and things as well as between things. We know the distance that separates us from the village because we have travelled similar distances before.

Butor's lived distances are expressed by the manipulation of those physical distances through various techniques borrowed from painting, photography and filmmaking. It should on this occasion be noted that Butor worked with an impressive number of artists throughout his writing career, mostly photographers and painters – curiously, it seems, no filmmakers – and produced over a thousand artists' books. He was therefore no stranger to these artistic practices and embraced them wholeheartedly. In *L'espace du roman*, he compares the novelist to a painter and writes:

Plantant son chevalet ou sa caméra dans un des points de l'espace évoqué, le romancier retrouvera tous les problèmes de cadrage, de composition et de perspective que rencontre le peintre. Comme lui, il pourra choisir entre un certain nombre de procédés pour exprimer la profondeur, l'un des plus simples étant la superposition claire de plusieurs de ces vues immobiles.

(1964, 53)

[Planting his easel or his camera in one of the parts of the space evoked, the novelist will rediscover all the problems of framing, of composition, and of perspective encountered by the painter. Like him, he may choose among a certain number of methods in order to express depth, one of the simplest being the obvious superimposition of several of these motionless views.]

(1970, 34)

In a 2008 interview, Butor notes that the writers associated with the movement of the *Nouveau Roman* were greatly aware that cinema had changed the way we see and perceive the world. He makes no secret of the use of cinematographic techniques in his work. I would, in this instance, question the translation of the French *caméra* into the English "camera" as he is probably referring to the moving image and the film camera – and not the *appareil photo*. We will see in the second part of this chapter how Butor depicts movement in the novel, but let us first bring our attention to the way in which he projects objects and people alike, located at various distances or depths, onto a single plane in the following extract:

> De retour à votre compartiment de première classe où vous étiez seul, apercevant la mer de temps en temps, vous avez repris les lettres de Julien l'Apostat que vous aviez laissées sur l'étagère, mais vous avez gardé le livre entre vos mains sans l'ouvrir, regardant passer la gare de Tarquinia et la ville au loin avec ses tours grises devant les montagnes arides, par la fenêtre ouverte qui laissait entrer quelque-fois une bouffée de sable avec l'air frais, puis fixant cette tache de soleil en forme de couperet qui s'étalait de plus en plus grande sur l'un des coussins.
>
> (1957, 205)

> [Back in your first class compartment where you were alone, with an occasional glimpse of the sea, you took up once more the letters of Julian the Apostate, which you had left on the shelf, but you held the book in your hands without opening it, looking out through the open window which sometimes let in a whiff of sand or the cool breeze, and watching the station of Tarquinia go by and the town in the distance with its grey towers outlined against the arid moun-tains, then staring at the wedge-shaped patch of sunlight that was gradually spreading over one of the cushions.]
>
> (1958a, 190)

Here, Butor gives us the immensity of the sea, the empire of Julian the Apostate, Tarquinia's train station, the grey town in the distance and the cushion of the seat in front of us, all in the space of a single sentence, as if to eventually flatten all distances into a single picture, a single plane. He uses the train window like the painter might use the surface of the can-vas or the photographer his photosensitive film, but he also makes use of the architecture of the train carriage *à compartiments* and its many surfaces. The train carriage is divided up into smaller compartments of six passengers distributed along a side corridor, and all the division pan-els would have windows through which you can see the adjacent space.

> En face de vous, entre l'ecclésiastique et la jeune femme gracieuse et tendre, à travers la vitre, à travers une autre vitre, vous apercevez as-sez distinctement l'intérieur d'un autre wagon de modèle plus ancien

aux bancs de bois jaune, aux filets de ficelle, dans la pénombre au-delà des reflets composés, un homme de la même taille que vous, dont vous ne sauriez ni préciser l'âge, ni décrire avec exactitude les vêtements, qui reproduit avec plus de lenteur encore les gestes fatigués que vous venez d'accomplir.

(1957, 10)

[Opposite you, between the cleric and the graceful, gentle young woman, through one window and another window beyond it, you can dimly make out, in another less up-to-date coach with yellow wooden seats and string racks, in the half darkness beyond the composite reflections, a man of your height, whose exact age you could not guess and whose clothes you could not describe with any precision, reproducing even more slowly than yourself the weary movements you have just made.]

(1958a, 12)

Furthermore, some of those surfaces also have mirrors and, indeed, the previous extract in which the man in front repeats "your own" movements may be seen as a *delayed* mirror. Lucien Dallenbach (1977, 16) writes extensively about Butor's use of mirrors in *Le récit spéculaire*. He describes the use of mirrors as a process of *mise en abyme* and interprets them as signs and symbols, which were often associated with the *Nouveau Roman* at the time. But he also explicitly rejects upfront any reference to the idea of depth, infinity or vertigo in his analysis, which I think are quintessential to Butor's work. Butor is very precise in his descriptions; in the above extract, for instance, the man seen through layers of glass in the compartment ahead is of the exact same height as the main protagonist, and repeats the exact same movements in the distance.

For Merleau-Ponty, depth is the most "existential" dimension as, contrary to height and width, it is not registered on the eye's retina, and is the result of our experience of space.

[La profondeur] est, pour ainsi dire, de toutes les dimensions, la plus "existentielle", parce que – c'est ce qu'il y a de vrai dans l'argument de Berkeley – elle ne se marque pas sur l'objet lui-même, elle appartient de toute évidence à la perspective et non aux choses [...] elle annonce un certain lien indissoluble entre les choses et moi par lequel je suis situé devant elles, tandis que la largeur peut, à première vue, passer pour une relation entre les choses elles-mêmes où le sujet percevant n'est pas impliqué.

(1945, 305)

[[Depth] is, so to speak, the most 'existential' of all dimensions, because (and here Berkeley's argument is right) it is not impressed upon the object itself, it quite clearly belongs to the perspective and not to things. [...] It announces a certain indissoluble link between things and myself by which I am placed in front of them, whereas breadth can, at first sight, pass for a relationship between things themselves, in which the perceiving subject is not implied.]

(1962, 298)

As noted earlier, the image captured by our eyes is a single image, very much like that of a screen, without any indication of depth. An object in the distance will appear to our eye smaller than it really is and we can only infer its true dimensions by assessing its distance from us. Merleau-Ponty shows a certain admiration for the work of Descartes on optics, which he often returns to. For Merleau-Ponty, it is the effort of convergence our eyes need to make in order to see the object in focus which enables us to assess this distance. From the rotation angle of our eyes reaching the object, we conclude its distance from us and effectively take note of our relationship and motivation to the object (Figure 11.2).

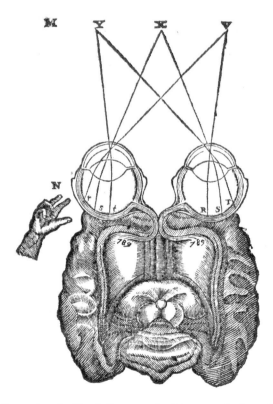

Figure 11.2 Engraving in René Descartes's *Discours de la méthode* (Paris: Théodore Girard, 1667).

However, limiting our understanding of depth and distances to our eyes alone seems rather reductive and neglects the complexity of our bodily and spatial experience. In *Phénoménologie de la perception*, Merleau-Ponty dedicates a whole chapter to what he calls "La spatialité du corps propre et la motricité," translated as "The Spatiality of One's Own Body and Motricity," where he shows that our understanding of space is the result of our experience of movement. For him, "it is clearly in action that the spatiality of the body is brought about, and the analysis of movement itself should allow us to understand spatiality better" (Merleau-Ponty 2012, 105).

Recent neurological studies confirm this idea and, in his book *Le sens du mouvement*, physiologist Alain Berthoz (1997) explains how various parts of the body are involved in spatial cognition and also, of course, our sense of movement. He repeatedly acknowledges the relevance of Merleau-Ponty's theories and also quotes eminent mathematician Henri Poincaré, whose essays on the philosophy of science are particularly enlightening. Poincaré clearly demonstrates the idea, which Berthoz later validates, that to localize an object in space *"we represent to ourselves the movements that must take place to reach that object"* (1905, 67; emphasis in original), i.e. we imagine the sensations of the muscular efforts we would have to make to get to the object. Our understanding of space is not purely geometrical and regulated by optical laws, it is also generated by motor activity and we take measure of our relation to things through bodily sensations.

In parentheses, I would like to note the relevance of the imperial measuring system. It uses feet and inches, i.e. bodily units, rather than the somehow remote ten-millionth part of one quarter of the meridian as a unit of measure, which is the basis of the metric system. The metre, which no longer takes the body as frame of reference but the earth on which we live, is the result of an empirical strategy in which the earth becomes the object of study and the focus of investigations, but where we ultimately forget our relationship to it. The foot, in comparison, constitutes not only a bodily unit of reference, but is also in direct contact with the earth it measures. The foot, as well as being a measuring unit, is also an essential part of the body's motricity.

So we have seen that taking measure of distances calls for an active participation of the reader to reach that which is described and involves more than vision alone; it calls for an active *effort* on the part of the reader. When we see the grey town in the distance, beyond the station of Tarquinia, not only do our eyes converge, but we also *represent* the *muscular efforts* necessary to reach [rejoindre] the town, we make what I will call, for the time being, an *effort of projection*.

After having published *La modification*, Butor decided to abandon the novel to the great dismay of his publishers, and also distanced himself from the literary movement of the *Nouveau Roman*, preferring instead to embrace other forms of writing. But in the essay *L'espace du roman*, published a few years later in 1964, he writes that every novel is in fact a form of travel:

> Toute fiction s'inscrit donc en notre espace comme voyage, et l'on peut dire à cet égard que c'est là le thème fondamental de toute littérature romanesque; tout roman qui nous raconte un voyage est donc plus clair, plus explicite que celui qui n'est pas capable d'exprimer métaphoriquement cette distance entre le lieu de la lecture et celui où nous emmène le récit.
>
> (Butor 1964, 50)

> [All fiction, then, is inscribed in our space as a voyage, and we may say in this regard that this is the fundamental theme of all novels; every novel which describes a journey is thus clearer, more explicit, than one which is not capable of expressing metaphorically that distance.]
>
> (Butor 1970, 32)

Butor's choice of the train journey for *La modification* can be seen as a direct application of the novel as travel, yet his essay introduces another travelling dimension: it establishes a link between the place of reading and the place where the story takes us. Butor explains how at the time of reading a spatial translation or displacement of the reader occurs. But what follows is more intriguing, if not slightly puzzling. In the next paragraph he writes: "A partir du moment où le lointain me devient proche, c'est ce qui était proche qui prend le pouvoir du lointain, qui m'apparaît comme encore plus lointain" (1964, 50) ["The moment what is distant becomes near to me, it is what was near that assumes the power of what was distant, that seems even more distant to me" (Butor 1970, 33)]. The analogy with the *mise au point* or focal adjustment of a camera springs to mind, with its ability to focus on what is far whilst rendering what is near blurry and vice versa. But as we have seen earlier in this chapter, the shift between what is near and what is far is not purely visual but also involves an effort of projection on the part of the reader, who will represent to himself the muscular efforts required to reach a certain point. If we project ourselves to the village in the distance, we 'forget' about our immediate surroundings; we effectively shift our frame of reference from the chair we sit on to that new point in the distance, which in turn becomes the new point zero of reference. Once we locate our own body in the village, all new measures are taken from that new point of departure.

In *Intentionality and Intersubjectivity*, Oppenheim (1980, 87) suggests that the reader experiences two types of spatial displacements: one which she claims is *outside* the text, whilst the other is *inside* the text. I would argue that there is no such clear distinction between displacement outside and inside the text and instead would suggest considering the successive shifts of frame of reference in the act of reading as a continuous series of *repositionings*, much like the various stops of an itinerary.

Eventually the distance, as Butor explains, is measured between the reader and the text and we have seen that a displacement within the text involves a repositioning of the reader, which is felt through his body if he is to be spatially aware. So the reader or, in the case of *La modification, you* travel and project yourself from your chair to the city of Rome and, throughout the story, a succession of shifts and repositionings occur from your place of reading and back again. You follow an itinerary, a certain trajectory.

A distinction between various types of displacements, however, may be seen in the *effectuation* of movement and muscular effort as opposed to their *representation*. The reader keeps moving whether it is inside or outside the text, and whether he be physically moving or not. Some movements require muscular effort, others the *representation* of muscular effort, whilst others still require no effort at all. Instead of the categorization proposed by Butor for his *itérologie* – where he writes about nomadism, exodus, emigration, the return trip, the leisure trip, the business trip, the foreign country, the return to the home country or pilgrimages – I therefore suggest studying movements according to their degree of *effort*.

Merleau-Ponty in *Phénoménologie de la perception* marks a distinction between relative movement and absolute movement, and concludes that it is our ability to shift between frames of reference which enables us to experience relative movement: "The relativity of movement is reduced to the power we have of changing domains within the large world" (2012, 293). Merleau-Ponty uses the words "domain" and, in the following sentence, "milieu," which are indeterminate and do not necessarily reflect the egocentric nature of the phenomenon. When we change position, we do not simply enter a pre-existing milieu but create a new environment, with new relationships with the surrounding elements, which is unique and particular to us. For this reason, I would rather use the term 'frame of reference,' and centre that frame – here not intended as two-dimensional but multidimensional – on the body. Merleau-Ponty further uses the word "power," which seems stronger than "ability" and also suggests a degree of intentionality. To explain this notion, he writes about the movement of the train:

> Je peux voir à volonté mon train ou le train voisin en mouvement si je ne fais rien ou si je m'interroge sur les illusions du mouvement. Mais "quand je joue aux cartes dans mon compartiment, je vois bouger le train voisin, même si c'est en réalité le mien qui part; quand je regarde l'autre train et que j'y cherche quelqu'un, c'est alors mon propre train qui démarre". Le compartiment où nous avons élu

domicile est "en repos", ses parois sont "verticales" et le paysage défile devant nous, dans une côte les sapins vus à travers la fenêtre nous apparaissent obliques.

(1945, 331)

[I am free to see my train or the neighboring train moving, whether I do nothing or whether I examine myself on the illusions of movement. But: "When I am playing cards in my compartment, I see the train move on the next track even if it is in reality my own train which is moving, but when I am looking at the other train, searching perhaps for an acquaintance in the coach, then it is my own train that seems to be moving." The compartment where we take up residence is "at rest," its walls are "vertical," and the landscape passes by in front of us; on one side the fir trees seen through the window appear to us as diagonal.]

(2012, 292)

Merleau-Ponty's description of the train in movement, in which he quotes psychologist Kurt Koffka, is one many readers will have experienced. Here he proposes an explanation of the phenomenon, which I would like to expand upon and relate to our reading of *La modification*. We have already seen how Butor deals with the departure of the train at the Gare de Lyon in Paris; how the protagonist first settles in the train carriage; how the departure is felt through the protagonist's body instead of being described purely visually. We see now why 'settling in' is such an essential phase to the spatial experience and appreciation of movement. By settling into the carriage, Butor invites the reader to move away from his place of reading and take his place in the carriage, which itself is about to move. He has invited you to shift your frame of reference onto the train. But in the end, we can equally see the train of Leon Delmont, the main character, moving, or the landscape in the window moving, depending on whether we choose to return to the chair we are reading in or remain in Leon's seat in the carriage, whether we *feel* our body on the chair in the library or whether we *feel* that it is in the carriage. This shift is exemplified in the following extract:

De l'autre côté du corridor, une onze chevaux noire démarre devant une église, suit une route qui longe la voie, rivalise avec vous de vitesse, se rapproche, s'éloigne, disparaît derrière un bois, reparaît, traverse un petit fleuve avec ses saules et une barque abandonnée, se laisse distancer, rattrape le chemin perdu, puis s'arrête à un carrefour, tourne et s'enfuit vers un village dont le clocher bientôt s'efface derrière un repli de terrain. Passe la gare de Montereau.

(Butor 1957, 20)

[Beyond the corridor, a small black car starts off in front of a church, follows a road alongside the railway, races the train, draws near, moves away, disappears behind a wood, reappears, crosses a little river with willow trees and a deserted boat, drops behind, catches up, then halts at a cross-road, turns off and escapes towards a village the steeple of which soon vanishes behind a fold of land. Montereau station has gone by.]

(Butor 1958a, 20)

Here, Butor uses the cinematic technique of the 'cut' to splice two 'shots' together when the dynamic landscape suddenly gives way to Montereau station. The *onze chevaux* is the subject of the first sentence, and to understand its movement, we need to make an effort of projection, take a seat in the car and drive alongside the tracks, but in the same breath, we are briefly reminded ("rivalise avec vous de vitesse") that we are in fact in the train and that the train is moving; the reminder is short-lived, though, and we find ourselves back on the road.

Passe la gare de Montereau. This sentence is the last of the paragraph and produces a strange feeling. In itself the statement is not unusual and could easily be read and understood, although of course we know that the train station itself does not move. The uncanny feeling comes from the fact that one's position has abruptly and surreptitiously shifted. Consecutive shifts of the point of reference have taken place in this paragraph. The train station, which we know to be static, is presented as moving; this can only mean that we have moved back into the carriage, which is rendered as static, immobile, for this is where the author wants us to take residence again. The shift is abrupt, brutal, and requires an active participation from the reader. What appears like a simple juxtaposition of times and places actually demands of the reader an effort of translation, of readjustment, of repositioning. The effort we make to move between the outside of the train and back into the carriage is contained in the effort we make to move between (and even within) paragraphs. The novel is awash with these juxtapositions, carefully crafted along specific patterns, and with each and every new paragraph the reader undergoes yet a further spatial displacement.

Finally, the distinction between relative and absolute movement referred to by Merleau-Ponty has become hazy, for every movement, relative or absolute, is lived and felt through our own body, whether it be through direct effective effort or through an effort of projection. Movement, as Merleau-Ponty has shown, is never inherent to an object and is understood, as Poincaré notes, through the 'correlative' movement of the viewer, so one might argue that there is no absolute movement and only a plethora of relative movements.

In *Phénoménologie de la perception*, Merleau-Ponty notes that some subjects suffering from cerebral pathologies lack the essential ability to

imagine themselves elsewhere or are unable to 'mime' a simple action –
of cutting a piece of paper with scissors, for instance, when they are perfectly able to cut it if they hold the scissors in their hand. Merleau-Ponty
infers that the normal subject has the ability to 'project' himself into a
situation, whether it be in time or space:

> La fonction normale qui rend possible le mouvement abstrait est une
> fonction de "projection" par laquelle le sujet du mouvement ménage
> devant lui un espace libre où ce qui n'existe pas naturellement puisse
> prendre un semblant d'existence.

> (1945, 142)

> [The normal function that makes abstract movement possible is
> a function of "projection" by which the subject of movement orga-
> nizes before himself a free space in which things that do not exist
> naturally can take on a semblance of existence.]

> (2012, 114)

Beyond the window, Butor develops [ménage] a space where the reader is
able to project himself. So by measuring the distance that separates him
from the town of Tarquinia, the reader is also able to reach it [la rejoindre],
to *join it in the distance*, and the gust of sand that enters the compartment
no doubt adds to the sensory experience. The juxtapositions and manipulations of distances that were referred to in the earlier parts of this chapter are
pushed to their paroxysm when, towards the end of the novel, Butor proposes to *actually* superimpose the cities of Rome and Paris, one under the
ground of the other, linked to one another by a series of hatches (1957, 280).
   This new geographic paradigm in which the two cities are directly
connected is the result of the realization by the author that the world
has lost its centre, that the Roman Empire is no more and that Paris
has lost its lustre. The psychological shift described in the book as the
main protagonist decides against his initial plan to abandon his wife
and live with his mistress is in fact accompanied by an important geographical shift. *La modification* is above all a spatial – and temporal –
modification in which distances are problematized. When Butor finally
decides against his radical scheme to superimpose the two cities, he argues that the distance between them is essential and should be kept. The
distance travelled is not only part of the experience, but it has made the
experience of travelling possible. Without the distance, there would be
no train journey, without the distance there would be no book: the novel
would not exist, nor would the idea of it. The distance has made the
book happen. *La modification* ends with these words:

> Le mieux, sans doute, serait de conserver à ces deux villes leur rela-
> tions géographiques réelles et de tenter de faire revivre sur le mode de

la lecture cet épisode crucial de votre aventure, le mouvement qui s'est produit dans votre esprit accompagnant le déplacement de votre corps d'une gare à l'autre à travers tous les paysages intermédiaires, vers ce livre futur et nécessaire dont vous tenez la forme dans votre main.

Le couloir est vide. Vous regardez la foule sur le quai. Vous quittez le compartiment.

(1957, 285–286)

[The best thing, surely, would be to preserve the actual geographical relationship between these two cities, and to try and bring to life in the form of literature this crucial episode in your experience, the movement that went on in your mind while your body was being transferred from one station to another through all the intermediate landscapes, towards this book, this future necessary book of which you're holding in your hand the outward form.

The corridor is empty. You look at the crowd of people on the platform. You go out of the compartment.]

(1958a, 264)

So the journey will take the form of the book, the form of the novel, the novel as travel. And again, in the last sentence of the novel, the spatial paradigm is brought back to the reader, point zero of the spatial paradigm. We leave the compartment to return to the space of reading, and Butor leaves the novel to explore other forms of writing.

References

Berthoz, Alain. 1997. *Le sens du mouvement*. Paris: Odile Jacob.
Butor, Michel. 1957. *La modification*. Paris: Editions de Minuit.
———. 1958a. *Second Thoughts*. Translated by Jean Stewart. London: Faber & Faber.
———. 1958b. *Le génie du lieu*. Paris: Grasset.
———. 1964. *L'espace du roman*. Paris: Les Editions de Minuit.
———. 1970. *The Space of the Novel*. Translated by Gerald Fabian. London: Jonathan Cape.
———. 1974. "Le voyage et l'écriture." In *Répertoire IV*. Paris: Les Editions de Minuit.
———. 2006. *Michel Butor: L'écriture nomade*. Edited by Marie Odile Germain and Marie Minssieux-Chamonard. Paris: Bibliothèque Nationale de France.
———. 2008. TV interview with Sumana Sinha. Auteurs TV.
Dallenbach, Lucien. 1977. *Le récit spéculaire*. Paris: Editions du Seuil.
Merleau-Ponty, Maurice. 1945. *Phénoménologie de la perception*. Paris: Gallimard.
———. 1962. *Phenomenology of Perception*. Translated by Colin Smith. London: Routledge.
———. 1964a. *L'œil et l'esprit*. Paris: Gallimard.

————. 1964b. "Eye and Mind." In *The Primacy of Perception and other Essays on Phenomenological Psychology*, edited by James M. Edie and translated by Carleton Dallery, 159–190. Evanston: Northwestern University Press.

————. 1969. *La prose du monde*. Paris: Gallimard.

————. 2012. *Phenomenology of Perception*. Translated by Donald A. Landes. London: Routledge.

Oppenheim, Lois. 1980. *Intentionality and Intersubjectivity: A Phenomenological Study of Butor's La modification*. Lexington: French Forum Publishers.

Poincaré, Henri. 1905. *Science and Hypothesis*. London: The Walter Scott Publishing Co. Ltd.

Van Rossum-Guyon, Françoise. 1970. *Critique du roman: Essai sur La modification de Michel Butor*. Paris: Gallimard.

Part V
Late Modernity and the Spatialized Self

12 The Reader, the Writer, the Text
Traversing Spaces in Frank McCourt's *Angela's Ashes*

Elizabeth Kollmann

If Frank McCourt's *Angela's Ashes* (1996) is not to be regarded as a return to the modern as such, Irish literary scholars would certainly agree that, at the least, it is a return to James Joyce. James Phelan, for example, has maintained that "one of the important precursor texts for *Angela's Ashes* is *A Portrait of the Artist as a Young Man*" (2005, 75) and Peter Lenz that "the protagonist's psychological development calls to the reader's mind several parallels from Joyce's autobiographical novel" (2000, 412). To be sure, they are not identical – while Lenz argues that in *Angela's Ashes* precedence is given to childlike narration over artistic sophistication (412), Phelan posits that McCourt uses different literary devices from Joyce to depict the maturation of the subject (76). In addition to drawing parallels with Joyce in particular, theorists have claimed that McCourt's writing features elements of the Irish literary tradition in general. This includes the way in which "McCourt employs syntactical and idiomatic elements of Anglo-Irish writing" (Lenz 2000, 411) as well as the fact that he portrays "stereotypical Irish characters and the woes that beset them" (Mitchell 2003, 615).

While it clearly lies beyond the scope of this chapter to analyze the various ways in which McCourt has perpetuated the Irish narrative tradition at large, I would like to briefly address the similarities between *A Portrait of the Artist as a Young Man* and *Angela's Ashes*. Comparing these narratives reveals how the interplay of the real and the fictitious conveys the protagonists' sense of displacement. It also brings to the fore the fact that both authors went into voluntary exile, Joyce leaving Ireland for continental Europe and McCourt seeking his fortunes in America. A further analogy that can be made, and which is of greater significance than the condition itself, is the *effect* exile had on these artists and their work. Both Joyce and McCourt, it seems, drew inspiration from the places they grew up in and used it as the main source for their writing. Martin Tucker, for one, has argued that "in his new surroundings in the metropolis [the colonized writer] gains strength from his memory of what he has fled, and he uses material of early life for the substance of his work" (1991, xx). As an example he mentions Joyce: "[this] pattern is suggestive of James Joyce who, adopting the creed of silence, exile, and cunning, wandered through Europe but never forsook the land of his birth" (1991, xx).

Because memories of their youth are stimulated by the condition of exile, it is only natural that authors like Joyce and McCourt write about their home. *Angela's Ashes* is an exemplar of letting the home you leave behind be the inspiration for your writing. Such was the extent to which he was fuelled by the memory of what he had left behind that McCourt, a late starter, shot to fame and fortune at the age of 66. The book enjoyed tremendous success, both in public and literary circles. It was on the *New York Times* Best Seller list for more than two years and won numerous prizes, including the Pulitzer Prize for Biography/Autobiography and the National Book Critics Circle Award (Mitchell 2003, 608). In 1999, it was made into a feature film directed by Alan Parker, and by February 2014 it had, according to Heather Greenwood Davis, sold "tens of millions of copies and [been] translated into more than 30 languages" (2014, par. 3).[1]

As intimated before, this immensely popular book was not only written in exile, but is also about exile. Subtitled *A Memoir of a Childhood*, it is a recollection of the author's years of growing up with a despairing mother, a mostly inebriated father and six scabby-kneed siblings in the Ireland of the 1930s and 1940s. Frank McCourt's story begins (for all intents and purposes)[2] in New York in 1930, the year of his birth. This is where his Irish parents have emigrated to in the hope of a better future, and where the protagonist spends the first four years of his life. But the constant struggle to get by financially, combined with the tragic death of Frankie's baby sister Margaret, leads to the family's returning to Ireland. While life in Brooklyn was marked by hardship, back in Limerick the situation is hopeless. Frankie's father drinks up most of their income and finally deserts his family for good, leaving his mother, Angela, to eke out an existence for her family by relying on charity and favours. Frank's twin brothers Oliver and Eugene die in short succession of each other, while the remaining four children (Frank, Malachy, Michael and Alphie) have to fight to survive in a town rife with squalor, disease and abject poverty. To make matters worse, Frank comes up against self-righteous Catholicism, a tyrannical school system and other forms of the establishment. The only thought that keeps him going is that he will get out of Limerick one day and go back to America, where he came from.

From the foregoing it may be gleaned that the way in which spatiality affects the individual's sense of self plays a significant role in the narrative. While the protagonist's sense of displacement will then also be the starting point of my argument concerning the performative nature of McCourt's text, this is not what I will be focusing on in this chapter. Instead, what I want to pay special attention to is the way in which the space that is created – or better said, re-created in the text – affects *the reader,* should he or she discover any inaccuracies or inconsistencies in its portrayal, and how this ties in with the protagonist's own experience of spatiality. To this end, I will argue that the strong reactions *Angela's Ashes* invoked when it first was published are, in the first place, an effect of the way in which McCourt conflates fact and fiction and plays with the autobiographical pact.[3] Further, I posit that the reader's dissatisfaction with the space created in the text mirrors the narrator-protagonist's own discontent with his spatial surroundings and, with that, his sense of unease.

Despite receiving predominantly favourable reviews, the reaction to *Angela's Ashes* was not unanimously positive. In fact, when the book came out, there were some Limerickians who made strong objection to its contents and accused McCourt of making libellous claims and of saying disparaging things about their town and its people. In response to the online magazine *Slate*, who asked a number of memoirists to write (among others) about how they handled readers who had a different recollection of the events they wrote about in their narratives, McCourt answered thus:

> When the book was published in Ireland, I was denounced from hill, pulpit, and barstool. Certain citizens claimed I had disgraced the fair name of the city of Limerick, that I had attacked the church, that I had despoiled my mother's name, and that if I returned to Limerick, I would surely be found hanging from a lamppost.
> [...].
> The only way around all this nervousness is the novel—and that's what I'm trying now. Yes, yes, I still have to cover my tracks—and my ass—but I'll have greater freedom.
>
> (McCourt 2007, par. 2–4)

Confronted with the problem of referentiality,[4] McCourt decides to make his next project a novel (albeit one he does not complete). By making such a decision, what he is effectively saying is that crossing the boundaries between fact and fiction is more complicated and has more far-reaching consequences when writing an autobiography than when creating a novel. As will become apparent, this idea has to do primarily with the complexities surrounding the notion of autobiographical truth. In order to provide some explanation as to why exactly McCourt's narrative might have unsettled some readers, in what follows I discuss the reactions to his memoir in detail as well as look at the problematic relationship between truth and autobiography. I ask if and to what extent this exilic text, located somewhere between the real and the fictional world, manages to convey the subject's sense of displacement, and finish off by analyzing the relationship between exile, the shiftiness of the text and the reader's discomfort.

A good starting point is the discontent surrounding the alleged fictionality of (parts of) *Angela's Ashes*. *Slate* (quoted before) is just one
of many online sources interested in McCourt and the notion of truth.
Another is *Mail Online*, who asked in their heading whether "Frank
McCourt [was] REALLY telling the truth" or whether he was "A miserable liar" (Brennan 2009). The article, which revolves around the anger that manifested itself when *Angela's Ashes* first came out, quotes
inhabitants of Limerick as accusing McCourt of being "'a conman and
a hoaxer' [who had] 'prostituted' his own mother in his quest for literary stardom, by turning her into a downtrodden harlot who committed
incest in his book" (2009, par. 5). Further the report reveals how the
lobby had added up the number of fabrications or inconsistencies in the
text to come up with "a total of '117 lies or inaccuracies' in the 426-
page book" (2009, par. 23). One major concern was Limerick's portrayal as filthy and dilapidated, another was defamation. In addition
to "wrongly accusing one local man of being a Peeping Tom" (2009,
par. 23), *Angela's Ashes* tainted the reputation of a young woman by
purporting that she had had sex with Frank when she was already in
advanced stages of tuberculosis. In addition, townspeople demanded
an embargo on the movie based on McCourt's book (2009, par. 23)
while "Limerick broadcaster Gerry Hannan spearheaded a campaign
against Angela's Ashes" (2009, par. 28). In his article "Memoir Lashed,
and Loved," Kevin Cullen writes that "[Hannan's] literary retort to
McCourt's book is one of his own called 'Ashes,' a title that he says [...]
was a coincidence" (1997, A.1). Other instances that underscore the indignation over the memoir[5] include an episode in which an erstwhile
schoolmate of Frank McCourt, Paddy Malone, encountered the writer at a
book-signing event and "denounced him while tearing up a paperback
copy of the book" (1997, A.1) and the fact that "[t]he local newspaper,
The Limerick Leader, has made disparaging McCourt a regular feature"
(1997, A.1).[6]

One might wonder how the newspaper, for one, could have missed the
significant detail that McCourt's book was designated a *memoir*. Shannon Forbes believes it is important that *Angela's Ashes* was published
with the subtitle *A Memoir of a Childhood* after it "was at first alter-
nately identified as fiction and as autobiography" (2007, 474). This shows
that the author realized that there was a distinction between autobiography and memoir, the latter, according to Forbes, referring to the way past
experiences are fashioned in our subjective memory. Further, by designating his work as memoir, McCourt managed to exempt himself from any
claims to its truth-value, since it is a non sequitur that a memoir – that
is, a subjective account of what we recall – can be fallacious (473–474).
That Forbes is right in assuming McCourt made an informed choice
regarding the classification of his text has been corroborated by the author himself: "In many ways I was guided by Gore Vidal, who said in

his memoir, *Palimpsest*, that an autobiography is the attempt to recreate the facts of your life – your memoir is your impression of your life. The facts are there, but then what impression did they leave?" (quoted in Mitchell 2003, 614).[7] Though Forbes, then, clearly has a point, it has to be stressed that the difference between the terms *memoir* and *autobiography* is academic,[8] and although McCourt might have been aware of it, the majority of his readers evidently was *not*, which may partly explain the vehement protest he came up against. In hindsight, he might have avoided some of the unpleasantness by furnishing his writing with some sort of precautionary note, like Laurie Lee does in *Cider with Rosie*:

> NOTE
> Some parts of this book were originally published in *Orion, Encounter, The Queen* and *The Cornhill*, and two other fragments have been adapted from pieces first written for *Leader Magazine* and *The Geographical Magazine*. The book is a recollection of early boyhood, and *some of the facts may be distorted by time.*
>
> (1965, 8, emphasis added)

But maybe McCourt did not *want* to shun confrontation. His official response to the rigorous criticism was that he could not allow himself to bother about such matters. He had related the events as he saw them, as *Mail Online* reports (Brennan 2009, par. 35). While *Mail Online* asks if "McCourt [crossed] the line between fact and fiction" (2009, par. 22), my own interest does not lie in determining whether parts of *Angela's Ashes* are fake or not, nor in deciding if the citizens of Limerick were harsh in their condemnation of McCourt. The question I would like to ask is *why* there was such a degree of indignation about the truth-value of the book.[9] Why, in other words, does the truth matter so much, and why is the border between fact and fiction patrolled so heavily? More pertinent still, is there any correlation between the reader's discontent and that of the author? Put differently, does the intertwining of fact and fiction undergird the writer's sense of displacement to such an extent that his unease becomes palpable, so much so that it is transferred to the reader?

In his work on twentieth-century British literary autobiography, Brian Finney looks at the complex nature of veracity with specific reference to life writing. He observes the evolution of "what is seen as the truth" (Finney 1985, 21), and looks at how it has impacted on autobiography from the Middle Ages up to the contemporary period (1985, 21–23). He starts off with St Augustine's *Confessions*, which upholds the medieval doctrine of giving precedence to religion over one's self and of being true to God. According to Finney, the first real breach with this way of viewing the world came only much later when Jean-Jacques Rousseau in the late eighteenth century conveyed, in and through his writing, that what ultimately mattered was to focus on and defer to the self. In the following era, however, "this defiantly individualist definition of the truth" (1985, 22) fell out of favour with the Victorians, who preferred "to focus on a historically factual and publically shared conception of the self" (1985, 22). This manner of thinking was, however, completely reversed with the arrival of Freud and his work on the unconscious. Freud radically changed the way man saw himself, and in the twentieth century it was no longer believed that the subject can be known in its entirety. That is, since there is always some part that will remain foreign and inaccessible to us, we as subjects can never access the whole truth about our selves. This, says Finney, is the reason why modern autobiographers doubt the truth-value of their memories and do not believe it possible to write a comprehensive narrative about their past. Instead, they opt for highlighting certain past happenings while commenting on the significance these have had for them in order to impart their true character.

Autobiographical truth is justifiably complex, not only because it has undergone major conceptual changes through the ages, but also because it is concerned with the meaning a writer attributes to facts or past happenings, and not just with the events themselves. Another facet of life writing that complicates the already dubious nature of truth pertains to the fragile nature of the virtual pact between the writer and the reader. In "Otobiographies: The Teaching of Nietzsche and the Politics of the Proper Name," Jacques Derrida depicts autobiography as "a secret contract" that needs to be "honored [...] by another" (1985, 9), thus implicating the reader. Developing this idea, one might posit that without the other (that is, the writer without the reader and vice versa), there *is* no life. In order to validate a life lived and recounted, then, both parties need to respect the autobiographical agreement – the writer needs to write about his life and the reader needs to be receptive to what is being said in order to decipher and understand the text. To Barrett Mandel, since the truth of a piece of life writing lies not so much in the events described as in "the writer's intention to tell the truth" (1980, 72), the reader of an autobiographical narrative should "cocreate [the] context that allows autobiography to speak the truth" (1980, 72). But while such an argument seems reasonable in theory, it is not always endorsed by the parties concerned. As Brian Finney (1985, 21) and Jerome Bruner (1993, 39–41), among others, have rightly noted, referentiality often has a very different meaning for those who are producing and those who are interpreting a text. This means that the expectations and intentions of the author do not always coincide with those of the reader, in which case there is a clash of desires and often a sentiment of having been deceived.[10]

For the purposes of analyzing the discrepancy between the reader and the writer's expectations in more depth, it is instructive to look at Paul John Eakins's work on referentiality in autobiography and on reader response. In *Touching the World*, Eakin points out the irony of the fact that we go on reading and writing autobiography even though we are aware of "theory's deconstruction of reference" (1992, 30). In an attempt to account for this seemingly paradoxical behaviour, Eakin posits that "readers and the autobiographers who write for them seem prepared to defend the existence of a generic boundary between biography and fiction despite knowledge that this distinction [...] may well partake more of fiction than fact" (1992, 30). Further he claims that their clinging to the truth-value of autobiography is "a kind of existential imperative, a will to believe" (1992, 30).

In *Fictions in Autobiography*, Eakin reiterates that we are enticed to, but also that we *want* to believe that what we are reading is factually accurate (1985, 56). This is why we wish for autobiography to reflect the author's life and why we feel deceived if we detect traces of fiction (1985, 9–10). Eakin alludes more overtly to the covenant between the autobiographer and the reader in *Living Autobiographically*; here he states that "[w]e don't [...] read autobiographies in the same way that we read novels [...]. I believe that our life stories are not merely *about* us but in an inescapable and profound way *are* us" (2008, x, emphasis in original). To elucidate the sacredness of this pact, Eakin refers to the immense controversy surrounding James Frey's *A Million Little Pieces* (2008, 21). When it came to light that the book, which was published as a memoir, contained fabrications about Frey's past, there was a public outcry. Eakin believes this is because writers that scorn autobiographical etiquette – of which, he says, "telling the truth is the cardinal rule" (2008, 21) – cannot dictate the way they will be read. He adds, however, that readers are fickle in this regard and more willing to oversee little inconsistencies "when they are having fun" (2008, 21).

Ironically (considering the foregoing discussion), Eakin cites *Angela's Ashes* as an example of a work where readers are tolerant of inaccuracies.[11] This is because although it is clear that Frank could not have recalled and recorded the precise conversations he had witnessed as a child of preschool going age, it is precisely by using "this imaginative reconstruction" (2008, 21) of the past – or what George O'Brien has called McCourt's "imaginative embellishment" (2000, 242)[12] – that "writers impress us as trying to tell the fundamental biographical truth of their lives" (Eakin 2008, 21).[13] If I have understood Eakin correctly, it seems that readers are able to tell the difference when a writer uses fiction to enhance past events and convey the 'essence' of who they are, and when they (as in Frey's case) take things too far and make their audience feel as if they have been tricked (2008, 21). It might then very well be, as Brian Finney has argued, that "[t]he autobiographer can shape, dramatize or stylize his material, but he cannot knowingly invent it" (1985, 71). Considering the degree of protest *Angela's Ashes* met with in Limerick, one can only assume that in this case those literally closest to home felt

that McCourt had not merely enhanced events but had deliberately fabricated lies about his family and about their town, and that in doing so
he had sold them out.

To understate the case, the notion of autobiographical truth is complex. Since the whole extent of the self can never be known, writers
interpret and disclose selected events in their lives. But these writerly
expectations and intentions do not always correlate with those of their
readers, who quickly feel that their pact with the autobiographer has
been violated and who consequently condemn the writer for giving false
testimony. What is more, a contemporary readership still seems to cher-
ish the truth-value of an autobiographical text, as it reflects and helps
them to understand the world they are living in. When this is meddled
with and the truth of a life narrative exposed as being nothing but an
illusion, readers are fundamentally shaken and can no longer make sense
of their own reality.

Of course in the instance of *Angela's Ashes* and the hostility it en-
gendered, things need not be so complicated. Perhaps locals felt slighted
because of the way their town was portrayed. Or perhaps they still remembered old Frankie and just didn't like his guts. This, however, would
not explain the *extent* of their outrage. Taking into account the severity
of their criticism as well as the fact that similar patterns of behaviour
have been found in the cases of Frey and Binjamin Wilkomirski,[14] I
believe their anger would be better understood if one considered the vol-
atile nature of the autobiographical pact as well as the desire to believe
that the world in the text resonates with their own. To my mind, it is
the writer's moving between different worlds (the virtual and the real)
which disturbs and unsettles the reader. My contention, then, is that the
author's homelessness, the shiftiness of the text and the reader's sense of
unease are inseparably and inescapably bound up with each other. This
claim requires that at some point in his life the writer finds himself in exile and consequently experiences feelings of displacement and alienation.
He determines to write a book and to recount the major events of his
formative years; he calls it a memoir. Writing about himself he marries
two worlds, the fictional and the factual. He does so firstly by embellish-
ing certain characters and events, and secondly by appropriating narrative elements normally associated with fiction.[15] Evidently, we can never
know what he ultimately wanted to achieve by interweaving the fictional
and the real, or whether the ensuing effects were intended or not, but
that does not seem to be terribly important here. What *is* relevant is that
the text has now become ambiguous, and when the reader engages with
it, he or she is disturbed by the fact that it does not explicitly belong to
either the fictional or the non-fictional world. The exact extent of the
reader's unease depends on how much importance is placed on the autobiographical pact, but it is doubtful whether there is anyone who will

feel totally indifferent once they ascertain that the memoir reads like a novel, or once they discover that not all of it is completely accurate; that is, when they realize that they cannot unequivocally categorize the text. If one, then, accepts that the reader is left feeling ill at ease about the interplay of fictionality and factuality, one can claim that the memoirist uses the text as a vehicle to relay his unease. In this way – so my wager – the text acts as go-between or, to use a spatial metaphor, as a vessel that traverses time and space in order to convey to the reader the narrator's sense of displacement and discontent, and his deep dissatisfaction with his spatial surroundings.

Notes

1 As concerns the impact the text has had, Abdullahi Osman El-Tom remarks that *Angela's Ashes* "has been given almost mythical importance by equating the author with Charles Dickens" (1998, 78). He goes on, however, to argue that "[a] rigorous critique of a book like McCourt's is necessitated by its power within modern literary discourse" as it is "steeped in racist discourse that has so far gone uncontested" (1998, 78).

2 Although there is an analepsis when, after a very short introduction, we are given an account of why Frank's parents are wed, this is almost as brief as their courtship, and takes up but seven of the four hundred-odd pages (McCourt 1996, 2–8).

3 Reference here is, of course, to Philip Lejeune's work. Julie Rak explains:

> Philip Lejeune is mainly known in the English-speaking world as the inventor of 'the autobiographical pact,' a tacit agreement a reader makes with the author of a text which has non-fictional truth claims. The reader has to assume that the author's proper name in the world outside the text matches the name on the cover of the book, and the first-person pronoun within the narrative itself. If any of these elements do not match, the book is considered to be fictional.
>
> (2009, 17)

4 To avoid any confusion, I would like to adopt Alun Munslow's definition of the term, namely that "[referentiality means] the accuracy and veracity with which the narrative relates what actually happened in the past" (2006, 5).

5 Cullen also points out, however, that not all Limerick's inhabitants objected to the memoir:

> It wouldn't be Irish if there wasn't a split, and the split here is between those who see 'Angela's Ashes' as an exaggerated, mean-spirited attack on the city and its people, and those who embrace the book's art, humanity, and the attention, whether good or bad, it has brought Limerick.
>
> (1997, A.1)

6 Cullen writes that "Brendan Halligan, editor of the Limerick Leader, denied that the paper was engaged in an ongoing campaign to discredit McCourt, even while citing recent stories that purported to do just that" (1997, A.1).

7 Before this quote, Mitchell points out that "[i]n an interview, McCourt offers some remarks on the processes of remembering and compiling that his books withholds" (2003, 614).

8 In *Reading Autobiography,* Smith and Watson note that the distinction between the original and present-day use of *memoir* has all but disappeared:

> [...] the memoir directs attention more toward the lives and actions of others than to the narrator. [...]. In contemporary parlance *autobiography* and *memoir* are used interchangeably. [...]. Currently, the term refers generally to life writing that takes a segment of a life, not its entirety, and focusing on interconnected experiences.
>
> (2010, 274)

On this matter, Timothy C. Baker argues that

> while the distinction between autobiography and memoir is traditionally understood to be one of relative completeness, in which the former recounts the subject's whole life and the latter focuses on a particular aspect or moment, it is difficult to imagine how any self-account could be other than partial or anecdotal.
>
> (2010, 219)

9 Ivan Cañadas believes that "[r]esponses to *Angela's Ashes* are perhaps symptomatic of a broader, widespread phenomenon in contemporary letters" (2006, 17). Further he posits that despite present-day interest in knowing the truth, "in looking, at *Angela's Ashes* [...] it seems that current trends ironically point back to the very inception of the novel form, reproducing the claims to marginal truth of the picaresque genre" (2006, 17).

10 This brings to mind Wolfgang Iser's reception theory. Robert Holub writers that "[Iser] wants to see meaning as the result of an interaction between text and reader" (2010, 83).

11 We need to keep in mind that the reaction to *Angela's Ashes* was divided. See note 5.

12 In "The Last Word: Reflections on *Angela's Ashes,*" O'Brien takes issue with the portrayal of Limerick in the memoir. Though he does not deny the socially deplorable conditions Frank McCourt grew up in, he questions what he regards to be an exaggerated account of the events:

> [...] it is not that people in Limerick did not invoke the Famine, the English, the Protestants, the faith of their fathers, Freedom, Northerners, and all the rest of it. But they did not do so as consistently as they are said to have done. Nobody could. No community does.
>
> (2000, 242)

13 Other critics who have written on why tweaking the truth in this way does not detract from the text include Shannon Forbes and James Phelan. Forbes has coined the term "the Performance as Fabricator technique," which she uses to describe instances "when McCourt-as-Author tells readers that which readers know he could not possibly know firsthand" (2007, 487). She moreover argues that "[i]t is improbable, in such a case, that McCourt-as-Author is asking his readers to accept as truth this obvious unlikelihood" (2007, 489). James Phelan believes that the discrepancy between the adult voice and the child's voice adds to the narrative:

> The unreliable narration is itself one of the means of heightening the mimetic component of the narrative: the gap between the child's understanding and evaluation of events and those of the mature author is crucial to McCourt's construction of Frankie as a plausible nonfictional character.
>
> (2005, 73)

14 In *Autobiography*, Linda Anderson addresses the contention created by Wilkomirski's *Fragments: Memories of a Wartime Childhood 1939–1948*, purportedly the memoirs of a Nazi concentration camp inmate, but later generally considered to be fiction. When the text's fictionality was discovered, there was widespread and vehement objection among readers (despite the fact that the author stuck to his original story). Anderson ascribes the protest the book came up against to the fact that "shifting from one genre to another [was] profoundly disturbing to readers" (2001, 132).

15 In her essay "Fiction, Autobiography and Memoir Intertwined: The Writings of Frank McCourt and Lozje Kovačič," Alenka Koron deals with the complexity of referentiality in *Angela's Ashes* as well as in Kovačič's *Prišleki*. In response to the long-standing debate whether fiction can categorically be distinguished from non-fiction, Koron posits that texts have authenticity markers or "orientation signals" (2006, 160) which we use to guide us in our reading. In short, this means that we determine a book's fictionality by deferring, among others, to what we know of the world and of other texts. Koron then goes on to offer a further interpretation of McCourt's story by virtue of applying "the pragmatic model for distinguishing between fiction and non-fiction" (2006, 160) as proposed by Irmgard Nickel-Bacon, Norbert Groeben and Margrit Schreier in their paper "Fiktionssignale pragmatisch: Ein medienübergreifendes Modell zur Unterscheidung von Fiktion(en) und Realität(en)" (2000). Koron writes that what Nickel-Bacon et al. suggest is that a text should be examined according to a triangular scheme, i.e. analyzed on "[t]he pragmatic [...] the semantic [and] the syntactic level" (2006, 160). She posits that *Angela's Ashes* may be rated as non-fictional on the first level as well as on the semantic tier. Analyzed for its syntax, however, McCourt's text classifies as fiction. This is because in its "narrative transmission" (2006, 162) it implements techniques usually associated with fiction writing; not only does it make use of external focalization and the historical present, but it also displays an intricate "temporal ordering, with its ellipses and condensation of episodes" (2006, 162).

References

Anderson, Linda. 2001. *Autobiography*. London: Routledge.

Baker, Timothy C. 2010. "The Art of Losing: The Place of Death in Writers' Memoirs." In *Life Writing: Essays on Autobiography, Biography and Literature*, edited by Richard Bradford, 219–233. Basingstoke: Palgrave Macmillan.

Brennan, Zoe. 2009. "A Miserable Liar? *Angela's Ashes* Inspired a New Literary Genre – But Was Frank McCourt REALLY Telling the Truth?" *Mail Online*. July 21, 2009. www.dailymail.co.uk/debate/article-1201062/A-miserable-liar-Angelas-Ashes-inspired-new-literary-genre--Frank-McCourt-REALLY-telling-truth.html.

Bruner, Jerome. 1993. "The Autobiographical Process." In *The Culture of Autobiography: Constructions of Self-Representation*, edited by Robert Folkenflik, 38–55. Stanford: Stanford University Press.

Cañadas, Ivan. 2006. "Lazarillo in Limerick: *Angela's Ashes* and the Shadow of the Picaresque Tradition on Contemporary Literature." *Inter-Cultural Studies: A Forum on Cultural Change & Diversity* 6: 9–19.

Cullen, Kevin. 1997. "Memoir Lashed, and Loved: Angela's Ashes Author Finds Foes, Friends in Limerick." *The Boston Globe*. October 29, 1997. A.1.

Derrida, Jacques. 1985. "Otobiographies: The Teaching of Nietzsche and the Politics of the Proper Name." In *The Ear of the Other: Otobiography, Transference, Translation*, edited by Christie MacDonald and translated by Avital Ronell, 8–39. Lincoln: University of Nebraska Press.

Eakin, Paul John. 1985. *Fictions in Autobiography: Studies in the Art of Self-Invention*. Princeton: Princeton University Press.

——. 2008. *Living Autobiographically: How We Create Identity in Narrative*. Ithaca: Cornell University Press.

——. 1992. *Touching the World: Reference in Autobiography*. Princeton: Princeton University Press.

Finney, Brian. 1985. *The Inner I: British Literary Autobiography of the Twentieth Century*. London: Faber and Faber.

Forbes, Shannon. 2007. "Performative Identity Formation in Frank McCourt's *Angela's Ashes: A Memoir*." *Journal of Narrative Theory* 37 (3): 473–496.

Greenwood Davis, Heather. 2014. "Travel Ireland, Limerick: Angela's Ashes Author, Frank McCourt, Lives On in His Hometown." *The Star*. February 25, 2014. www.thestar.com/life/travel/ireland_travel/2014/02/25/travel_ireland_limerick_angelas_ashes_author_frank_mccourt_lives_on_in_his_hometown.html.

Holub, Robert C. 2010. *Reception Theory: A Critical Introduction*. London: Routledge.

Koron, Alenka. 2006. "Fiction, Autobiography and Memoir Intertwined: The Writings of Frank McCourt and Lozje Kovačič." In *Fiction and Autobiography: Modes and Models of Interaction*, edited by Sabine Coelsch-Foisner and Wolfgang Görtschacher, 155–166. Frankfurt am Main: Peter Lang.

Lee, Laurie. 1965. *Cider with Rosie*. London: The Hogarth Press.

Lenz, Peter. 2000. "'To Hell or to America?': Tragi-Comedy in Frank McCourt's *Angela's Ashes* and the Irish Literary Tradition." *Anglia: Zeitschrift für englische Philologie* 118 (3): 411–420.

Mandel, Barrett J. 1980. "Full of Life Now." In *Autobiography: Essays Theoretical and Critical*, edited by James Olney, 49–79. Princeton: Princeton University Press.

McCourt, Frank. 1996. *Angela's Ashes: A Memoir of a Childhood*. London: Flamingo.

——. 2007. "When Irish Tongues Are Talking." *Slate*. March 27, 2007. www.slate.com/id/2162499.

Mitchell, James B. 2003. "Popular Autobiography as Historiography: The Reality Effect of Frank McCourt's *Angela's Ashes*." *Biography: An Interdisciplinary Quarterly* 26 (4): 607–624.

Munslow, Alun. 2006. *Deconstructing History*. Second edition. London: Routledge.

Nickel-Bacon, Irmgard, Norbert Groeben and Margrit Schreier. 2000. "Fiktionssignale pragmatisch: Ein medienübergreifendes Modell zur Unterscheidung von Fiktion(en) und Realität(en)." *Poetica* 32 (3/4): 267–299.

O'Brien, George. 2000. "The Last Word: Reflections on *Angela's Ashes*." In *New Perspectives on the Irish Diaspora*, edited by Charles Fanning, 236–249. Carbondale and Edwardsville: Southern Illinois University Press.

Osman El-Tom, Abdullahi. 1998. "McCourt's *Angela's Ashes* and the Portrait of the Other." *Irish Journal of Anthropology* 3: 78–89.

Phelan, James. 2005. *Living to Tell About It: A Rhetoric and Ethics of Character Narration*. Ithaca: Cornell University Press.

Rak, Julie. 2009. "Dialogue with the Future: Philippe Lejeune's Method and Theory of Diary." In *On Diary*, edited by Philippe Lejeune, Jeremy D. Popkin, and Julie Rak, 16–26. Honolulu: University of Hawai'i Press.

Smith, Sidonie and Julia Watson. 2010. *Reading Autobiography: A Guide for Interpreting Life Narratives*. Second edition. Minneapolis: University of Minnesota Press.

Tucker, Martin, ed. 1991. *Literary Exile in the Twentieth Century: An Analysis and Biographical Dictionary*. New York: Greenwood Press.

13 Narrative, Space and Autobiographical Film in the Digital Age

An Analysis of *The Beaches of Agnès* (2008)

Deirdre Russell

In a review of Jerome Bruner's book *Making Stories: Law, Literature, Life* (2002), the British philosopher Galen Strawson (2004) denounced what he called the "narrativist orthodoxy" in the humanities and human sciences. He was referring to the widespread notion, posited by philosophers like Paul Ricœur (1990) as well as numerous psychologists, sociologists and others, that the self is constructed by stories. However, coinciding with the postmodern 'spatial turn' heralding an intellectual shift from history to geography, this orthodoxy faces a profound challenge in a computer-based culture where many of narrative's principles and properties are marginalized; where hypertext, for example, threatens sequential reading and writing. As the philosopher Richard Kearney notes, "[w]e can hardly deny that the notion of continuous experience, associated with traditional linear narrative, has been fundamentally challenged by current technologies of the computer and Internet" (2002, 125–126). These technologies, according to much new media theory, privilege *space* over *time*, recalling Michel Foucault's oft-quoted claims that

> [w]e are now in the epoch of simultaneity: we are in the epoch of juxtaposition, the epoch of near and far, of the side-by-side, of the dispersed [...] our experience of the world is less of a long life developing through time than that of a network that connects points and intersects with its own skein.
>
> (quoted in Manovich 2001, 325)

We might anticipate, then, the displacement of the dominant model of 'narrative identity' by, say, concepts of 'network identity.'

To explore these contentions, this chapter examines the French filmmaker Agnès Varda's autobiographical film *The Beaches of Agnès* (*Les plages d'Agnès* 2008), a transitional text straddling the supposedly time-based 'old' media of cinema and space-based new media. Travelling between Belgium, France and the United States via China and Cuba, this documentary eschews conventional narrative patterns in favour of geographic configurations and digital compositions, including collage and other spatial forms. The film thus suggests that space, rather than time, may be its governing dimension of self-exploration and -representation. By examining an autobiography – a genre traditionally associated with time and narration – I consider whether notions of lives and selves as stories are supplanted by, or can be reconciled with, the spatial orientations of a computer-based culture. The article draws, then, on long-standing debates regarding the relative dominance of historic and geographic intellectual frameworks and seeks to synthesize these with insights into digital spatiality. I will begin by briefly exploring the concept of narrative identity before probing how narrative's status may be threatened by technologies that encourage spatial thinking and representation, before turning to explore some of these issues in Varda's film. Focusing on key computer forms such as database, navigable space and hypertext, this chapter ultimately argues for narrativity's continued importance in audiovisual autobiography, but also its remodelling in the light of these spatially oriented forms.

Narrative Identity and Life as a Journey

Concepts of narrative selfhood arose from a shift in interest, across the humanities and beyond, from narrative as a representational mode, examining its formal properties and functions, to narrative as a *psychological* and *social* phenomenon. With roots in hermeneutic phenomenology, theories of narrative identity are grown in several strains and varieties, but all stress the centrality of *time*, in which narration's status as a process for articulating time responds to the self's supposed temporal construction. Narrative is posited as our way of making meaningful connections among past, present and future; among memories, actions and intentions, both personal and collective. The concept also stresses the intersubjective nature of identity, which is formed through narrative interactions and in cultural contexts of shared narratives. A broad definition might state, then, that *we make sense of our experiences and the world and develop a sense of self through the narrative interpretation of our lives*. Like much life-writing scholarship, the concept is indebted to Wilhelm Dilthey's notion of *Zusammenhang des Lebens* – the nexus or interconnectedness of life – and highlights how narrative organization can respond to desires to find or forge coherence in self-experience (1976, 212–216).

The affinities between these theories and autobiography also chime with that richest of root metaphors: life stories as *journeys*, identified by Susanna Egan (1984, 106) and Wendy Everett (2005, 112) as key tropes of autobiographical literature and film, respectively, and by Stella Bruzzi (2000, 99–114) as prominent narrative structuring devices in many contemporary documentaries; the autobiographical documentaries *Tarnation* (Caouette 2003), *My Winnipeg* (Maddin 2007), *Waltz With Bashir* (Folman 2008), *Photographic Memory* (McElwee 2011) and *Stories We Tell* (Polley 2012) all feature literal and figurative journeys (and all share traits with Varda's film in various ways).

The relationships among travel, identity and narrative are also addressed by postcolonial, migration and diaspora scholars. Many narrativists declare that all known cultures are story-telling cultures (e.g. Brockmeier and Harré 2001, 41), and much postcolonial scholarship aims to recover suppressed stories. Other critics, however, such as Dipesh Chakrabarty (1992), have argued that our narrative models of History are European inventions and typically Eurocentric constructions. For some, the narrative impulse of historiography indeed rides tandem with colonialism, both asserting linear and progressive development, and underpinned by mythical ideals of universalism and mastery of knowledge. This arguable "Western-ness of history" (Curthoys and Docker 2006, 8) asks us to consider whether apprehending lives and selves as narrative, rather than being universal, might be a cultural (perhaps specifically Judeo-Christian) proclivity.

Debates regarding the 'naturalness' of narrative have a long history. Identity narrativists generally maintain that storytelling is a fundamental feature of the human mind, perhaps what makes us human above all else, and that it is only *through* narrative that experience can be grasped (e.g. Carr 1986, 65; Kerby 1991, 8; Manusco and Sarbin 1983, 245; Turner 1996, 7). Conversely, 'narrative sceptics' like the philosopher of history Louis Mink (1970) and the literary critic Frank Kermode (1967) have treated the notion that narrative is a feature of life before art suspiciously. For these sceptics, attributing narrative coherence to real life – resulting from desires to organize and find meaning in the world – is not inevitable and constitutes a naïve escape from reality at best, and dangerous myth-making in the interests of power and manipulation at worst (Carr 1986, 15–16).

Identity, Narrative and New Media

We can summarize this debate in terms of narrative being deemed either inherent to, or artificially imposed on, the raw material of experience. Do novels and films mimic essential ways of thinking and being? Or do we conceptualize ourselves narratively *because of* the ubiquity of these story forms? In this light, if 'narrative identity' lends itself to a culture grounded in books and films – in sequential reading and watching – the concept may be undermined in the digital age, which supposedly privileges non-sequential forms.

The mid-1980s is a reasonable marker for the emergence of 'new media,' signalling the computerization of culture and the increasingly intimate interweaving of technology into everyday life. There are of course inherent challenges to studying anything 'new,' and an 'upgrade culture' means that technology and its effects are always in flux; we must also be wary of simplistic technological determinism regarding such effects on subjectivity and society. Most new media scholarship, in any case, stresses that there has been no sudden, absolute rupture between old and new, between analogue and digital. Nonetheless, for many critics, the increasingly fuzzy boundaries between material and virtual realms herald genuine and profound changes regarding personal and social identity. From Sherry Turkle's (1995) early work on anonymity and performance to recent scholarship devoted to social network identities (e.g. Papacharissi 2010), the lines of enquiry regarding new media and identity are numerous, though a common thread is a conceptualization of the self as a "networked presence" (Lister et al. 2009, 210).

My concern here is the relative position of narrative in these reconfigurations of identity formation and expression, and more broadly whether we are living through a general decline in storytelling as a mode of discourse and of thought. It is often remarked that 'narrative' and 'knowledge' have a shared etymological root and are intimately connected (e.g. Manusco and Sarbin 1983, 236), and yet we cannot ignore that knowledge in the 'information age' is often generated, organized and accessed in distinctly non-narrative ways; as Caroline Bassett – whose book *The Arc and the Machine: Narrative and New Media* (2007) is ultimately a defence of narrative – concedes, databases and algorithms are among the forms of information to have emerged as crucial elements of contemporary culture (2007, 2). In her book *How We Think: Digital Media and Contemporary Technogenesis* (2012), which charts the emergence and implications of the 'digital humanities,' N. Katherine Hayles concurs that the "ability to access and retrieve information on a global scale has a significant impact on how one thinks about one's place in the world" (2012, 2). Consequent predictions of the end, decline or radical reshaping of narrative abound in new media scholarship, most famously in Lev Manovich's influential book *The Language of New Media* (2001), on which I will be drawing substantially. Manovich argues that whereas in the modern age, literature and cinema advanced narrative as the dominant form of cultural expression, the computer age's equivalent is the *database*, defined as a collection of unordered individual items. Indeed, he contends that "database and narrative are natural enemies. Competing for the same territory of human culture, each claims an exclusive right to make meaning out of the world" (2001, 225).

Narrative, New Media and Spatiality

Hayles (2012, 180) and Manovich (2001, 238) both note that whereas narrative is associated with temporality, databases are inclined towards spatial organization and display. And Manovich cites the second key computer-based form as *navigable space*. Together, he sees database and virtual space as "true cultural forms – general ways used by the culture to represent human experience, the world, and human existence in this world" (2001, 215). In these and other ways, he identifies computer culture as spatializing all representations and experiences (2001, 252). These contentions neatly cohere with the academic 'spatial turn.' As Robert T. Tally's recent account elucidates (2013, 11–43), after the nineteenth-century dominance of temporality and historiography rooted in Enlightenment values, and the preoccupations with time and memory in modernist projects in the early twentieth century,[1] spatial discourses and practices gained ground after the Second World War amid crumbling beliefs in History as progressive and teleological, confirmed by the realities of postcolonialism. For thinkers and artists exploring and expressing the postmodern condition, the shifting spatial dimensions of the world in the twenty-first century demand ever more attention, whether due to mass migrations or global corporations. That technologies also play a pivotal role in redefining contemporary space scarcely needs stating. More compelling, though, are suggestions that spatiality is inherent to such technologies. As Manovich states:

> In the 1980s many critics described one of the key effects of 'postmodernism' as that of spatialization—privileging space over time, flattening historical time, refusing grand narratives. Computer media, which evolved during the same decade, accomplished this spatialization quite literally. It replaced sequential storage with random-access storage; hierarchical organization of information with a flattened hypertext; psychological movement of narrative in novel and cinema with physical movement through space.
>
> (2001, 78)

More broadly, spatial metaphors like *browsing, searching, surfing, exploring* and *immersion*, in *realms, spheres* and *environments,* dominate the ways we discuss interaction with computerized data, especially through the Internet. And while the term 'cyberspace' is arguably increasingly redundant with the growing integration of technology into every aspect of life, it points to how, as Bassett notes, the Internet entered public consciousness as a promise of space (2007, 132).[2]

For commentators such as Sean Cubitt (2002, 6), the spatial rather than temporal structures of data storage and retrieval (from spreadsheets to geographical information systems) mean that multimedia and networked communication marginalize narrative. Manovich (2001, 323) cites the cultural geographer Edward Soja's analysis that the nineteenth-century rise of history entailed a decline in spatial imagination, which (for Manovich, Soja and many others) has in recent decades made a significant comeback. Indeed, there is a body of scholarship devoted to historicizing new media in terms of a powerful revival of earlier spatial modes of expression and communication that were marginalized by the dominant nineteenth- and twentieth-century forms of knowledge and culture (i.e. the historical paradigm and the pre-eminence of novels and films). For example, Benjamin Woolley (1992) draws parallels between the "spatial data management" of computer desktop icons and classical and medieval mnemonic traditions (quoted in Lister et al. 2009, 63).

Pertinent to both the academic and technological facets of the spatial turn, Tally identifies *mapping* as the key figure in contemporary spatiality studies and perhaps "the only really appropriate aesthetic and political process for the postmodern condition" (2013, 41). The art historian Söke Dinkla (2002, 35), meanwhile, cites cartography as an important metaphor for new media artists. Beyond mapping as a trope, Hayles notes the impact of geographic information systems (GIS) mapping and global positioning systems (GPS) in creating a "culture of spatial exploration in digital media" (2012, 14). More specifically, she notes that the emerging field of "spatial history"[3] (within a discipline traditionally grounded in time and narrative of course) is one manifestation of the spatial turn in the digital humanities: by deploying tools like GIS, researchers are "rethinking and re-representing the problematic of history in spatial terms. Accordingly, historians have moved into alliance with geographers in new ways" (2012, 183). Seen in these ways, cartography seems to replace narrative – both are modes of knowledge (and often power) that seek to create order and meaning out of chaos – in the spatial paradigm.

Spatiality studies and the spatiality of digital media also dovetail with regards to aspects of autobiographical identity. It is often noted that autobiographical reflection tends to draw on spatial metaphors such as *exploration* of inner *depths*; Mike Crang and Nigel Thrift also remark that the Western model of the autonomous self is often framed using a "language of spatial containers" (2000, 7). The significance of space to memory, meanwhile, has been widely asserted, from the childhood home's inscription in memory and imagination for Gaston Bachelard (1957) to the realms of collective memory for Pierre Nora (1984–1992). New technologies and media intensify these spatial impressions of the inner life. Much like claims regarding the fundamental storytelling structures of the mind, Manovich and others posit that computer forms and functions evoke or imitate (as well as potentially rewire) key cognitive processes. For example, the database becomes a new metaphor to conceptualize memory (Manovich 2001, 214). A particularly prominent form here is *hypertext*, a key way of organizing computer data and one which is defined by non-sequential connections. Indeed, a seminal contribution to the idea of hypertext is Vannevar Bush's 1945 essay "As We

May Think," which calls for a system of sorting and classifying knowledge that emulates cognitive activity:

> The human mind operates by association. With one item in its grasp, it snaps instantly to the next that is suggested by the association of thoughts, in association with some intricate web of trails carried by the cells of the brain.
>
> (quoted in Lister et al. 2009, 27)

Bush's ideas have arguably manifested in hypermedia, where clicking on hyperlinks resembles the associative patterns of, say, memory and imagination. Like database, hypertext can be understood spatially since discussions and designs of hypertext emphasize *networks* (recalling Foucault's words cited in the introduction to this chapter). Indeed, George P. Landow identifies the "paradigm of the network" (1997, 42) and attendant rejection of linearity as a key shared concern for critical theory and hypermedia. Beyond claims that typical organizations of computer data have more natural affinities with the human mind than linear forms, research suggests that computer use and especially Web interactions actually modify neural circuitry (Hayles 2012, 2–3).

My question, then, is whether concepts of narrative autobiographical identity reliant on the supposed temporality of the human mind and experience are replaced, displaced or reformulated by a culture with renewed emphasis on spatiality and non-sequentiality. To explore these contentions, I would now like to turn my attention to Varda's film.

Space and Database in *The Beaches of Agnès*

Themes of memory, identity and subjectivity dominate Varda's work, both fictional and documentary, but *The Beaches of Agnès* is her most thoroughly autobiographical film. From the vantage point of her eightieth year, she reviews her life and work in this very playful and inventive film that interweaves material from earlier projects with contemporary footage revisiting key locations including Brussels, Sète, Paris, Avignon, Noirmoutier and Los Angeles.

Varda previously aligned her cinema with literary forms, coining the term *cinécriture* ('cinewriting'); for *The Beaches*, however, she draws parallels with new media. Recalling claims that narrative gives way to database as a means of grasping experience, Varda states, in the film's press kit, that "[t]he excerpts from my films were treated as if they had come from a database of my life's work, from which I could take a scene of fiction or documentary, and use it out of context" (quoted in Conway 2010, 134). Furthermore, the film and its subject are ostensibly coordinated geographically rather than historically, structured according to the significant sites of her life and work. In these ways, the film arguably foregrounds cinema's latent cartographic qualities (as asserted by Tom Conley 2007). In fact, the relationship between place and identity is a long-standing preoccupation of Varda's oeuvre, from her debut film *La pointe courte* (1955) devoted to the town of Sète, where Varda spent some of her childhood, to *Daguerréotypes* (1976), a documentary about the Parisian street where Varda has lived since the 1950s. The title of her last film, *The Beaches of Agnès*, of course connotes autobiography-as-geography, and this is underscored in the film's opening monologue where Varda declares:

> This time, to talk about myself, I thought:
> If we opened people up, we'd find landscapes.
> If we opened me up, we'd find beaches.[4]

The film's and the subject's geographic composition means that experiences of Varda's life that occurred at different times are presented simultaneously. For example, Varda's account of her wartime childhood in Sète accompanies her discussion of *La pointe courte* made some fifteen years later. Similarly, in sequences devoted to her home on rue Daguerre, images from her early days in the courtyard in the 1950s feature alongside those from *Daguerréotypes* and her 1988 film *Jane B. par Agnès V.* Such coexistence of different events and eras inhabiting one place is explicitly articulated when, in Venice Beach (her sometime home in the 1960s and 1970s), Varda says, "On this beach, I like seeing friends from all eras."[5] Also in L.A., recalling the productions there of *Lions Love (... and Lies)* in 1968 and her 1981 documentary *Mur Murs*, she declares that "when I think about it, all the eras get mixed up."[6]

But it is also digitally crafted compositions which produce this spatial simultaneity; images and sounds from various sources and times appear within, beside or overlapping one another. For example, a sequence detailing *Cléo de 5 à 7* (1962) begins with present-day images of Varda laid over footage from the film, followed by various split screen formats depicting archival and contemporary still and moving images. In these ways, Varda's enterprise recalls Manovich's prophesies that see digital cinema as

> a new cinema in which the diachronic dimension is no longer privileged over the synchronic dimension, time is no longer privileged over space, sequence is no longer privileged over simultaneity, montage in time is no longer privileged over montage within a shot.
>
> (2001, 326)

He also argues that such "spatial montage" (2001, 322–330) reflects the experience of several windows or applications open on a computer screen, and that we may thus come to find multiple streams of information more satisfying than the single stream of traditional cinema (2001, 328).

In *The Beaches*, these strategies paint a self-portrait that is seemingly more *collage* than *narrative*. This postmodern attitude is accentuated by the prominence of art history images: reproductions as well as playful reconstructions of paintings. Many of these come from earlier films (such as the performance of Titian's Venus of Urbino in *Jane B.*), perhaps suggesting a proto "database imagination" (Manovich 2001, 235). And, of course, collage is in itself not a new form, but it is promoted by computer technologies; as Manovich argues, the avant-garde strategy is revived through the most basic of operations to be performed on digital data: cut-and-paste (2001, 306–307). In these ways, such techniques are in tune with postmodern notions that, with the demise of history as continuous progress, the past has become a vast archive of content and styles available for recycling and quoting.

The Beaches remains, of course, a film, and as such it involves temporal sequencing. However, in tune with its spatial structure, the connections between scenes and themes are typically orchestrated through graphic rather than narrative associations. An exemplary sequence concerns the rue Daguerre courtyard. Varda recounts a photography exhibition held there in 1954, which included a photo of a heart-shaped potato. This is followed by footage of her 2003 video installation *Patatutopia* featuring similar potatoes, and of Varda, promoting the work at the Venice Biennale, with a series of images digitally layered over her head (a cat, a ceramic portrait), followed by a shot of a mosaic – "my first official self-portrait"[7] – which leads to a discussion of the links between art history and her choice of actors – "Mosaics or frescoes, I loved old art, and the women of Piero della Francesca led me to Silvia Monfort"[8] – and finally the production of *La pointe courte*. So, the current of images sweeps, in little over one minute, from 1950s Paris to Venice in 2003, to her artistic inspirations and back to the 1950s and the production of her debut film. The cumulative effect of such playful associations leaping across time and space is a sense of a network of infinite connections between her life, her work, and the lives and works of others. These arrangements also evoke *hyperlinking*. We should be clear that Varda's film is not a hypertext, but it evokes hypermedia's non-linear, networked procedures. Recalling claims that this is closer to the workings of the human mind than narrative, the atemporal associative patterns of ideas and memories in *The Beaches* are indeed reminiscent of what Ryan identifies as hypertext's potential for the "*simulation of mental activity— dreams, memory, stream of consciousness*" (2006, 145; emphasis in original). The constant (sometimes unmarked) cutting between contemporary and archive still and moving images (Varda's own and others') is also suggestive of how hypertext is, according to George P. Landow, "a fundamentally intertextual system" (1997, 35).

In these ways, the film does suggest Varda's life as, in Foucault's words, a "network that connects points and intersects with its own skein." The impression of 'networked' rather than concatenated links is expressed in the recurrent motif of *un puzzle,* a jigsaw. However, rather than a definitively completed jigsaw, the film's logic points to a puzzle whose pieces can be endlessly rearranged. Interestingly, Ryan suggests that hypertext can be usefully approached "like a jigsaw puzzle" (2006, 109); albeit "faithful to postmodern aesthetics, hypertexts may prevent the formation of a complete picture" (2006, 144). Examples of this trope in *The Beaches* include, in a sequence devoted to an exhibition in Avignon, the assembly of huge tiles of photographs of Jean Vilar and Gérard Philippe, about which Varda asks "is it possible to reconstitute this character?"[9] and later states "it's the puzzle side of things that appeals to me."[10] The (self-)portrait as jigsaw is a useful way of conceiving of Varda's film, and again one which points to a spatial rather than temporal composition.

Narrativity and Navigable Space in *The Beaches of Agnès*

I would now like to explore how Varda's project is not as de-narrativized as initially implied by its new media inflections. Manovich himself concedes that narrative shows few signs of disappearing, and that many new media artists pursue an interest in storytelling (2001, 264). He explains this in part by underlining the continuities rather than ruptures of cultural history. He thus suggests that, given the dominance of database in computer software and design,

> perhaps we can arrive at new kinds of narrative by focusing our attention on how narrative and database can work together. [...] *How can our new abilities to store vast amounts of data, to automatically classify, index, link, search, and instantly retrieve it, lead to new kinds of narrative?*
>
> (2001, 237; emphasis in original)

Bassett, meanwhile, argues that "narrative remains *central* to what we do in an information-saturated world" (2007, 8; emphasis in original), but that it may indeed require redefinition in this context. Similarly, Hayles suggests that "[r]ather than being natural enemies, narrative and database are more appropriately seen as *natural symbionts.* Symbionts are organisms of different species that have a mutually beneficial relation" (2012, 176; emphasis in original). I hope now to suggest how Varda's film may be indicative of these redefinitions and reconciliations of narrative and computer forms.

To do so, we can usefully turn to Manovich's account of *navigable space*. Citing literary archetypes of the European *flâneur* and the American explorer as templates, and video games as examples, Manovich argues that space functions as a *trajectory* rather than an area in computer culture (2001, 279). Moreover, he describes database and navigable space as complementary regarding narrative:

> On the one hand, a narrative is 'flattened' into a database. A trajectory through events and/or time becomes a flat space. On the other hand, a flat space of architecture or topology is narrativized, becoming a support for individual users' trajectories.
>
> (2001, 284)

Consequently, in many video games, narrative is equated with moving through space in ways which revive ancient forms of plot driven by a hero's spatial journey (2001, 245–246). This finds echoes in Tally's account of spatiality in literary and cultural studies; he notes that whereas narrative seems primarily temporal, "the very idea of plot is also spatial, since a *plot* is also a plan, which is to say, a map" (2013, 49). Manovich's analysis of navigable space and his emphasis on such space as dynamic and traversed rather than static (2001, 279) coheres with intellectual shifts (initiated by Henri Lefebvre's seminal work *La production de l'espace* in 1974) in Western conceptualizations of space: from an absolute category to, as Crang and Thrift put it, "*space as process* and *in process*" (2000, 3; emphasis in original). Manovich's emphasis on navigation is also directly indebted to Michel de Certeau's (1980) emphasis on apprehending space in terms of trajectories. So, such notions of navigation, process and trajectory revive a temporal, potentially narrative, dimension of space, as indicated by the aforementioned association of 'life stories' and 'journeys.'

Just as Varda's film is not a hypertext, nor a navigable space in the manner of, say, a computer game, it nonetheless expresses a "navigable space imagination" (Manovich 2001, 279). Firstly, its central trope of beaches connects with the more familiar autobiographical figure of journeys, not least via recurrent transport imagery – especially boats and bridges – used to transition between the different places and times of Varda's life. As the film travels from Belgium to the South of France, then to Paris, L.A. and elsewhere (including a "leap" [un bond] to China and a "stop" in Cuba), a sense of spatial wandering is clear. Furthermore, while locations provide its main contours, the film does have a loosely chronological 'macro'-structure which can be seen as a voyage of discovery: Varda broaches her childhood early in the film ("In the direction of my childhood home"[11]), and her later years towards the end ("Back to France"[12]). Beyond travel motifs, 'navigable space' is evoked in the presence and pertinence of Varda's multimedia installations: as well as footage of actual exhibitions, the genre influences the film as a whole in its variety of source materials and its spatial structure. Manovich cites this genre of modern art as particularly relevant to virtual spaces. He refers to the artist Ilya Kabakov, whose immersive installation practice blends spatial and temporal art forms by carefully structuring the viewer's navigation of an enclosed space:

> On the one hand, it belongs to the plastic arts designed to be viewed by an immobile spectator – painting, sculpture, architecture. On the other, it also belongs to time-based arts such as theatre and cinema. We can say the same about virtual navigable spaces.
>
> (Manovich, 2001, 266)

Varda's gallery work similarly suggests the combination of spatial structure and narrative in inventive ways. For example, at the end of *The Beaches*, she presents her piece *La cabane de l'échec*: a hut composed of strips of celluloid from her 'failed' film *Les créatures* (1966); the installation is a 'navigable space' and it 'spatializes' cinematic time, but Varda also states that this "*Cabane du cinéma* a une histoire," it has a story.

Much the same could be said about all of the film's locations. Each calls forth memories or fantasies, or stories from past films. For example, while in a sailing boat on the Seine and recounting her student days, Varda states, "I remember: I went to read [art books from the library] on the banks of the Seine,"[13] which leads to footage of her short film *Nausicaa* (1970) at the same location. At Venice Beach, meanwhile, Varda announces that "I'd like to tell a little beach love story"[14] about two close friends. In these ways, Varda imbues all the places she visits with *meaning*, and it is arguably this which guarantees the continued significance of narrative in the film despite the influence of computer forms; as Tally reports, "what makes a *place* noteworthy is often the narratives that give it meaning" (2013, 51; emphasis in original).

It is narrative's meaning-making functions that Hayles stresses in her critique of the database-narrative binary:

> Because database can construct relational juxtapositions but is helpless to interpret or explain them, it needs narrative to make its results meaningful. Narrative, for its part, needs database in the computationally intensive culture of the new millennium to enhance its cultural authority and test the generality of its insights. If narrative often dissolves into database, [...] database catalyzes and indeed demands narrative's reappearance as soon as meaning and interpretation are required.
>
> (2012, 176)

Manovich summarizes the binary thus: "Narrative (= hierarchy) – database, hypermedia, network (= flattening of hierarchy)" (2001, 284). Varda may have conceptualized the project in terms of database; it bears traces of this form as well as of hypermedia and network, but it also *narrativizes*. In addition to the multitude of mini-narratives emerging from each location, she adopts a storyteller role in how she selects and arranges the elements of her life and work, and always explains the causes, consequences and connotations of the 'data.' Whereas narrative is stripped here of associations with linearity, sometimes even temporality, it retains its function of determining the relative *significance* of events and of places.

Conclusions

Whilst not structured according to typical narrative patterns, a storytelling impulse still permeates *The Beaches of Agnès* and, despite the collage aesthetic, the film ultimately constructs a thoroughly *coherent* landscape. One explanation for this resides in the hermeneutic notion, following Dilthey, that "life interprets itself" (Gadamer 2004, 229). Having already rendered prominent features of her life and subjectivity in previous projects, the meaningful coherence to which narrative aspires is already encoded in the harmonious nature of Varda's 'data': the consistent themes of memory, Western art and locations, for example. In this light, we might see the film's seemingly 'non-narrative' qualities as a testament to a subject that can bear endless reconfigurations since the parts are all consonant with the whole. In this respect, Dilthey's concept of the 'nexus' of life arguably harmonizes narrative and network (and the temporal and spatial dimensions of each).

Geography and history prove to be complementary means of grasping and expressing the climates and currents of the autobiographical subject's life. This is manifested through the *combination* of temporal-narrative and spatial-data properties; such an analysis coheres with an approach to cultural history that stresses its continuities, rather than radical epistemological breaks. Seeing Varda's film as synthesizing the narrative qualities of life and its spatial orientations promoted by new media leads me to conclude that the computer age need not signal an end but perhaps a redefinition of what is meaningfully implied by 'narrative' in audiovisual autobiographical discourse, perhaps increasingly liberated from conditions of linearity and sequentiality and increasingly embracing notions of networked association. Whereas linearity may have been a dominant property of narrative and narrative selfhood in particular technological and ideological contexts (the printing press, the celluloid reel, the industrial revolution and Enlightenment ideals of progress), new technologies and contexts may foreground other qualities expressing the human mind's propensity to make nonlinear, but still narratively meaningful, connections. Perhaps the insights from new media scholarship suggest that narrative identity must now be theorized in terms of *space* as much as time.

Notes

1 See Andrew Thacker's *Moving Through Modernity* (2003) for an alternative account stressing the spatial dimensions of modernism.
2 It should be noted, however, that, as Bassett outlines, "the status of virtual space as a form of space is disputed: some understand it to 'negate geometry' altogether" while others argue that "a particular kind of geometry is no longer operational in virtual space" (2007, 134).
3 A key example cited by Hayles is The Spatial History Project at Stanford University, whose projects "operate outside of normal historical practice in five ways: they are collaborative, use visualization, depend on the use of computers, are open-ended, and have a conceptual focus on space." http://web.stanford.edu/group/spatialhistory/cgi-bin/site/page.php?id=1.
4 "Cette fois-ci, pour parler de moi j'ai pensé:
   si on ouvrait les gens, on trouverait des paysages.
   Moi si on m'ouvrait, on trouverait des plages."
5 "C'est sur cette plage que j'aime retrouver mes amis de toutes les époques."
6 "Quand je réfléchis, toutes les époques se confondent."
7 "Celle de mon premier autoportrait officiel."
8 "Mosaïques ou fresques, j'aimais l'art ancient et les femmes de Piero della Francesca m'ont amenée à Silvia Monfort. "
9 "Est-ce qu'on peut reconstituer ce personnage?"
10 "C'est le côté puzzle des choses qui me plaît."
11 "Direction, ma maison d'enfance."
12 "Retour en France."
13 "Je me souviens: j'allais les lire sur les quais."
14 "Je voudrais raconter une petite histoire d'amour et de plage."

References

Bachelard, Gaston. 1957. *La poétique de l'espace*. Paris: Presses Universitaires de France.

Bassett, Caroline. 2007. *The Arc and the Machine: Narrative and New Media*. Manchester and New York: Manchester University Press.

Brockmeier, Jens and Rom Harré. 2001. "Narrative: Problems and Promises of an Alternative Paradigm." In *Narrative and Identity: Studies in Autobiography, Self and Culture*, edited by Jens Brockmeier and Donal Carbaugh, 39–58. Amsterdam: John Benjamins.

Bruner, Jerome. 2002. *Making Stories: Law, Literature, Life*. New York: Farrar, Straus and Giroux.

Bruzzi, Stella. 2000. *New Documentary: A Critical Introduction*. London and New York: Routledge.

Caouette, Jonathan, dir. 2003. *Tarnation*. New York: Wellspring, 2005. DVD.

Carr, David. 1986. *Time, Narrative and History*. Bloomington: Indiana University Press.

Conley, Tom. 2007. *Cartographic Cinema*. Minneapolis and London: University of Minnesota Press.

Conway, Kelley. 2010. "Varda at Work: *Les Plages d'Agnès*." *Studies in French Cinema* 10 (2): 125–139.

Chakrabarty, Dipesh. 1992. "Postcoloniality and the Artifice of History: Who Speaks for 'Indian' Pasts?" *Representations* 37 (Winter): 1–26.

Crang, Mike and Nigel Thrift, eds. 2000. *Thinking Space*. London and New York: Routledge.

Cubitt, Sean. 2002. "Spreadsheets, Sitemaps and Search Engines: Why Narrative is Marginal to Multimedia and Networked Communication, and Why Marginality is More Vital than Universality." In *New Screen Media: Cinema/Art/Narrative*, edited by Martin Reiser and Andrea Zapp, 3–13. London: BFI.

Curthoys, Ann and John Docker. 2006. *Is History Fiction?* Sydney: University of New South Wales.

de Certeau, Michel. 1980. *L'invention du quotidien*. Paris: Gallimard.

Dilthey, Wilhelm. 1976. *Selected Writings*. Translated by H. P. Rickman. Cambridge: Cambridge University Press.

Dinkla, Söke. 2002. "The Art of Narrative: Towards the *Floating Work* of Art." In *New Screen Media: Cinema/Art/Narrative*, edited by Martin Reiser and Andrea Zapp, 27–41. London: BFI.

Egan, Susanna. 1984. *Patterns of Experience in Autobiography*. Chapel Hill and London: University of North Carolina Press.

Everett, Wendy, ed. 2005. *European Identity in Cinema*. Second edition. Exeter: Intellect Books.

Folman, Ari, dir. *Waltz with Bashir*. 2008. Sydney: SBS1, 2009. DVD.

Gadamer, Hans-Georg. 2004. *Truth and Method*. Revised second edition. Translated by Joel Weinsheimer and Donald G. Marshall. London: Bloomsbury.

Hayles, N. Katherine. 2012. *How We Think: Digital Media and Contemporary Technogenesis*. Chicago: The University of Chicago Press.

Kearney, Richard. 2002. *On Stories*. London and New York: Routledge.

Kerby, Anthony Paul. 1991. *Narrative and the Self*. Bloomington: Indiana University Press.

Kermode, Frank. 1967. *Sense of an Ending: Studies in the Theory of Fiction*. Oxford: Oxford University Press.

Landow, George P. 1997. *Hypertext 2.0: The Convergence of Contemporary Critical Theory and Technology*. Baltimore: The John Hopkins University Press.

Lefebvre, Henri. 1974. *La production de l'espace*. Paris: Editions Anthropos.

Lister, Martin, Jon Dovey, Seth Giddings, Iain Grant and Kieran Kelly, eds. 2009. *New Media: A Critical Introduction*. Second edition. London: Routledge.

Maddin, Guy, dir. *My Winnipeg*. 2007. Irvington: The Criterion Collection, 2015. Blu-ray.

Manovich, Lev. 2001. *The Language of New Media*. Cambridge, MA: MIT Press.

Manusco, J. C., and T. R. Sarbin. 1983. "The Self-narrative in the Enactment of Roles." In *Studies in Social Identity*, edited by Theodore R. Sarbin and Karl E. Scheibe, 233–253. New York: Praeger Press.

McElwee, Ross, dir. *Photographic Memory*. 2011. New York: Films Media Group, 2015. E-video.

Mink, Louis O. 1970. "History and Fiction as Modes of Comprehension." *New Literary History* 1 (3): 541–558.

Moretti, Nanni, dir. *Dear Diary (Caro Diario)*. 1993. UK: Arrow, 2009. DVD.

Nora, Pierre, ed. 1984–1992. *Les lieux de mémoire*. Paris: Gallimard.

Papacharissi, Zizi, ed. 2010. *A Networked Self: Identity, Community, and Culture on Social Network Sites*. New York: Routledge.

Ricœur, Paul. 1990. *Soi-même comme un autre*. Paris: Seuil.

Ryan, Marie-Laure. 2006. *Avatars of Story*. Minneapolis and London: University of Minnesota Press.

Polley, Sarah, dir. *Stories We Tell*. 2012. Santa Monica: Lionsgate, 2013. DVD.

Strawson, Galen. 2004. "Tales of the Unexpected." *The Guardian*. January 10, 2004. www.theguardian.com/books/2004/jan/10/society.philosophy.

Tally Jr, Robert T. 2013. *Spatiality*. The New Critical Idiom. London: Routledge.

Thacker, Andrew. 2003. *Moving Through Modernity: Space and Geography in Modernism*. Manchester: Manchester University Press.

Turkle, Sherry. 1995. *Life on the Screen: Identity in the Age of the Internet*. New York: Simon & Shuster.

Turner, Mark. 1996. *The Literary Mind*. New York and Oxford: Oxford University Press.

Varda, Agnès, dir. *The Beaches of Agnès (Les plages d'Agnès)*. New York: Cinema Guild, 2010. DVD.

———, dir. *Daguerréotypes*. 1976. Paris: Ciné Tamaris, 2006. DVD.

———. *Cléo de 5 à 7*. 1962. Paris: Ciné Tamaris, 2006. DVD.

———. *Jane B. par Agnès V*. 1988. Los Angeles: Cinelicious Pics, 2016. Blu-ray.

———. *Lions Love (... and Lies)*. 1969. Irvington: The Criterion Collection, 2015. DVD.

———. *Mur Murs*. 1981. Irvington: The Criterion Collection, 2015. DVD.

———. *Nausicaa*. 1970. Paris: Ciné Tamaris, 2012. DVD.

———. *La pointe courte*. 1955. Paris: Ciné Tamaris, 2012. DVD.

Woolley, Benjamin. 1992. *Virtual Worlds: A Journey in Hype and Hyperreality*. Oxford: Blackwell.

Index